Accountability and the Law

This book discusses contemporary accountability and transparency mechanisms by presenting a selection of case studies.

The authors deal with various problems connected to controlling public institutions and incumbents' responsibility in state bodies. The work is divided into three parts. Part I: Law examines the institutional and objective approach. Part II: Fairness and Rights considers the subject approach, referring to a recipient of rights. Part III: Authority looks at the functional approach, referring to the executors of law. Providing insights into increasing understanding of various concepts, principles, and institutions characteristic of the modern state, the book makes a valuable contribution to the area of comparative constitutional change.

It will be a valuable resource for academics, researchers, and policy-makers working in the areas of constitutional law and politics.

Piotr Mikuli is a full professor at the Jagiellonian University in Kraków, where he is head of the Chair in Comparative Constitutional Law. His interests include constitutional and administrative justice, political systems, and constitutional principles in comparative perspective. He is the author or co-author of a number of publications dealing with constitutional issues. He has served inter alia as a visiting professor at Oxford University, an honorary visiting scholar at Leicester University, and a guest researcher at Dalarna University (Sweden) and the University of Lucerne (Switzerland).

Grzegorz Kuca is an associate professor in the Chair in Comparative Constitutional Law and a member of the Center for Interdisciplinary Constitutional Studies at the Jagiellonian University in Kraków. He has worked at the Office of the Constitutional Tribunal. He is currently an attorney at law, a member of the Krakow Bar Association of Attorneys-at-Law, a member of the Polish Association of Constitutional Law, and a fellow of the European Group of Public Law. His interests include constitutional law and public finances.

Comparative Constitutional Change

Series editors: Xenophon Contiades is Professor of Public Law, *Panteion University*, Athens, Greece and Managing Director, Centre for European Constitutional Law, Athens, Greece.

Thomas Fleiner is Emeritus Professor of Law at the *University of Fribourg, Switzerland*. He teaches and researches in the areas of Federalism, Rule of Law, Multicultural State; Comparative Administrative and Constitutional Law; Political Theory and Philosophy; Swiss Constitutional and Administrative Law; and Legislative Drafting. He has published widely in these and related areas.

Alkmene Fotiadou is Research Associate at the Centre for European Constitutional Law, Athens.

Richard Albert is Professor of Law at the *University of Texas at Austin*.

Comparative Constitutional Change has developed into a distinct field of constitutional law. It encompasses the study of constitutions through the way they change and covers a wide scope of topics and methodologies. Books in this series include work on developments in the functions of the constitution, the organization of powers and the protection of rights, as well as research that focuses on formal amendment rules and the relation between constituent and constituted power. The series includes comparative approaches along with books that focus on single jurisdictions, and brings together research monographs and edited collections which allow the expression of different schools of thought. While the focus is primarily on law, where relevant the series may also include political science, historical, philosophical and empirical approaches that explore constitutional change.

Also in the series:

Illiberal Constitutionalism in Poland and Hungary
The Deterioration of Democracy, Misuse of Human Rights and Abuse of the Rule of Law
Tímea Drinóczi and Agnieszka Bień-Kacała

Courts and Judicial Activism under Crisis Conditions
Policy Making in a Time of Illiberalism and Emergency Constitutionalism
Edited by Martin Belov

For more information about this series, please visit: www.routledge.com/Comparative-Constitutional-Change/book-series/COMPCONST

Accountability and the Law
Rights, Authority and Transparency
of Public Power

Edited by Piotr Mikuli
and Grzegorz Kuca

LONDON AND NEW YORK

First published 2022
by Routledge
2 Park Square, Milton Park, Abingdon, Oxon OX14 4RN

and by Routledge
605 Third Avenue, New York, NY 10158

Routledge is an imprint of the Taylor & Francis Group, an informa business

© 2022 selection and editorial matter, Piotr Mikuli and Grzegorz Kuca; individual chapters, the contributors

The right of Piotr Mikuli and Grzegorz Kuca to be identified as the authors of the editorial material, and of the authors for their individual chapters, has been asserted in accordance with sections 77 and 78 of the Copyright, Designs and Patents Act 1988.

All rights reserved. No part of this book may be reprinted or reproduced or utilised in any form or by any electronic, mechanical, or other means, now known or hereafter invented, including photocopying and recording, or in any information storage or retrieval system, without permission in writing from the publishers.

Trademark notice: Product or corporate names may be trademarks or registered trademarks, and are used only for identification and explanation without intent to infringe.

British Library Cataloguing-in-Publication Data
A catalogue record for this book is available from the British Library

Library of Congress Cataloging-in-Publication Data
A catalog record for this book has been requested

ISBN: 978-0-367-76733-4 (hbk)
ISBN: 978-0-367-76735-8 (pbk)
ISBN: 978-1-003-16833-1 (ebk)

Typeset in Galliard
by Apex CoVantage, LLC

Contents

List of contributors   vii

1 **Introduction**   1
PIOTR MIKULI AND GRZEGORZ KUCA

PART I
Law   7

2 **Accountability in the globalised digital age: online content moderation and hate speech in the European Union**   9
KYRIAKI TOPIDI

3 **Economic crises and transformation to the theoretical model of budget process: a comparative constitutional analysis via an example of EU Member States**   28
GRZEGORZ KUCA

4 **Financial accountability and transparency of public sector institutions in the Republic of Serbia**   46
JELENA KOSTIĆ AND MARINA MATIĆ BOŠKOVIĆ

PART II
Fairness and rights   61

5 **Disciplinary liability of judges: the Polish case**   63
PIOTR MIKULI AND MACIEJ PACH

vi *Contents*

6 **Transparency and accountability versus secrecy
   in intelligence operations: an Italian case study**   80
   ARIANNA VEDASCHI

7 **Non-judicial legal accountability: the case of the Chilean
   comptroller-general**   102
   GUILLERMO JIMÉNEZ

PART III
Authority   127

8 **Presidents' (mis)use of public accountability: going-public
   tactics in European semi-presidential regimes**   129
   THOMAS SEDELIUS

9 **Ministerial criminal liability in the Greek legal order:
   a concise critical review**   156
   EUGENIA KOPSIDI AND IOANNIS A. VLACHOS

10 **Transparency and accountability of the Italian public
    administration in the context of public procurement:
    the case of below-threshold contracts**   174
    FRANCESCA SGRÒ

11 **Transparency and government accountability
    in Brexit negotiations**   193
    NATALIE FOX

Index   221

Contributors

Natalie Fox is an assistant professor in the Chair in Comparative Constitutional Law of Jagiellonian University in Kraków. She is a principal investigator in the research project 'The British Constitutional Law and the Membership in the European Union', financed by the Polish National Science Centre. The aim of the project is to analyse British constitutional law in the context of membership of the UK in the EU.

Guillermo Jiménez is an assistant professor of public law at Universidad Adolfo Ibáñez (Chile). He holds a PhD in law from University College London (2018). His research interests include constitutional and administrative law, administrative justice, socio-legal studies, legal and political theory, regulatory theory, and comparative law.

Eugenia Kopsidi is currently a postdoctoral researcher at Aristotle University of Thessaloniki and a lecturer at Democritus University of Thrace. From 2016 to 2019 she served as legal advisor to the Greek Ministry of Foreign Affairs, and she is a member of the National Registry of Lawyers at the Asylum Service since 2017.

Jelena Kostić is a research fellow at the Institute of Comparative Law, Belgrade, Serbia, researching financial and criminal law, including financial management and control, and internal and external audit.

Grzegorz Kuca is an associate professor in the Chair in Comparative Constitutional Law and a member of the Center for Interdisciplinary Constitutional Studies at the Jagiellonian University in Kraków. He has worked at the Office of the Constitutional Tribunal. He is currently an attorney at law, a member of the Krakow Bar Association of Attorneys-at-Law, a member of the Polish Association of Constitutional Law, and a fellow of the European Group of Public Law. His interests include constitutional law and public finances.

Marina Matić Bošković is a research fellow at the Institute for Criminological and Sociological research in Belgrade, Serbia. She has extensive experience as a justice reform consultant working predominantly for the World Bank and EU in the Western Balkans and Eastern Partner countries. She has been the

viii   *Contributors*

president of the Program Council of Serbian Association of Public Prosecutors since 2007.

Piotr Mikuli is a full professor at the Jagiellonian University in Kraków, where he is head of the Chair in Comparative Constitutional Law. His interests include constitutional and administrative justice, political systems, and constitutional principles in comparative perspective. He is the author or co-author of a number of publications dealing with constitutional issues. He has served inter alia as a visiting professor at Oxford University, a honorary visiting scholar at Leicester University, and a guest researcher at Dalarna University (Sweden) and the University of Lucerne (Switzerland).

Maciej Pach is a researcher in the Chair in Comparative Constitutional Law of Jagiellonian University in Kraków. Since 2016 he has worked as a freelance journalist dealing with constitutional topics and is currently publishing most frequently on popular Polish websites. Leading Polish newspapers also have published his texts.

Thomas Sedelius is a professor of political science at Dalarna University, Sweden. His speciality is political institutions in Eastern Europe, and he has published widely on semi-presidentialism. Professor Sedelius is a Steering Committee member of the Standing Group on Presidential Politics in the European Consortium of Political Research. He is currently the co-director of the Research Profile Intercultural Studies at Dalarna University, where he also teaches comparative politics and supervises PhD students.

Francesca Sgrò has had the Italian national scientific qualification as Associate Professor of constitutional law since 2017. She holds a PhD in constitutional law (2010) and has been a researcher in constitutional law since 2016. Sgrò was a research fellow in constitutional law at the University of Milan from 2011 to 2015, where she also taught constitutional law and administrative law.

Kyriaki Topidi, is a senior research associate and the head of the culture and diversity cluster at the European Centre for Minority Issues in Flensburg, Germany. She holds a degree in law from the Robert Schuman Faculty of Law in Strasbourg, a master's in international studies from the University of Birmingham, and a PhD in European studies from Queen's University Belfast. She has undertaken extensive research in the areas of minority rights, EU law, and public international law.

Arianna Vedaschi is a full professor of public comparative law at Bocconi University and has a PhD in law-drafting techniques and law-evaluation methods from the University of Genova. She served as a visiting researcher professor at Trinity College (Dublin, Ireland) and the Max Planck Institute for Comparative Public Law and International Law (Heidelberg, Germany); a visiting professor at the Universities of Valencia (Spain), Lima (Peru), Austral and La Matanza (Buenos Aires, Argentina), and Monterey (Nuevo León, Mexico);

and a visiting scholar at Fordham University (New York, USA) and Exeter University (UK).

Ioannis A. Vlachos holds a degree in law from the Aristotle University of Thessaloniki and a bachelor of arts in business studies (finance and accounting) from the University of Sheffield. He earned his master of laws in criminal law and criminology from the School of Law of the Aristotle University of Thessaloniki and is a PhD candidate in the same faculty.

1 Introduction

Piotr Mikuli and Grzegorz Kuca

This book analyses and discusses issues related to the accountability and transparency of public power and mutual interactions between the two concepts.

We believe that the term 'accountability' is quite elastic and inclusive. One has to remember that conceptualising this term may present difficulties due to the lack of a proper equivalent in other languages. We argue, however, that it includes various procedures for assessing individual behaviours of incumbents of state organs in the performance of their duties (including punitive ailments that may befall them but also rewards), many mechanisms involving reporting on this performance (reporting), and various instruments that refer to material (organisational) substrates of a state organ or the whole branch of government. Thus, the notion of accountability includes some kind of relationship between either an individual (i.e., an incumbent of a state organ) and an institution endowed with competences in this respect or between two institutions. The spectrum of these relations may include specific elements described by using expressions (apart from accountability) such as 'responsibility' or 'liability'. In the sphere of constitutional and legal norms in a national state or at the level of a supranational organisation, the aforementioned relationship undoubtedly has normative significance, including legal consequences of applying accountability measures. Nevertheless, some legally prescribed accountability procedures may not evoke an immediate legal effect, or these legal effects may be more general and limited to a particular branch of the law. Within such an approach, one can mention, for instance, the so-called political accountability mechanisms, such as deciding upon a vote of no-confidence motion by a chamber of parliament. In turn, the legal accountability of state organs' incumbents may also signify applying a direct, repressive legal sanction for breaching the constitution or a statute (a constitutional tort).

The direct link between accountability and transparency has at least a twofold meaning. First, we have to assume that all measures connected with holding people and institutions accountable must be straightforward, clear, and open to eliminate illegal behaviour and the possibility of corruption. Second, both notions interact with each other as they constitute important public values connected with the idea of democracy and the rule of law, and with other critical constitutional components such as separation of powers and checks-and-balances mechanisms (Harlow 2014). The sovereign can make conscious electoral decisions only when the activities of those who are in power are transparent. In turn, 'good transparent policies contain methods of accountability', and 'transparent policies also provide information to citizens and improve their ability to make choices about the services they receive' (Ball 2009, p. 300). Thus, transparency and accountability interrelate with fundamental constitutional principles, which are also characteristic features of the idea of good governance (Harlow 2006, p. 204ff.). On the other hand, Kosař and Spáč observe that transparency does not necessarily contribute to public institutions' proper and desirable actions, which is why accountability and transparency should be treated separately. Nevertheless, they rightly add that transparency is a prerequisite for accountability, and the former is a separate concept that 'operates as the contingent circumstance that might influence whether a certain form of accountability will bring about a particular set of results' (Kosař and Spáč 2018, p. 42).

The contributions included in this collective volume have been divided into three parts: the institutional and objective approach (Part I: Law); the subject approach, referring to a recipient of rights (Part II: Fairness and Rights); and the functional approach, referring to the executors of law (Part III: Authority).

In Chapter 2, Kyriaki Topidi argues that the traditional framework governing the relationship between the state and citizens has changed radically in the 21st century. Instead of a binary structure between the two main actors—the state and citizens—the present setting involves multiple state and non-state actors as well as transnational ones, all involved in the process of producing public goods. The shift is also connected to the extension of the public space to the digital sphere. One of the core questions in terms of governance, therefore, relates to the ways the state can position itself in the battle for accountability that occurs in the media, including social and alternative media. These trends are most evident in the regulation of online content at the EU level. The exercise of free speech can be offensive and can contribute to a climate of prejudice and discrimination against certain groups. Kyriaki's chapter engages with the normative dimensions of the balance between the need to control and limit incitement to violence and the fundamental right to freedom of expression as it is exercised in online contexts.

In Chapter 3, Grzegorz Kuca concentrates on the impact of economic crises on the budget process. Specifically, the author states that the budget process is now beginning to vary from its traditional theoretical model, which entrusts the government with the power to prepare and execute and parliament to adopt and control a state budget. This transformation refers to both formal and substantive matters; that is, it concerns form and content as well as the actual course of the budget process. It also changes the control of both the parliament's and government's actions with judicial review. Therefore, from the perspective of public debt and budget deficits, numerous essential questions must be answered, including those referring to the change in the central bank's role. The author attempts to identify these issues and propose possible solutions to some of them.

Introduction 3

In Chapter 4, Jelena Kostić and Marina Matić Bošković raise the issue of financial accountability and transparency of public sector financial operations in the Republic of Serbia. Financial accountability in the public sector in this context includes accountability to ensure efficient, economical, and effective public spending. Transparency of public spending is part of accountability to citizens since they contribute to public revenues. The authors explain key challenges for financial accountability and the key reasons for the development of such challenges, and the behaviour of financial control institutions in Serbia that frame challenges. Based on an analysis of the Supreme Audit Institution's reports of the Republic of Serbia, the authors highlight the problems that exist in practice and propose recommendations for improving the current situation.

In Chapter 5, Piotr Mikuli and Maciej Pach focus on the current legal measures concerning disciplinary accountability of judges in Poland. The authors focus on solutions applied in Poland after several legal modifications that the Law and Justice Party introduced between 2015 and 2020. The Polish case constitutes a warning that the concept of accountability, especially related to judicial power, may be applied in an abusive way. The disciplinary liability measures were introduced in this country under the guise of ensuring greater efficacy of such procedures and judicial power transparency, but they de facto aim to intimidate the entire judicial system. This must also be perceived in light of the systematic breach of the rule of law in Poland.

In Chapter 6, Arianna Vedaschi explains how the tensions between transparency and accountability and state secrecy implied in security-related operations are addressed by Italian legislators and courts, especially in times of severe political stress; namely, those characterised by the ongoing threat of international terrorism. As a first step, the chapter explains the choice of the Italian jurisdiction as the main context for the research from a methodological perspective, and it defines the notions of transparency and accountability from a theoretical perspective. Vedaschi's research focuses on mechanisms designed to ensure oversight of intelligence operations and accountability of agents, and on the relationship between intelligence services and the executive as framed by laws that courts interpret. She also highlights some challenging issues emerging from the described background and discusses whether and how some aspects of the Italian intelligence framework could be improved to achieve a better balance between the values at stake.

In Chapter 7, Guillermo Jiménez explains that this institution, established in the late 1920s, has played a critical role in the Chilean constitutional landscape. It operated for decades as a court substitute and complemented judicial review in the task of ensuring executive branch accountability. The chapter describes this office's main structure and functions, emphasising its monocratic organisation and its combination of a variety of auditing, binding legal interpretations, and internal review powers, as well as its close interaction with both bureaucracy and the legislature. The chapter concludes by placing the Chilean comptroller-general in the broader context of Latin American struggles to ensure legality and subject governments to the rule of law.

4 *Piotr Mikuli and Grzegorz Kuca*

In Chapter 8, Thomas Sedelius refers to accountability in the semi-presidential system of government. Despite an increasing amount of research about the formal role and prerogatives of the presidency in these systems, we still know little about the various channels for public accountability in dual executive systems. Sedelius' study partly addresses this gap by empirically examining how presidents in semi-presidential systems utilise their option to *go public* to establish citizen support to pursue their agendas. Aware of their popular support, presidents can effectively use the option of public addresses to compensate for their formally weaker powers. Sedelius uses a comparative case study design that includes two Central European countries (Lithuania and Romania) and Finland as long-lasting cases of European semi-presidentialism. He explains the interplay between executive power and citizens. Each country represents a unique semi-presidential path: high levels of institutionalisation and the weakening of a historically strong presidency in Finland in 2000; general intra-executive stability under a personalised political system in Lithuania; and party system instability, strong presidential influence, personalised politics, and high institutional tensions in Romania.

In Chapter 9, Eugenia Kopsidi and Ioannis A. Vlachos contend that the relationship between elected officials' political and criminal—or more broadly, legal—responsibility is linked inextricably to the quality of the rule of law. According to Article 86:

> Only the Parliament has the power to prosecute serving or former members of the Cabinet or Undersecretaries for criminal offences that they committed during the discharge of their duties, as specified by law. The institution of specific ministerial offences is prohibited.

In this sense, as the authors emphasise, the legislature seems to substitute the judiciary, which is a constitutional deviation from the foundational principle of separation of powers. Combined with the explicit prohibition of establishing specific ministerial offences, such as procedural immunity, seems to craft a rather entitled and privileged legal framework that encourages impunity among high-ranking political figures. Moreover, the parliamentary majority at any time can revoke impeachment resolutions or suspend prosecutions and relevant investigatory proceedings. Although officially intended to safeguard cabinet members from groundless complaints and politically driven prosecution, this special procedure governing criminal ministerial liability in Greece has led to constitutionally controversial solutions. The authors argue in this context that the vague notion of *political responsibility* tends to absorb its criminal counterpart, essentially leading to penal exoneration and escalating mistrust in political institutions.

In Chapter 10, Francesca Sgrò examines the constitutional value and legislative implementation of transparency and accountability concerning the public administration, with a particular emphasis on public contracts. She assesses how transparency and accountability—which are traditionally expressions of the constitutional principle of public administration's 'impartiality' according to the Italian Constitution's Article 97—have experienced progressive implementation; that is,

Introduction 5

they have acquired an autonomous ontological relevance that partially emancipates them from the constitutional principle of impartiality, bringing them closer and functionalising them to other different constitutional principles that guide public action, such as 'good performance' (efficiency) and 'legality' (protection from corruption) within the public administration under Article 97. The chapter ends with some constitutional considerations about the highlighted evolution of the principles of transparency and accountability from the Italian perspective—from principles strictly linked to the public administration impartiality concerning autonomous principles and values that are open not only to administrative actions' legality but also to the good performance of the public administration.

In Chapter 11, Natalie Fox refers to the process of the UK's withdrawal from the European Union in the context of the Brexit negotiations started after the notification of Article 50(2) of the Treaty on European Union. The author wonders how accountability in the divorce process from the EU should be construed. This question is closely linked to the pro-Brexit campaign's main argument to 'take back control' and consequentially regain sovereignty. Parliament is obligated to monitor and control the negotiation process as a matter of accountability. The legal analysis is also complemented by an examination of the interpretation and application of the principle of transparency from a legal and political perspective. The 'maximum level of transparency' was embraced in the Brexit discussions, and the approach to openness was instrumental. Although the Brexit negotiations are a striking example of the rising importance of the concept of transparency, the UK government embraced the Brexit talks in a particular way. The UK sought to avoid the scenario called a 'no-deal' Brexit but consistently exposed a tough line on the issues where it was difficult to reach an agreement despite the fact it would result in the so-called hard Brexit.

To sum up, the chapters included in this volume contain reflections on the developments of the various accountability mechanisms and institutions in times of rapid change. We believe that these chapters, therefore, answer questions concerning the efficiency of accountability and transparency mechanisms from the perspective of consolidated democratic systems as well as various tendencies of democratic decay and infringement on the rule of law.

References

Ball, C. (2009). What is transparency? *Public Integrity*, 11(4), pp. 293–307.

Harlow, C. (2014). Accountability and constitutional law. In: Bovens, M., Goodin, R. E. and Schillemans, T. eds. *The Oxford Handbook of Public Accountability*. Oxford: Oxford University Press, pp. 195–210.

Harlow, C. (2006). Global administrative law: The quest for principles and values. *The European Journal of International Law*, 17(1), pp. 187–214.

Kosař, D. and Spáč, S. (2018). Conceptualization(s) of judicial independence and judicial accountability by the European network of councils for the judiciary: Two steps forward, one step back. *International Journal of Court Administration*, 18(3), pp. 37–46.

Part I
Law

2 Accountability in the globalised digital age

Online content moderation and hate speech in the European Union

Kyriaki Topidi

2.1 Introduction: a new accountability environment

The traditional framework governing the relationship between the state and its citizens has radically changed in the 21st century. Instead of a binary structure between the two main actors, the present setting involves multiple actors—both state and non-state as well as transnational—all involved in the process of production of public goods. This multiplicity/plurality has inevitably affected the locus and operationalisation of accountability.

The digital era and the challenges that it brings fit quite well in this complex, multilateral framework. Whether a researcher refers to the presence and the role of corporate (private) actors or to the levels of regulation in various (relatively new and still developing) policy areas, such as online speech regulation, the implications for accountability are real and pressing. The regulation of online content, particularly in connection to the exercise of the right to freedom of expression, is a powerful reminder of the perennial constitutional (and governance) question of how power should be distributed and regulated in the digital ecosystem. With online expression becoming easier and more plural than ever, it is worth considering how the power to regulate such expression is handled, often in the service of (not always benevolent) political aims that will likely influence and ultimately determine who shall govern (Joshi 2017).[1]

In classical constitutional studies, the concept of accountability has signified compliance with and respect for the principles of legality and due process (Bamforth and Leyland 2013). It involves the justification of an actor's performance of one's duties towards others to whom accounts are owed, through the use of standards to measure one's performance and with possible consequences for the actor if the standards are not met (Bovens 2004, pp. 447–448; Nollkaemper and Curtin 2007, p. 4). Accountability has traditionally operated on two levels: the practical and the ethical (Bishman 2016, p. 2). As digital technology has essentially reconfigured the features of the constitutional environment and, more broadly,

---

1 Joshi (2017) mentions the examples of former President Donald Trump (United States), President Narendra Modi (India), and President Rodrigo Duterte (Philippines).

10 *Kyriaki Topidi*

the relation between society and technology, accountability is also firmly connected at present to the degree to which regulatory systems that are applicable online consider public values and ethical commitments. Additionally, with private entities emerging alongside states as actors involved in the governance of online public space, the process of being called to account for one's actions becomes equally relevant for both sets of actors but within a different governance constellation when compared with a state-citizen frame. This new constellation requires new normative perspectives on principles and processes that are applicable to the digital setting, which is of interest to this discussion (Marshaw 2006). In more contemporary terms, holding one to account not only carries the obligation to disclose information and justify one's actions; it also presupposes a social relationship between the actor and the relevant accountability forum (Nollkaemper and Curtin 2007, p. 8). As an inherently relational concept, accountability is built around transparency, control, punishment, and restoration.

Particularly for the purposes of this contribution, transparency is approached as the degree of asymmetry of information between the actor that owes accountability as opposed to the actor to which the account is owed (Bishman 2016, p. 3). The transparency objective more specifically allows access to the way that an actor exercises decision-making and attains certain outcomes. In other words, it operates as a criterion for the extent to which accountability is pursued. Normatively, transparency can also be connected to the improvement of the quality of decision-making by actors, an increase in citizen participation and the cultivation of trust, and (legal) empowerment and the realisation of individual rights (Buijze 2013, pp. 4–5, 7). When applied to digital governance, legal scientific knowledge of the empirical functions of transparency (along with its effects), as discussed in this chapter, is incomplete and still evolving. Ultimately, the concept of accountability is used as extending beyond describing a process to exploring a practice linked to democracy, dialogue, responsibility, and responsiveness (Rock 2017).

From the perspective of fundamental rights, the digital age has particularly affected the way(s) that freedom of expression is exercised. In more ways than one, social media platforms are now in a position to moderate the flow of information in the digital public square. In the words of Mark Zuckerberg, 'in a lot of ways Facebook is more like a government than a traditional company' (cited by Langvardt 2018, p. 1357), touching even intimate aspects of its users' lives. Through digital methods of surveillance of citizens using the internet or through ways to censor online expressions, accountability is currently also linked to the 'manufacture [of] consent, sabotage [of] dissent', and the broader shaping of public opinion (Joshi 2017). Within such a framework, online platforms are the battlefields of such accountability concerns. However, to what extent does a digital society relying on algorithms challenge democratic frameworks? More specifically, in what ways does the role of content moderation afforded to (private) social media companies constitute a challenge to accountability? To address these questions, it is useful to first approach the concept of *content moderation*. According to Flew et al. (2019, p. 40), content moderation can be defined as 'the screening, evaluation, categorization, approval or removal/hiding of online content

Accountability in the globalised age 11

according to relevant communications and publishing policies'. Such moderation can occur before or after the publication of online content. The constitutional dimension of moderation is directly linked to accountability mechanisms. This is because of its heavy reliance on both automated resources (e.g., prioritisation, geo-blocking) and human ones to fulfil its moderation tasks, with limited clarity on the division of tasks between humans and machines. However, for accountability assessment purposes, the constitutional tension in most instances arises from information technology (IT) platforms' commitment to protect free speech while fulfilling a business purpose (De Gregorio 2020, p. 3). The combination of the concern to maintain a business-friendly digital ecosystem with the upholding of fundamental rights is precisely the starting point of accountability concerns.

Nevertheless, it should be noted that online platforms, understood (for the purposes of this analysis) as providers hosting third-party content, have a responsibility but not a full-fledged duty to guarantee fundamental rights and freedoms, in contrast to states. As such, the need to balance various constitutional interests, particularly in the European context, has effectively led to the transformation of the online public space from an opportunity to exercise such rights/freedoms to a potential risk of curtailing them (Pollicino 2019). The activation of such risk is triggered not only by the special characteristics of the online public sphere or the change in the regulating actors but also by the concentration of online moderation powers to a limited number of online platforms, coupled with the expanding use of artificial intelligence (AI).

The evolution of the role of online platforms in online content governance is understandably in flux at present; private entities, such as Facebook, have begun to acknowledge their 'broader social responsibility' to combat polarisation and extremism (Zuckerberg 2018). This task should also be placed in correlation to the amount of content in need of moderation.[2] The magnitude of the produced content has provoked numerous discussions around the subjectivity of decision-making related to the vast number of online expressions, particularly in the sensitive areas of hate speech and the fight against misinformation.

The idiosyncratic character of online speech moderation does not stop here. The speed, anonymity, volume, and platform dependence of online expressions make enforcement through state judicial mechanisms unrealistic. Instead, moderators in international call centres, typically located in the Philippines, Ireland, Singapore, India, or Eastern Europe (Langvardt 2018, p. 1362), are called to assess and qualify online speech. In sum, the current governance dynamics in online content moderation point to systemic deficiencies in the aspects of rule of law and due process guarantees and, by extension, to accountability and transparency.

Specifically, in the field of freedom of expression, content moderation requires the exercise of judicial balancing (between competing rights and interests) and public enforcement of measures, usually carried out by state actors (de Gregorio

---

2 According to Zuckerberg (2018), Facebook alone has reviewed two million pieces of content on a daily basis.

2019). Several layers of accountability concerns emerge as a result of the delegation of powers from the state to private actors of this nature: when regulating online speech, private companies (i.e., social media platforms) propose and apply their own standards of protection, usually in the form of their own internal community standards, terms of use, or policies. These standards, including the ways that they are applied by content moderators, often remain obscure and unsuitable for a democratically accountable public activity (Langvardt 2018, p. 1356). Furthermore, as the balancing of rights and interests is performed and enforced by social media companies themselves, they also indirectly decide which right prevails in each case. Per the current European Union (EU) legal framework, these same non-state actors can be held neither accountable nor responsible for hosting third-party content[3] (provided that certain conditions are met), thus indirectly allowing the risk of proliferation, expansion and flourishing of hateful expressions. In terms of the review of platforms' decisions to remove content, there is often little in terms of transparency on how appeal processes are performed and reviewed (Culliford 2020). Resolving disputes between users and platforms then becomes an element that is tightly connected to accountability. Appeals on any contested decisions submitted to independent bodies also require the existence of dispute resolution procedures, guaranteeing transparency and impartiality. This last concern appears to be reconsidered by measures such as the recent appointment of Facebook's Oversight Board, which will act as an *appeals instance* and will be able to overturn the company's decisions on whether individual pieces of content should be allowed on Facebook and Instagram.[4] Overall, responding to accountability concerns seems to be an ongoing, multifaceted process, where platforms are developing and refining their rules and standards as circumstances require and in the light of evolving events.

This contribution focuses on one of the core values of contemporary constitutionalism in a digital society: accountability. Through the discussion of practices adopted in the regulation of hate speech online, the analysis employs a methodological approach that combines governance with the emerging digital constitutionalist frame to reflect on both the value of accountability as a normative concept and the more empirical elements of its practice, as adopted by private actors. The analysis aims to offer insights on the articulation of the web of rights, governance norms, and limitations that regulate the exercise of accountable power on the internet.

To do so, this chapter first considers in more detail the implications of the shift in online content moderation from states to online platforms in the fast-developing area of digital constitutionalism. The second part of the analysis examines more closely how the most common tools of online content moderation pose a challenge to accountability in order to explore the current trends in the European legal landscape regarding the question. The chapter concludes with a consideration of the challenges ahead.

---

3 Articles 14–15 of the E-Commerce Directive.

4 See indicatively, BBC, 'Facebook unveils its plan for Oversight Board', 17 September 2019, www.bbc.com/news/technology-49735795 [Accessed 24 November 2020].

2.2 Digital constitutionalism and the regulatory shift

As 'architects of public spaces' (Gillespie 2017, p. 25), digital platforms are expected to become more accountable in making and amending the rules concerning online expressions and interactions. Their legitimacy, in classic constitutional terms, is inevitably connected to legality and commitment, particularly to values of the rule of law such as consent, procedural fairness, or predictability (Suzor 2018, p. 2).

This alignment to liberal constitutional values presupposes a number of procedural safeguards. Namely, it requires a core body of clear, consistent, and fair rules governing online content, allowing due process guarantees in case of disagreement between the involved parties. This growing and evolving body of rules is connected to the standards of legitimacy for governing online content in the digital age, appropriately labelled *digital constitutionalism* (Douek 2019, p. 1; Suzor 2018, p. 2).

It is noticeable that in the case of online content moderation, private actors are the ones responsible for setting such rules. This complicates the requirements for accountability as it involves 'a diverse, contested environment of agents with differing levels of power and visibility: users, algorithms, platforms, industries and governments' (Crawford and Lumby 2013, p. 279). Nevertheless, the importance of accountability standards cannot be underestimated for broader governance and democracy purposes; the present generation lives in a world where false news travels faster than verified news (Vosoughi et al. 2018) and where hate speech circulates in manifold layers.

The modalities of digital expression are unprecedented in terms of constitutionality and freedom of expression. The use of the internet to produce online speech now offers the possibility to do so anonymously, concealing the speaker's location and his/her humanity (i.e., the 'bot' problem) (Wojcik 2018).[5] These features that are specific to online speech not only have governance implications (e.g., potential harm to democratic regimes and processes) but also affect the levels of accountability in the digital sphere, as the rules/standards devised by private IT companies are required to determine the nature of a fast-growing proportion of speech produced online. In terms of accountability, of equal concern is the gradual development of automated filters that pre-emptively regulate content prior to publication.

However, there is no uniformity across national jurisdictions or international bodies on whether the classic offline constitutional framework can be applied to the online legal sphere by analogy (Suzor 2018, p. 3). The focal point of the constitutional uncertainty is the issue of the platforms' liability to third parties for content placed on their networks. Of course, this comes with the broader concern about whether these platforms are simple 'hosts' as opposed to

---

5 According to Twitter, 10% of US accounts and perhaps a greater percentage in other countries are 'bots'. Bots repeat and distribute messages, increasing their contents' online visibility (Wojcik 2018).

14   *Kyriaki Topidi*

'regulators' of content, in which case they have to set rules on how their systems are used. In Europe, pressure and legislative initiatives towards platform regulation are intense. In essence, the trend is towards 'forced self-regulation' of the platforms (Persily 2019, p. 22), imposing on them the duty to remove content that is illegal or contrary to their internal standards, provided they are notified of its existence on their networks. The German approach to the question has been widely discussed, with some criticism.[6] It has opted for the imposition of a (statutory) duty on social media companies to establish a mechanism to consider complaints. This duty raised a number of policy concerns, including the fear that IT platforms will 'over-block' content to avoid fines, and the persistent discriminatory effects of blocking/deleting content on some groups more than others. It also carries the risk of privatisation of the judiciary due to the review and interpretation function of criminal law being passed to non-state entities (Heldt 2019, p. 5).

Superimposed on the issue of the platforms' function is the nature of digital media platforms as private business entities with the discretion to manage their private properties. However, this discretion has encountered scepticism insofar as platforms are not neutral (i.e., their technical features, such as algorithms, shape the type of information that users can access; Suzor 2018, p. 3; Persily 2019, p. 5)[7] and relies on the assumption that users are rational and autonomous actors in the digital marketplace (Suzor 2018, p. 3). How then does a regulator address bias in algorithmic selection and content moderation, censorship, or abuse/harassment occurring through online media?

Consequently, the call for the establishment of users' rights against online platforms has become more pressing and, within it, the setting of limits in the exercise of the power of platforms in the context of digital constitutionalism. After all, accountability mechanisms assume a certain defensible vision of the common good (Allan 2001), which then leads to the establishment of rules against which such accountability should be measured.

In the case of online content moderation, the terms of the setting of such limits face two basic, interconnected conceptual hurdles. The first concerns the division between private and constitutional law, which becomes of limited use in this case since private entities regulate online space, as mentioned. Second, the current rule-of-law guarantees have been devised for states, not private actors. Additionally, from the perspective of equality, any rules that will be devised should be applied in clear, equitable, and predictable terms for users. However, these features would only satisfy the formal aspects of equality. Most current controversies on the impact of online content moderation concern indirect discriminatory effects, whereby groups of users promoting

---

6 The Law for the Improvement of the Legal Regulation of Social Networks (Netzwerkdurchsetzungsgesetz—NetzDG) came into force on 1 October 2017 and has been fully implemented since 1 January 2018.

7 Virality is connected to the placement and prevalence of information. It prioritises 'popular' communication.

certain opinions are affected disproportionately due to race, gender, religion, or sexual characteristics.

In parallel, platforms are gradually adopting 'state-like' characteristics when attempting to regulate online content. Given the constant evolution of the digital regulatory regime and the characteristics of online speech (particularly its speed and volume), legal formulations covering comprehensively dangerous and authoritarian online speech have yet to be identified. Ultimately, for private companies that are responsible for online content moderation, what places them in a special position is their impact on both individual rights and matters central to democracy (Douek 2019, p. 1). In this sense, the question of the direction of self-regulation rules represents an important constitutional moment for the digital era.

2.3 Content moderation instruments and accountability

Any restriction to freedom of speech—which is not in itself an absolute right—should be publicly explained and justified to limit arbitrariness. The accountability dimension of online speech governance thus includes both the *processes* through which platforms decide on content and the *substantive rules* they use to do so.[8] Equally important, when pushing for regulation, governments should also consider the impact of the use of technological tools (AI tools, filters, etc.) in the process of speech moderation on society and other fundamental rights. As experience has shown so far, the rapid evolution of the nature of online disputes due to technological developments and the use of new practices online will likely complicate the task, especially when states have to negotiate the governance of the digital expression with private online platforms.

From a regulatory perspective, the main question remains whether states should regulate platform censorship or leave it to the market in order to balance accountability concerns in the first case and protect the right to business in the second. Behind this dilemma lie two competing visions of freedom of expression. One claims that based on political realism and out of the concern to allow the marketplace of ideas to function, reduced levels of regulation are desirable. The other is in favour of a stricter framework in the exercise of freedom of expression to avoid harm. In the European legal space, there is a growing preference for states to impose additional legal duties on online platforms in order to mitigate the current situation, where a limited number of private companies determine the content of and implement the right to freedom of expression.

As mentioned, content moderation policies are usually spelt out in a platform's internal rules. Transparency and accountability concerns have often been raised in connection to the consistency in the application of such standards.[9] These

---

8 For a different view, see Douek (2019, p. 7), who argues that government regulation should focus on processes rather than substantive rules.
9 See, e.g., Facebook's Civil Rights Audit Progress Report, 30 June 2019, p. 7.

16   *Kyriaki Topidi*

concerns involve not only appeals' processes to correct content reviewing errors but also other substantial accountability concerns, such as the opaque character of decision-making during reviews or decisions to bar users temporarily or permanently for content violating the terms of use.

In connection to hate speech, platforms either rely on users to report such an incident or on automated means to detect it. More sophisticated tools are also being developed in an attempt to counter the spread of online hate more efficiently. The example of Facebook's most recent initiatives is illustrative; since 2019, Facebook has introduced a policy 'banning the explicit praise, support, or representation of white nationalism and white separatism' (Facebook Civil Rights Audit 2019, p. 9). However, at the current stage of its development, the policy has been deemed too narrow as it relies on the use of 'white nationalism' while excluding other wording with the same or similar effect (Ibid.). Similarly, the popular platform has adopted a policy that discourages attempts to organise events targeting minority groups or vulnerable people and has maintained its ban on organisations that meet hate/violence criteria (Ibid. pp. 9–10).

The link between transparency and accountability is difficult to miss. The openly stated rules and values governing content moderation address, at some length, the platforms' successes and failures in self-regulation in measurable terms (Douek 2019, p. 12), but the rule of due process guarantees also require consideration. An illustrative case in this context concerns the ways that social media platforms treat content that violates their own standards when issued by governments themselves. Accountability is at stake, especially when a platform interferes between a government and its citizens,[10] where consistency and clarity are necessary against risks of arbitrariness.

As online expression has become a 'borderless experience' (Douek 2019, p. 13), the issue of diverging standards and norms of various national jurisdictions has also turned into a real concern for online platforms as international business corporations. The aim here is not necessarily to reach uniformity or unanimous agreement across states but to encourage reasoned disagreement in a Rawlsian sense (Rawls 2005), achieved through decisional transparency, ideally within a relational approach to dispute resolution among a platform, its users, and states in some of these instances. It is only through processes similar to this that it may be possible to limit abuses of online expression, such as hate speech or misinformation, and gradually move towards shared norms among users.

---

10 The recent controversy between Trump and Twitter is a good example. Twitter took action by fact-checking some of Trump's tweets and issued warning labels that they were in violation of the site's policies due to their content that glorified violence. In retaliation, Trump signed an executive order threatening to narrow legal protection for platforms that would censor speech on ideological grounds. Until the end of May 2020, Trump had enjoyed a privileged relationship of permissiveness with most platforms, including Twitter (Roose 2020).

2.3.1 Automated social media content moderation tools and accountability

It is widely acknowledged that the use of AI to moderate online content is currently limited in its efficiency (Duarte et al. 2017). This is because the use of algorithms in language moderation tends to reproduce, if not amplify, bias. Often, the broad implication of such bias is to disproportionately censor minority/vulnerable groups.

From the perspective of accountability, algorithmic content moderation poses a challenge. Algorithms are essentially operationalised to identify and classify data deemed harmful/illegal. Some algorithms produce accurate results (e.g., in facial recognition), but it remains questionable how accurate they are vis-à-vis the identification of hateful speech, for example. In the case of speech, they consistently fail to identify dialects, nuances, and cultural contexts (Duarte et al. 2017, pp. 4, 15).[11] With hate speech being notoriously hard to define, automated tools cannot successfully target this type of speech, as it can be distinguished only with great difficulty from satire, news reporting, or political activism, among others.[12]

Despite social media companies' efforts to moderate online hateful content using automated means (combined with human moderation), hate speakers' patterns of expression are also evolving to bypass detection.[13] Hate speech in itself is also not a uniform form of expression; it has several sub-types (anti-Muslim hate speech, hate speech against women, etc.) and requires varied automated tools according to each type. It can also be used in a large variety of languages where no equivalent algorithms are available (Duarte et al. 2017, p. 14).[14]

In theory, algorithms constitute enforcement means to apply a country's laws and/or a platform's terms of service, thus setting the limits of permitted/lawful speech. When such tools miss hateful speech or disproportionately target a sub-type of speech, accountability and transparency (along with efficiency) levels drop significantly. Given that the scientific reliability of these tools is also at issue, the identification of hate speech must ultimately be treated as a non-binary decision, requiring cultural appraisal prior to final assessment of context (Duarte et al. 2017, pp. 17–18).[15] In this sense, the use of automated content tools cannot be mandated by law insofar as their exclusive use poses considerable challenges, at their present stage of development, to efficiency and transparency.

---

11 Duarte et al. (2017) explain how natural language processing tools misidentify African American English as non-English.

12 Duarte et al. (2017, p. 5) cite a hate speech detection accuracy rate of 70%–80%.

13 Duarte et al. (2017, pp. 6, 20) refer to the examples of using triple parentheses on Twitter to indicate Jewish origin in a derogatory way or to the use of the names of technology companies (Yahoo, Google, and Skype) as racial/ethnic slurs.

14 For English, French, Spanish, German, or Chinese, the tools are widely available, while for Bengali, Indonesian, or Punjabi, among others, they are less so.

15 Cultural appraisal is also multifaceted; a majority view of the meaning of a statement is not always conclusive.

18   *Kyriaki Topidi*

Human moderators—also semantically labelled 'human agency'—consequently become crucial in automated content moderation. Their role is more widely connected to the discussion on the hotly contested topic of 'function allocation' in hate speech detection. The Council of Europe's *Study on the Human Rights Dimensions of Automated Data Processing Techniques and Possible Regulatory Implications* (Wagner 2017) has highlighted the concern about the integration of human rights into internet moderation; it has argued in favour of shared decision-making between humans and automated tools. In the interest of both human rights protection and accountability (but also transparency), human decision-making becomes a constituent element of online speech moderation and by no means redundant in the digital era. However, given the volume of online content in need of moderation for the purpose of hate speech detection, it is worth questioning whether human moderation—reduced to making decisions within seconds, without adequate training on whether or not a particular post constitutes hate speech—indeed represents an instance of exercise of human agency (Wagner 2019, pp. 11–12).[16]

Faced with the limited impact of the use of AI tools, especially in cases where human judgement is needed, platforms have additionally considered effective ways to limit the spread of information by reducing the distribution/virality of such content and by removing fake accounts.[17] The prioritisation (according to virality, among other factors) is often presented as an option in order to avoid the more radical alternative of taking down content,[18] with the censoring risks and the procedural challenges posed by content removal. In this way, the potential for algorithmic bias (particularly with discriminatory impact) is partially offset, while 'algorithmic fairness' is expected to increase.

2.3.2 *Appeals system*

Further to the use of AI tools, also taking the form of indirect means of moderation, such as filtering and prioritisation of content, an appeals system directed at decisions to remove content is gradually being considered by some platforms. Facebook's recently formed 'Oversight Board' is expected to consider appeals on content decisions (Douek 2019, p. 1). The body's role is aligned with the need to provide a basis of accountability for decisions to remove content. The board's decision-making is stated to be guided by the best interests of the users' community as opposed to the commercial interests of the company (Zuckerberg 2018).

---

16 Wagner (2019, at 11–12) identifies seven criteria determining a decision: amount of time invested by the human operator, required degree of qualification of the human operator, degree of liability of the human operator, level of support provided to the human operator to fulfil the task, level of adaptation to the system by the operator, the human operator's access to information, and agency (i.e., authority to change the decision).

17 Facebook's Civil Rights Audit (2019, p. 18) provides evidence of foreign actor use of Facebook accounts during the 2016 US election period to target communities of colour through the use of fake accounts encouraging racial/religious tensions.

18 See, e.g., the Google Trust Project (Persily 2019, pp. 30–31), which prioritises content according to its authoritativeness, depending on a variety of factors.

Accountability in the globalised age 19

The advantages of such a solution are its interpretation as a contribution to a more accountable type of governance through a quasi-judicial type of oversight and the increasing visibility of community standards and norms that it may offer in specific contexts (Douek 2019, p. 14).

A timely appeal, particularly on decisions on content removal or suspension of accounts, is an element towards higher levels of accountability. Nonetheless, the feasibility of this procedural guarantee is jeopardised, first, by the number of appeals that platforms have to process,[19] and second, by the use of algorithmically reduced distribution (without removing the content) for expressions that are not explicitly 'sanctionable'. For this latter case, there is little disclosed information related to the number of posts or the procedural criteria applied; therefore, any type of review on how/why these posts are distributed less widely is precluded in the present state of affairs.

2.4 Online platforms' accountability in a European context

In the European context, there is a plurality of approaches, even at the supra-national level, to the interpretation of and the limits to freedom of expression, particularly in connection to online content moderation. The essential human rights references to freedom of expression include Article 10 of the European Convention on Human Rights (ECHR) and Article 11 of the European Charter of Fundamental Rights.[20]

Based on the above-mentioned normative standards, freedom of expression is a right in need of constant balancing and carries duties and responsibilities. Article 10(2) of the ECHR explicitly states that the right can be

> subject to such formalities, conditions, restrictions or penalties that are pre-scribed by law and are necessary in a democratic society, in the interests of national security, territorial integrity or public safety, for the prevention of disorder or crime, for the protection of health and morals, for the protec-tion of the reputation or rights of others, for preventing the disclosure of information received in confidence, or for maintaining the authority and impartiality of the judiciary.

It is clear from the formulation of the second paragraph of Article 10 that free speech is understood as assessed in the light of other competing constitu-tional rights and interests. Within this frame, the jurisprudence of the Euro-pean Court of Human Rights (ECtHR) in the pre-digital era has indicated an

---

19 Douek (2019, p. 9) cites data from Facebook, stating that the company received 25 million requests for appeal of content in the first quarter of 2019.

20 Council of Europe, European Convention for the Protection of Human Rights and Fun-damental Freedoms, as amended by Protocols Nos. 11 and 14, 4 November 1950, ETS 5; European Union, Charter of Fundamental Rights of the European Union, *OJ C 326, 26.10.2012, pp. 391–407.*

20 Kyriaki Topidi

understanding of freedom of expression that has dissociated protected speech from social approval.[21] As such, any expression, even when likely not offering a significant contribution to public opinion and the exchange of information, is protected in principle.

In the European constitutional review, the main instrument for assessing the activities of these platforms appears to be proportionality. Proportionality is linked to a broader attempt to balance competing interests.[22] For example, when the state intervenes to censor/limit individual speech, the ECHR can require the state to take both positive and negative measures and fulfil its obligations to protect free speech.[23] With the expansion of the use of the internet, the focus has shifted to preventing the potential harm that could be inflicted by online content and communications. This became visible in *Editorial Board of Pravoye Delo and Shtekel v. Ukraine*, where the ECtHR found that 'the risk of harm posed by content and communication on the Internet to the exercise and enjoyment of human rights and freedoms . . . is certainly higher than that posed by press'.[24]

In general terms, the EU legal and policy framework for online hate speech has placed a duty on intermediaries to remove hate speech, following complaints from users. The focus, different from those of the Council of Europe institutions, has been more centred on economic activities. The next step has been to require IT companies to provide a procedure for such complaints. The prevalent (moral) justification for these requirements is that given the companies' considerable power in regulating online content, an obligation to monitor and remove content appears as a fair counterweight. However, this almost transactional approach has not addressed the criticism that in this way, the platforms' power to interpret and enforce both national and European speech laws has also increased. For the purposes of the EU law, social media platforms are a priori regarded as 'hosts' in accordance with Article 14 of the E-Commerce Directive.[25] This implies that as intermediaries (i.e., hosts) of content, they cannot be held liable for illegal content uploaded by their users (e.g., hate speech, copyright infringement, child pornography).[26] Nonetheless, there remains the possibility to extend the same modalities of constitutional review of the fair balance of interests and proportionality to social media intermediaries when handling take-down notices that

---

21 *Handyside v. UK*, Appl. N. 5493/72 [1976]; *Jersild v. Denmark*, Appl. N. 15890/89 [1994].

22 The test of 'fair balance' between the public interest and users' fundamental rights applies both to state actors and private intermediaries (Leersen 2015). See also CJEU, C-314/12 *UPC Telekabel Wien GmbH v. Constantin Film Verein GmbH* (2014).

23 See, e.g., the findings of the ECtHR in *Ozgur Gundem v. Turkey*, Appl. N. 23144/93, 16 March 2000, or *Dink v. Turkey*, Appl. N. 2668/07, 14 September 2010, neither of which applies to the digital space.

24 ECtHR, *Editorial Board of Pravoye Delo and Shtekel v. Ukraine*, Appl. N. 33014/05 [2011].

25 Directive 2000/31/EC of the European Parliament and of the Council of 8 June 2000 on certain legal aspects of information society services, in particular electronic commerce, in the Internal Market ('Directive on electronic commerce'), *OJ L 178, 17.7.2000, pp. 1–16*.

26 CJEU, C-360/10 *SABAM v. Netlog NV* (2011), para. 27.

result in content removal. Whether this is practically feasible, given the volume of notice-and-takedown claims, is a separate yet important consideration. In practice, this would call for the consideration of both the interests of users and the platforms' freedom to conduct business.[27]

However, European case law is not entirely consistent and coherent regarding the contours of this duty of IT intermediaries. The ECtHR has found that compelling a news platform to police user comments in search of defamatory ones would have a 'chilling effect on the freedom of expression on the internet'.[28] However, in a similar earlier case, the same Court reached the conclusion that the national court could uphold a platform's strict liability for user comments (also in the context of forum comments) without violating the ECHR. The main difference between the two cases is that in the earlier one, the unlawful content constituted hate speech. The legal argument to justify the diverging outcomes of *Delfi* and *MTE* posited that given the strong public interest in regulating hate speech under European law, it was conceivable to limit freedom of expression, requiring a news site to constantly review (and remove, as appropriate) users' comments.[29]

In an equivalent case before the Court of Justice of the European Union (CJEU) about defamatory and hateful comments posted on Facebook, the Luxembourg court found that it was lawful for national courts to not only require the platform to remove the post but also impose on it the task to monitor and ensure that the same or similar hateful comments would not reappear in the future anywhere in the world.[30] The CJEU's approach therefore appears wider than that of the ECtHR, imposing a considerable additional burden on IT platforms for present and future purposes of content moderation. The same judgement also invoked the possibility that EU member states could require a 'duty of care' from IT intermediaries to prevent illegal speech/activities. Equally important, the judgement also implied that in the future, IT platforms would be required to define the limits of free expression more actively, under the persistent threat of liability. It can thus be argued that there is an evolving tendency towards an

---

27 See Article 16 of the Charter of Fundamental Rights, where the 'freedom to conduct a business in accordance with Community Union Law and national laws and practices is recognized'.

28 *MTE v Hungary*, Appl. N. 22947/13 EurCtHR 135 (2016, para. 86). The court ruled that Hungary failed to adequately balance the right to reputation and the right to freedom of expression when it awarded damages to a real estate website for injuries to its business reputation. The Hungarian courts imposed objective liability for unlawful comments made by readers on a website, and the ECtHR held that such reasoning unduly placed 'excessive and impracticable forethought capable of undermining freedom of the right to impart information on the Internet'.

29 ECtHR, *Delfi v. Estonia*, Appl. N. 64569/09, judgement of 16 June 2015, for example, paras. 115–116.

30 CJEU, C-18/18, *Eva Glawischnig Piesczek v. Facebook Ireland Limited*, 3 October 2019 [preliminary ruling]. The court found no general monitoring obligation on hosting providers to remove or block equivalent content, which covers only essentially unchanged content where the hosting provider does not have to carry out an independent assessment but can use automated technologies to identify it.

22 *Kyriaki Topidi*

enhanced liability regime of IT platforms in Europe, with the willingness to also increase the degree of their accountability to their users.

The *Facebook* case showcased the intention for a broader reform on EU liability law for IT platforms that will also affect online hate speech moderation. The Copyright Digital Single Market Directive[31] indeed introduced proactive content-filtering duties of platforms (Article 17), applicable in the copyright context. Should this approach be extended to hate speech, the use of pre-filtering would pose genuine threats to equality and non-discrimination. While giving rise to additional accountability concerns about the modalities of filtering, preliminary findings already suggest that erroneous filtering disproportionately affects racial and linguistic minority groups.[32] So far, IT platforms have often opted for removing lawful content or have used flawed enforcement tools to avoid liability or simply to please advertisers. Such choices, guided primarily by platforms' interests (as opposed to users' interests), have broader consequences. The upcoming EU Digital Services Act, set to replace the E-Commerce Directive, is expected to update the EU's liability and safety rules for digital platforms in the near future, towards the creation of EU-wide applicable rules against online hate speech and disinformation. The spirit of the new piece of regulation moves in the direction of shifting more responsibility for content to IT intermediaries, echoing the *Facebook* decision. It is reported to consider specific provisions for automated filtering technologies within a more transparent and accountable frame.

These plans follow up on the European Commission's 2018 recommendation on tackling illegal content online, which stipulates that in cases where hosting providers use 'automated means' to review content, 'effective and appropriate safeguards' (e.g., human review) should be used to ensure the well-founded nature of the effects of such decisions.[33]

However, on the ground, platforms operate in differentiated terms as private entities. EU law and national jurisdictions quickly reach the limits of their influence on the platforms as private actors in light of the technical features and challenges of online content moderation. For this reason, governments (and the EU in some instances) have opted for soft law approaches, pushing for corporate responsibility while maintaining (largely non-transparent) collaborative links with social

---

31 Directive (EU) 2019/790 of the European Parliament and of the Council of 17 April 2019 on copyright and related rights in the Digital Single Market and amending Directives 96/9/EC and 2001/29/EC, *OJ L 130, 17.5.2019, pp. 92–125.*

32 See, e.g., Enstrom, E. and Feamster, N. (2017). The limits of filtering: a look at the functionality and shortcomings of content detection tools (www.engine.is/the-limits-of-filtering).

33 European Commission, Commission Recommendation on Measures to Effectively Tackle Illegal Content Online (https://ec.europa.eu/newsroom/dae/document.cfm?doc_id=50095). The Council of Europe's Committee of Ministers had similarly stated in a 2018 recommendation: 'Due to the current limited liability of automated means to assess context, intermediaries should carefully assess the human rights impact of automated content management and should ensure human review where appropriate'. Cf. Council of Europe, Recommendation CM/Rec (2018) 2 of the Committee of Ministers to Member States on the Roles and Responsibilities of Internet Intermediaries, Committee of Ministers.

media platforms (Leersen 2015). The 2016 European Commission Code of Conduct on Countering Illegal Hate Speech Online,[34] the 2018 Code of Practice on Online Disinformation, the Communication on Tackling Illegal Content Online (European Commission 2017) and the Recommendation on Measures to Effectively Tackle Illegal Content Online (European Commission 2018) represent a group of soft law measures designed to enhance users' safeguards in online content moderation. The essence of these recommendations moves to emphasise procedural safeguards for users. However, most recommendations have focused on specific categories of content (e.g., copyright; De Gregorio 2020, p. 17). In parallel, the platforms' own 'terms of use' and 'community standards' step in to almost replace state legislation as the primary means of regulating their activities.

In this sense, the evolution and the implications of the continuing use of terms of use or community standards provide an additional layer of constitutional opacity. The removal of content (and in some cases, the elimination of users' accounts) does not require the state's control or review but allows autonomous content management of digital space on the part of online platforms (De Gregorio 2020, p. 11). It has even been argued that through this process, users consent to a withdrawal of their fundamental rights in exchange for services (Mackinnon 2013). The Santa Clara Principles on Transparency and Accountability in Content Moderation (2018), particularly Article 19 that proposes the creation of social media councils to oversee moderation, provide some suggestions on due process within content moderation and spell out the rights of users, though with legally non-binding force.

Given the dynamics of this particular regulatory environment, increasing the direct accountability of platforms still appears as the most viable solution to strike a balance between speech removal and freedom of expression and, more broadly, to assist platforms in observing free speech principles. As the 'public is private and the private is public' (Leersen 2015), private online content powers are unsurprisingly taking on more judicial features to be able to regulate public discourse at the same time as states are devising means to negotiate their regulatory goals with these same private entities, though not always in complete transparency.

The EU's approach to this crucial point is the acknowledgement that the mission of ensuring society's access to information and content comes with a 'wider responsibility' (European Commission 2016, p. 7). This responsibility amounts to not only protecting core values but also increasing transparency and fairness for users (Ibid.). Examples of required measures in this direction include ensuring human oversight in automated content decisions, the possibility to contest a removal decision within a reasonable time frame or the publication of criteria for removal of content.

In sum, accountability-enhancing measures concern three distinct phases of online moderation: notice, decision-making on content removal, and eventual

---

34 The Code of Conduct requires platforms to clarify the reporting process for hate speech, remove illegal contents within 24 hours of notification, and increase their transparency on how they deal with such content.

24 Kyriaki Topidi

redress (De Gregorio 2020, p. 19). Both before and after publication of content, users should have knowledge of the means by which content is prevented from circulating or even removed if already in circulation. Justifications of removal decisions, albeit brief, would be instrumental to assess alignment with ECHR balancing techniques, especially in relation to the grounds, the purpose, and the criteria used (proportionality) for removal. As for the phase of redress, the procedural expectation would be to provide the possibility for brief yet justified review of a removal decision within a reasonable time frame.

2.5 Concluding remarks

Across the globe, since the 2016 US presidential election, in more visible ways for the public, social media platforms have been used to promote populism, hate speech, fake news and misinformation, and as vehicles for governments to interfere with elections (their own and those of other countries) or target and silence opponents. Conversely, they have also been the object of contestation in connection to their moderation policies. The recent advertiser boycott of Facebook by a number of corporations based on the platform's non-intervention to moderate Donald Trump's 'abusive' posts illustrates the repercussions of hate moderation in the business world (*The Guardian* 2020).

Within such a complex and contested framework and from a more socio-legal perspective, online platforms have carved out a privileged position for themselves in public discourse. This is because they not only facilitate expression of opinion but also increasingly contribute to shaping public opinion when users access information and the news[35] (Pew Research Center 2018). They also serve as means to organise political and social movements (e.g., Arab Spring protests; Leersen 2015). Given these tremendous powers, their accountability is disproportionately measured for the most against the 'internal' aspect of these platforms' rules.

Ultimately, online content moderation of expressions of hate has broader implications than the consideration of legal liability rules and regimes. It concerns the responsibility for social cohesion (O'Brien 2018, p. 106). Hate speech online moderation carries the risk of allowing platforms to prioritise their own corporate interests (along with those of authoritarian governments, in some cases) to the detriment of individuals and the ethnic/cultural groups to which these individuals belong. In this sense, online speech moderation that fails to be efficient creates the preconditions for the flourishing of cultural relativism, particularly through the proliferation of hateful expressions. Therefore, while the digital space opens access to an innovative tool for public debate, it also requires pragmatic (not only legal) and active balancing of interests. The alignment of corporate purposes with

---

35 According to the Pew Research Center (2018), digital pathways to the news are gaining increasing preference by users. For Western Europeans, within their social media activity, most users are still exposed to a variety of political views. The 'echo chamber' effect is thus not confirmed for social media news consumers.

Accountability in the globalised age   25

societal expectations for accountable and transparent means of moderation of expression (O'Brien 2018, p. 109) stands a better chance to build trust and faith in how the entire system works.

References

Allan, T. R. S. (2001). *Constitutional Justice: A Liberal Theory of the Rule of Law.* Oxford: Oxford University Press.

Bamforth, N. and Leyland, P. (2013). *Accountability in the Contemporary Constitutions.* Oxford: Oxford University Press.

Bishman, A. (2016). *Accountability in the Digital Age: Social, Technological, Political and Commercial Implications* [Online]. Available from: www.academia.edu/ 28708751/Accountability_in_the_Digital_Age_Social_Technological_Political_ and_Commercial_Implications [Accessed 6 September 2020].

Bovens, M. (2004). Analyzing and assessing accountability: A conceptual framework. *European Law Journal*, 13(4), pp. 447–468.

Buijze, A. (2013). The six faces of transparency. *Utrecht Law Review* [Online], 9(3), pp. 3–25. Available from: www.utrechtlawreview.org/articles/abstract/10.18352/ ulr.233/ [Accessed 6 September 2020].

Council of Europe. *European Convention for the Protection of Human Rights and Fundamental Freedoms*, as amended by Protocols Nos. 11 and 14, 4 November 1950, ETS 5.

Crawford, K. and Lumby, C. (2013). Networks of governance: Users, platforms, and the challenges of networked media regulation. *International Journal of Technology Policy and Law*, 1, pp. 270–282.

Culliford, E. (2020, 6 May). Facebook names first members of Oversight Board that can overrule Zuckerberg. *Reuters* [Online]. Available from: www.reuters.com/ article/us-facebook-oversight/facebook-names-first-members-of-oversight-board-that-can-overrule-zuckerberg-idUSKBN22I2LQ [Accessed 24 November 2020].

De Gregorio, G. (2019, 26 November). Free speech in the age of online content moderation. *Voelkerrechtsblog* [Online]. Available from: https://voelkerrechtsblog. org/free-speech-in-the-age-of-online-content-moderation/ [Accessed 24 November 2020].

De Gregorio, G. (2020). Democratising online content moderation: A constitutional framework. *Computer Law and Security Review* [Online], 36, pp. 1–28. Available from: https://ssrn.com/abstract=3469443 [Accessed 24 November 2020].

Douek, E. (2019). *Verified Accountability: Self-Regulation of Content Moderation as an Answer to the Special Problems of Speech Regulation.* Aegis Series Paper No. 1903 [Online]. Hoover Institution. Available from: www.hoover.org/sites/default/ files/research/docs/douek_verified_accountability_aegisnstl1903_webreadypdf. pdf [Accessed 24 November 2020].

Duarte, N., Llanso, E. and Loup, A. (2017). *Mixed Messages? The Limits of Automated Social Media Content Analysis, Center for Democracy and Technology* [Online]. Available from: https://cdt.org/insights/mixed-messages-the-limits-of-automated-social-media-content-analysis/ [Accessed 24 November 2020].

Enstrom, E. and Feamster, N. (2017). *The Limits of Filtering: A Look at the Functionality and Shortcomings of Content Detection Tools, ENGINE.* Available from: https://www.engine.is/the-limits-of-filtering [Accessed 21 April 2021].

26 *Kyriaki Topidi*

European Commission. (2016). Online platforms and the Digital Single Market: Opportunities and challenges for Europe, COM (2016) 288 final.

European Commission. (2017). Communication on Tackling Illegal Content Online: Towards an enhanced responsibility of Online Platforms, COM (2017) 555 final.

European Commission. (2018). Recommendation of 1 March 2018 on Measures to Effectively Tackle Illegal Content Online, COM (2018) 1177 final.

Facebook. (2019, 30 June). *Facebook's Civil Rights Audit Progress Report* [Online]. Available from: https://about.fb.com/wp-content/uploads/2019/06/civilright-audit_final.pdf [Accessed 24 November 2020].

Flew, T., et al. (2019). Internet regulation as media policy: Rethinking the question of digital communication platform governance. *Journal of Digital Media and Policy*, 10(1), pp. 33–50.

Gillespie, T. (2017). Governance of and by platforms. In: Burgess, J., Poell, T. and Marwick, A. eds. *SAGE Handbook of Social Media*. London, pp. 254–278.

Heldt, A. (2019). Reading between the lines and numbers: An analysis of the first NetzDG reports. *Internet Policy Review* [Online], 8(2). Available from: https://policyreview.info/articles/analysis/reading-between-lines-and-numbers-analysis-first-netzdg-reports [Accessed 24 November 2020].

Joshi, A. (2017, 29 September). Seven challenges for accountability 2.0 [Online]. *Institute for Development Studies*. Available from: www.ids.ac.uk/opinions/seven-challenges-for-accountability-2-0/ [Accessed 24 November 2020].

Langvardt, K. (2018). Regulating online content moderation. *The Georgetown Law Journal*, 106, pp. 1353–1388.

Leersen, P. (2015). Cut out by the middle man: The free speech implications of social network blocking and banning in the EU [Online]. *JIPITEC*. Available from: www.jipitec.eu/issues/jipitec-6-2-2015/4271 [Accessed 24 November 2020].

Mackinnon, R. (2013). *Consent of the Networked: The Worldwide Struggle for Internet Freedom*. New York: Basic Books.

Mashaw, J. (2006). Accountability and institutional design: Some thoughts on the grammar of governance. In: Dowdle, M. ed. *Public Accountability: Designs, Dilemmas and Experiences*. Cambridge: Cambridge University Press.

Nollkaemper, P. A. and Curtin, D. (2007). Conceptualizing accountability in international and European law. *Netherlands Yearbook of International Law*, 36, pp. 3–20.

O'Brien, J. (2018). Letter from Sydney: Accountability in the digital age. *Law and Financial Markets Review*, 12(3), pp. 105–110.

Persily, N. (2019). *The Internet's Challenge to Democracy: Framing the Problem and Assessing Reforms* [Online]. Kofi Annan Foundation. Available from: https://pacs center.stanford.edu/publication/the-internets-challenge-to-democracy-framing-the-problem-and-assessing-reforms [Accessed 24 November 2020].

Pew Research Center. (2018, 14 May). *Many Western Europeans Get News Via Social Media, But in Some Countries, Substantial Minorities Do Not Pay Attention to the Source* [Online]. Available from: www.journalism.org/2018/05/14/many-western-europeans-get-news-via-social-media-but-in-some-countries-substantial-minorities-do-not-pay-attention-to-the-source/ [Accessed 24 November 2020].

Pollicino, O. (2019). Judicial protection of fundamental rights in the transition from the world of atoms to the world of bits: The case of freedom of speech. *European Law Journal*, 25(2), pp. 155–168.

Rawls, J. (2005). *Political Liberalism*. Expanded ed. New York: Columbia University Press.

Rock, E. (2017). Accountability: A core public law value? *Australian Journal of Administrative Law*, 24, pp. 189–203.

Roose, K. (2020, 29 May). The President versus the Mods. *New York Times* [Online]. Available from: www.nytimes.com/2020/05/29/technology/trump-twitter.html [Accessed 24 November 2020].

Santa Clara Principles on Transparency and Accountability in Content Moderation. (2018). Available from: www.santaclaraprinciples.org [Accessed 24 November 2020].

Suzor, N. (2018, July–September). Digital constitutionalism: Using the rule of law to evaluate the legitimacy of governance by platforms. *Social Media and Society*, pp. 1–11.

The Guardian. (2020, 24 June). Facebook to be hit by its largest ever advertiser boycott over racism [Online]. Available from: www.theguardian.com/business/2020/jun/24/ben-and-jerrys-joins-facebook-advertising-boycott-racism [Accessed 24 November 2020].

Vosoughi, S., Roy, D. and Aral, S. (2018, 9 March). The spread of true and false news online. *Science* [Online], 359(6380), pp. 1146–1151. Available from: https://science.sciencemag.org/content/359/6380/1146 [Accessed 24 November 2020].

Wagner, B. (2017). Algorithms and human rights: Study on the Human Rights Dimensions of Automated Data Processing Techniques and Possible Regulatory Implications. DGI (2017) 12. Strasbourg: Council of Europe.

Wagner, B. (2019). Liable, but not in control? Ensuring meaningful human agency in automated decision-making systems. *Policy and Internet*, 11(1), pp. 1–19.

Wojcik, S. (2018, 9 April). 5 things to know about bots on Twitter. *Pew Research Center: Internet Technology* [Online]. Available from: www.pewresearch.org/fact-tank/2018/04/09/5-things-to-know-about-bots-on-twitter/ [Accessed 24 November 2020].

Zuckerberg, M. (2018, 15 November). *A Blueprint for Content Governance and Enforcement* [Online]. Available from: www.facebook.com/notes/mark-zuckerberg/a-blueprint-for-content-governance-and-enforcement/10156443129621634/ [Accessed 24 November 2020].

3 Economic crises and transformation to the theoretical model of budget process

A comparative constitutional analysis via an example of EU Member States*

Grzegorz Kuca

3.1 Introduction

At the start of the 21st century, the world has faced two economic crises. Their origins differ, but their range is comparable to the Great Depression of the 1920s and 1930s. The economic crisis during the first decade of the 21st century (now known as the global financial crisis [GFC]) arose in the US banking system, causing the high-risk mortgage market to collapse and then infecting other elements of the financial market, resulting in a global recession. The crisis during the second decade of the 21st century has been caused by COVID-19, and its economic consequences are likely to exceed those of the GFC.

Though the COVID-19 crisis is far from over, and its final economic consequences are not yet known, the actions implemented during it to stabilise global economic growth are similar to those applied during the GFC. The macroeconomic policy that has been followed during the first two decades of the 21st century diverges from the theoretical model developed in the 1980s and 1990s. These changes apply to both fiscal and monetary policy. In the GFC and the COVID-19 crisis, unprecedented fiscal expansion has been applied alongside unconventional monetary policy, significantly impacting the budget process.

From the perspective of constitutional law, these economic crises have created a sustained threat to social relations. There are at least four reasons to suspect this is the case. First, such crises may paralyse parliamentary activity, which is otherwise aimed at exercising citizens' constitutional rights or extending the catalogue of these rights, which could pose a threat to economic security of the state. Second, economic crises may provide a reason for governments to restrict the execution of citizens' rights, which—in the context of the rule of law—would be impossible under normal conditions; they could also serve as a catalyst for these rights to be extended. Third, economic crises may be used to pressure constitutional courts to rule more favourably or more leniently towards the government and parliament. Fourth, such crises may lead countries to redefine the role of their central

---

* This chapter is an extended version of a paper titled 'Economic Crisis and Transformation to the Theoretical Model of Budget Procedure', presented at the 10th IACL-AIDC World Congress 2018, Seoul, June 18–22, 2018.

Economic crises and transformation 29

banks and shape new relations between political (government and parliament) and monetary powers (central bank).

All these factors lead states to change their budget process. In the context of public debt and the budget deficit, scholars of constitutional law face several significant questions regarding budget process. The main research problem boils down to answering this question: do the scope and manner of regulating a budget process provide optimal formal and substantive conditions for overcoming the consequences of economic crises consequences? Additional questions follow from this (as also posed by Gherghina 2013; Diamant and Emerik 2014; Zubik 2015, pp. 138–139; Kuca 2015, pp. 138–145):

1 Is the government required to include any budget items that cannot be altered or rejected by parliament in its budget bill, even in the face of economic crisis?
2 To what extent does passing a deficit budget limit the ability of the government or parliament to prepare drafts or pass laws that imply new spending or reduce taxes and other public levies?
3 Would the present rules for assessing constitutionally protected values be sufficient if a lawmaker were to limit one such rule to protect the state's economic security?
4 In the absence of a direct constitutional provision limiting state debt (e.g., numerical fiscal rules or a balanced budget rule), could the constitutional court declare a law that restricts economic and social rights to be unconstitutional on the grounds that it poses a threat to the state's economic security?
5 As a result of two financial crises, does the state of public finances enforce cooperation between political (government and parliament) and monetary powers (central bank)?

While these questions do not cover all issues that can determine changes in a budget process over the short or long term, they do cover the most significant issues.

3.2 The notion, phases, and course of budget process in the EU Member States

A budget process aims to establish a state's revenues and expenditures (Rubin 2015). On the grounds of constitutional law, this is a legislative process requiring the participation of parliament (or, at least, the house of parliament elected in general elections). The process is initiated and has its execution guaranteed by the government, takes place in precisely defined and restricted time limits, and secures the continuity of the state's financial management in cases of delay or failure to adopt a state budget (Kuca 2018, p. 42). According to von Hagen and Harden:

> The budget process describes how decisions concerning public resources are made: It is the answer to the question, who does what, when, and how in

the preparation and the implementation of the budget. The budget process is governed by formal and informal rules of behavior [*sic*] and interaction.

(von Hagen and Harden 1995, p. 772)

Thus, 'a budget process is a system of rules governing the decision-making that leads to a budget, from its formulation, through its legislative approval, to its execution' (Ehrhart et al. 2007, p. 279). The basic phases of a budget process are (1) creation (adoption) and (2) execution. However, a subjective criterion (the diversity of the participants in the budget process) gives reason for dividing the budget process into three parts: (1) preparation, (2) adoption, and (3) execution (Raundla 2010, p. 463). In other instances, budget control is also considered to be yet another phase (Kuca 2018, p. 112).

Formally, a budget is a list of revenues and expenses for a certain time period (von Hagen 1992). It has become standard, and even guaranteed by constitutional provisions, for a state's budget to be adopted as a statute. However, exceptions can be noted (Slovenia). According to the Constitutional Court of Slovenia, the budget does not define the rights and obligations of Slovenian citizens, and therefore it does not have to be adopted as a statute (Case U-I-40/96). When a state's budget is adopted as a statute, constitutional lawmakers recognise the significance of financial management and the necessity of maintaining proper financial management relationships between legislative power and executive power (Zubik 2001, p. 71). Parliamentary adoption of a budget is typically accompanied by tensions between the government and the parliament. This situation leads to solutions that can be approved by parliamentary majority on the one hand, and are best from the state's financial management perspective on the other (Bałaban 2007, pp. 143–144). It is worth noting that, according to Germany's Federal Constitutional Court, parliament cannot entrust its budget competences to other entities for an indefinite period of time through unspecified budgetary authorisations. The more financial responsibility is taken, the more effective must be parliament's authority to accept, reject, and control the state budget (Case 2 BvR 987/10). The following arguments oppose issuing a state budget in any form other than a statute:

1   The budget should not be issued by the government, as this approach gives the executive power full financial authority and arbitrary influence over the state's financial management policy.
2   The government can make expenditures, including credit and loans, without the consent of parliament, significantly limiting parliament's political position.
3   It is against the character of an executive power, which is responsible for *executing*, rather than *making*, the law.
4   It significantly changes the responsibility for public revenues, budget deficits, and the direction of the state's expenditures.

In the first phase of a budget process, a budget act is prepared. Doing so is the exclusive competence of the minister responsible for budget matters (most commonly known as the finance minister), who proposes the budget to the government. The government then exercises its right to take legislative action. This model is the most common and most widely approved. Across the EU, the government does exercise this legislated authority during the budget process, but it is formally the competence of the prime minister in France; the lower house of parliament in Ireland; the monarch in Denmark, the Netherlands, and the UK; and the minister responsible for the budget in Cyprus (Article 167(1) of the Constitution of Cyprus), Greece (Article 79(3) of the Constitution of Greece), Luxembourg, and Malta (Article 103(2) of the Constitution of Malta). In this context, it is also worth mentioning that, under the Constitution of Austria, the federal government may use its right to submit a bill concerning a budget act, but it is not the only entity entitled to do so. If the federal government does not submit the bill within the specified time frame, the right can be exercised by members of the National Council (Article 51a(1) of the Constitution of Austria). In most countries, work on the budget bill begins long before it is presented to parliament and lasts for several months. Preparation of the state budget is conducted in accordance with a process specified in an executive act or other act issued by the minister responsible for budget. This act must be updated annually due to changes in social and economic situations. Work on a budget bill must be completed on time to give certainty that the budget will be adopted before the commencement of the next fiscal year.

The second phase of a budget process is adopting the state budget. This competence is exercised by parliament or, in the case of bicameral parliaments, the house of parliament elected in general elections. Concerning bicameral parliaments, there are three basic models of relationships between the parliamentary houses: (1) a full balance between both houses (Romania and Hungary); (2) dominance of one house (France, Germany, and Poland); and (3) deprivation of participation by one house (Austria, Belgium, the Czech Republic, and Slovenia). Committees play key roles when working on a state budget in a parliament. There are two basic models: (1) one specialised committee (Austria, Finland, and Slovenia) or (2) one committee considering a budget bill based on reports drawn up by formal committees (Belgium, the Netherlands, and Sweden). The latter model presents more advantages, as it ensures prompt and efficient elaboration of a budget bill accompanied by proper coordination of the bill's elements by other committees (Kuca 2018, p. 303).

Other significant issues are the admissibility and scope of amendments to a budget bill, which should be considered one of the most significant impacting a state's finances (Gustafson 2003, p. 20). In the EU Member States, there are three basic models of introducing amendments to a budget act (Stapenhurst 2008, p. 56). The first model involves an unlimited right to introduce amendments. Entities entitled to do so may propose both decreasing revenues and increasing expenditures (e.g., Austria, Belgium, the Czech Republic, Denmark, and Finland). Another model involves a limited right to introduce amendments. Amendments should not introduce content entirely unrelated to the basic bill, as that could be considered an attempt to circumvent legislative initiatives (Cases:

32 Grzegorz Kuca

37/03, 45/05, 11/08). Therefore, it is generally acceptable to propose amendments whose substantive scope is restricted to what helps the government establish the bill's final content, achieving fiscal consolidation and a sustainable fiscal position. Restrictions may be (a) the prohibition of increasing the deficit or public debt (Croatia, Poland, Romania, and Italy); (b) the prohibition of sums proposed by the government (Bulgaria, France, Malta, and Germany); (c) the obligation to indicate financing sources (Estonia, Lithuania, and Latvia); and (d) the order of the government's acceptance (Spain and Germany). In the third model, no amendments may be introduced (Cyprus, Ireland, and the UK). Other important elements of the process are signing the budget act and ordering its publication in a proper, official journal, which makes it law. Entrusting parliament with the possibility to introduce amendments of limited subject scope, and ensuring that the government determines the amendments' final content, seems to be the most reasonable solution, as it allows the state to reach fiscal consolidation and balance its fiscal records (Wehner 2010a, p. 208).

In some cases, the head of state is entitled to veto all or part of a budget act. In other cases, the head of state is allowed no veto power over a budget act (Poland, Article 224(1) of the Constitution of Poland). However, in many states, this issue is not settled, which makes it much more difficult to determine whether such vetoes are possible. This concerns more than the proceedings necessary for ordinary statutes. A budget process must include a fall-back solution if the budget fails to be adopted. The most common, generally approved fall-back solution is prorogation. Its basic advantage is that no additional procedural actions must be taken to apply it, but its basic disadvantage is that the structures of revenues and expenditures in two subsequent budgetary periods are never identical. Therefore, it seems that, unlike a provisional budget, the possible application of prorogation means there is no need to introduce additional fall-back solutions.

Some countries have constitutional regulations allowing the dissolution of parliament (Croatia, Estonia, and Hungary) or the shortening of parliament's term (Poland) in case the state budget fails to be adopted. This is a voluntary action in Croatia, Poland, and Hungary, and obligatory in Estonia. These regulations apply to situations when the legislative power is unable to take steps important to the state's financial management, generally due to the lack of a stable parliamentary majority. Tensions between parliament and the government may arise as a result of a break-up in the parliamentary majority, which leads to discrepancies in positions regarding budget issues.

The third phase of a budget process is execution of the state budget. In this phase, public money is spent, and amendments to the budget act are introduced with parliamentary participation. Changes are made to the state budget, with the government playing a key role through the minister responsible for budget matters. It has recently become acceptable to exceed expenditures approved by parliament, what should be reflected in the constitution (Austria and Germany). Amendments to a state budget, introduced during its execution, are made in the form of a supplementary budget or budgetary amendments. Generally, there are no limitations concerning the number (frequency) of amendments that may be made or the moment (time of the fiscal year) at which they may be brought up. However, amendments to a state budget should certainly not become a rule; they should be an exception. When amending a state budget during a fiscal year becomes a rule (as it did in Italy and Belgium in 1980 and in Germany in 1990), the authorising entities cannot be expected to treat the budget act and its limitations as legally binding (von Hagen 2007, p. 42).

Budget control can be performed in the following forms: (1) ex ante (regarding the budget bill's conformity to national law [and to European regulations among EU Member States]); (2) current control (regarding the constitutionality of a budget act); and (3) ex-post control (regarding executing a budget act during a given fiscal year). The key role in budget control is played by supreme audit institutions (SAIs). Their position, functions, tasks, and competences have evolved over the years due to numerous factors, primarily political. From the very beginning, the basic task of SAIs has been to exercise control over government and administration, specifically for financial issues. In France, court authorities— the Court of Audit (Cour des Comptes)—act independently of the government and parliament. In Germany, chambers of audit are organised as administrative bodies (with a hierarchical structure and clerical dependency) but are outside the governmental structure and tend to strengthen their bonds with parliament. In the UK, budget control is within the competences of the auditor general, who is independent of the government but is responsible to the parliament.

Budget control is performed by qualified auditors and specialist in various fields (Mazur 2009, pp. 108–109). Also deserving of mention is the increasing role and significance of independent bodies that monitor a state's financial stability (fiscal councils and parliamentary budget offices) and prepare analyses and assessments (Debrun et al. 2009). Developing such institutions should be recommended and should provide them with constitutional frames; for instance, entrusting them with specified instruments of influence in the budgetary process. However, numerous doubts regarding the control of state budget execution have been raised, as parliaments are generally not bound by SAIs' critical assessments of the execution process. One problem with the budget process is that financial oversight may become too technically complex for politicians tasked with that oversight and too political for accountants with the necessary technical skills (Jacobs 2008, p. 67). This seems to undermine the effort involved in such control and questions whether fiscal control has become a myth (Wehner 2010b, p. 129). This should be considered, as even when there are significant differences in normative revenues and a state's expenditures presented in the budget act, this does not necessarily indicate refusal to discharge by a government acting alongside a stable parliamentary majority (Kuca 2018, p. 366).

3.3 Economic crisis and budget process

Coming to the core part of this study, it must be stated that a state's financing of its citizens' expectations is determined by its budget act, which, in addition to international agreements and other grounds resulting in third parties'

34   *Grzegorz Kuca*

claims against the state, outlines the execution of all other financial laws. As outlined above, budget acts are passed according to special process, which engages both government and parliament. After the economic crises of the 21st century, this process has strayed considerably from its previous theoretical model, which entrusted governments with the power to prepare and execute the state budget and parliaments with the power to adopt and control the budget legislation.

An increasingly significant role is played by the EU, which gives specific requirements for budget bills on the one hand and allows control instruments in Member States' governments on the other. Budgets in the EU are planned via medium-term budgetary frameworks (MTBFs) and within the financial framework of EU funds. EU funds are distributed among Member States based on Partnership Agreements, which are draw up individually with each Member State. Thus, the budget of an EU Member State is no longer its only instrument for the planned acquisition and disbursement of its public finances. Each EU Member State uses EU funds; however, they do so to varying degrees. This means that the EU has the option to control conditions of the Member State's public finances as its budget bill is being prepared. EU Member States must particularly implement into their budget bills the arrangements and policies included in the EU's MTBFs.

According to Council Directive 2011/85/UE of 8 November 2011, an element of the regulatory 'six-pack' defining requirements for the budgetary frameworks of EU Member States, the Member States must establish credible, effective MTBFs, providing for a fiscal planning horizon of at least three years, to ensure that national fiscal planning follows a multiannual perspective.[1] The objectives of Council Directive 2011/85/UE were developed by Regulation no. 473/2013 (part of the regulatory 'two-pack'), which implemented (in Article 4) a common budgetary schedule involving an elaboration procedure for both MTBFs and annual budgets. These regulations extend the surveillance mechanisms for states experiencing financial difficulties and introduce new procedures for the surveillance of national budgets (Armstrong 2014, pp. 68–69). EU funds are not always included in a budget act, though Member States generally design separate budgets for their EU funds. Therefore, EU Member States must follow obligations resulting from the Stability and Growth Pact, inter alia, the obligation to avoid an excessive budget deficit. By these measures, the EU participates in its

---

1 Significantly, budget process must also follow the European Semester, established by the Council (in the form of conclusions) on 17 June 2010, which was based on the Commission announcement of 12 May 2010 and was formally confirmed by the six-pack. The European Semester aims at wider consideration of the European dimension in the national economic strategies of EU Member States—planning and providing sources for the fulfilment of 'Europe 2020' goals in the Member States' budgets. This process involves three parallel, related paths: macroeconomic supervision, subjective coordination, and fiscal supervision. (The first two paths concern issues covered by National Reforms Programmes, while the third concerns issues covered by the Stability or Convergence Programme prepared via the Stability and Growth Pact.)

Member States' budget economies, significantly impacting the change that is taking place in the previous budget process model.

The course of the two 21st-century financial crises also offers examples proving that governments assume multiple competences in the passage[2] and amendment (flexible performance)[3] of a state budget—competences formerly considered to be within the purview of parliaments (Konrath and Berger 2014). They also ignore established limits for deficits and public sector debt set in effective EU provisions (Article 126 TFEU) and sometimes in their own constitutions (Germany, Hungary, Italy, Spain, and Poland). In reaction, the role of the legislature is changing (Posner and Park 2007), and parliaments are developing forms of cooperation with the government during budget execution. However, these have not provided a sufficient balance to government dominance. Therefore, parliamentary competences, such as the right to perform ex post control of budget performance or to vote about budget approval, have been deprived of real significance (Wehner 2010b). According to Schick:

> As legislatures enhance their budget role, one of the challenges facing budget architects will be to balance the impulse for independence with the need to be fiscally responsible. The future of legislative-governmental relations will be strongly influenced by the manner in which this balance is maintained.
>
> (Schick 2002, p. 14)

Thus, it seems essential to develop parliamentary forms of cooperation and ongoing monitoring in the state budget execution process, including the characteristic, and increasingly common, participation of parliamentary commissions. As Schick underscores, 'The legislature's new role in budgeting cannot come from government's weakness. . . . The legislature's role must be defined more in terms of policy, accountability, and performance, and less in terms of control and restriction' (Schick 2002, p. 17). It is, therefore, even more significant—given

---

2 In particular, there is the obligation to obtain the government's consent to introduce amendments to the state's budget bill. Such an obligation is applied, for instance, in Spain. In accordance with Article 134(6) of the Constitution of Spain, 'each non-governmental bill or amendment which cause[s] increase in expenditures or decrease in budget incomes, must be accepted by the government for its consideration'.

3 For instance, in accordance with Article 51b(1) of the Constitution of Austria, expenditures not included in the federal budget (unplanned expenditures) may be made, as can expenditures that exceed those accepted by the Federal Council (extra expenditures), only on the basis of authorisation expressed in the budget act. In case of delay, the following may be established, based on federal government regulations issued in consultation with the commission of the National Council: (1) unplanned expenditures in an amount not exceeding 1% of the total sum of expenditures provided for in the budget act and (2) extra expenditures in an amount not exceeding 2% of the total sum of expenditures provided for in the budget act. If the commission of the National Council does not make a decision within two weeks, it is assumed that consent is given. See Article 51b(2) of the Constitution of Austria. Excess authority given in the state budget is also constitutionally regulated in Germany; see Article 112 of the Constitution of Germany.

36   Grzegorz Kuca

that governments are increasingly obtaining the ability to make expenditures exceeding their states' budget acts—to identify what limits the position of parliament (Steger 2010). Generally, governments' competences within this scope are not based on constitutional provisions, although they should be (as in Austria and Germany). As Kopits and Craig write of transparency in the budgeting process, this requires 'ready access to reliable, comprehensive, timely, understandable, and internationally comparable information on government activities . . . so that the electorate and financial markets can accurately assess the government's financial position and the true costs and benefits of government activities' (Kopits and Craig 1998, p. 1).

In this context, there remains the question of the government's and ministers' liability for budget performance. They can be liable for unlawfully exceeding or failing to make budgeted expenditures; however, they cannot be liable for estimated public revenues turning out to be lower than those established in a budget act, nor can they be liable for all the money planned for budgetary expenditures not being disbursed. The problem is that there is a specific sequence of events and consequences. If a speaker in a parliament overlooks certain flaws in a budget bill submitted to the parliament, the parliament's faultiness may increase. The final budget will be burdened with flaws, and, if so, the question arises: will those who pass it in good faith remain liable for the budget's performance? If a parliament adopts a flawed budget, there is no guarantee that the flaw(s) will be noticed and corrected at the ongoing control stage (e.g., while controlling the budget act's constitutionality). It may even be that the constitutional court itself will avoid controlling the budget act or will not notice its flaws. Because a budget act is divided into normative and accounting portions, the chosen judicial instruments applied by the constitutional courts may prove problematic (Sinkevicius 2003; Granat 2017; Zubik 2015). In this context, a particularly significant issue is controlling the constitutionality of the normative acts related to budget execution, as well as other (potential) financial plans initiated by the state's public authorities, which can lead to questioning of the legal institutions threatening the state's economic security.

These challenges must be faced by constitutional courts, which—particularly in the context of controlling planning norms—must develop new juridical instruments that do not result in an economic interpretation of the law. Such mechanisms could easily be taken out of the context of constitutional rules and values, or even contrasted with those rules and values. The independent role of such mechanisms would be enormous. They could even be used to demand, for example, the closure of some medical healthcare units or public educational units for posing a threat to the state's economic security. This could lead to restrictions in citizens' ability to enjoy their freedoms and rights (Granat 2017, p. 22). Such mechanisms must, therefore, consider the differences between rules and principles. That is it is necessary to determine whether they should be conclusive (according to the 'all or nothing' rule) or inconclusive (being applied according to optimisation). In the latter case, rules indicate an ideal (a goal), and their level of performance depends on legal and actual possibilities. Consequently, it is important to determine whether is it possible to weight the rules or whether

Economic crises and transformation 37

they should remain solely a value under constitutional protection, as they are sometimes defined by constitutional courts.[4] Budget process must be adjusted to account for sequences of events such as this.

With this in mind, the government is also required to include any budget items that cannot be altered or rejected by parliament into its budget bill. This process differs between budget incomes and expenditures, and it also depends on whether the items are related to increasing or decreasing incomes/expenditures.[5] A comparative analysis of constitutional instruments suggests a few universal limitations. First, budget incomes are, in the vast majority, based on acts (i.e., legislations regarding taxes or other public levies), which determine a given type of income. Parliament may increase or decrease those incomes only by amending an act that is already in force. It is necessary to amend an act when budget incomes refer to a citizen's legal situation. Therefore, on the one hand, parliaments are not allowed to increase expenditures when amending governmental budget bills, and on the other hand, governments are entitled to propose incomes that have not been previously determined in acts passed by parliament. Therefore, the determination of budget incomes is mainly declaratory, involving estimating the effects of executing acts in force within the indicated system of relations. The authority of the legislative powers to independently act within that scope is limited to shaping incomes related to the management of the state's assets, as well as credit marketing.

Both government and parliament enjoy greater freedom with budget expenditures, certainly in the scope of decreasing expenditures. However, even in this case, their competences remain limited. First, the government is obliged to enter in a budget bill, and parliament to pass in a state's budget (budget act), expenditures that expressly result from other acts, international agreements, or other sources that result in legal claims from third parties.[6] This is required by both

---

4 Comparative analysis shows that Hungarian constitutional lawmakers have already approached this issue. In Article 37(4) of the Constitution of Hungary, there are direct control patterns (positive approach) that are the basis for controlling state budget constitutionality. This provision states: 'As long as state debt exceeds hall of the Gross Domestic Product, the Constitutional Court may, within its competence Set out in Article 24(2)(b-e), only review the Acts on the State Budget and its implementation, the central tax type, duties, pension and healthcare contributions, customs and the central conditions for local taxes for conformity with the Fundamental Law or annul the preceding Acts due to violation of the right to life and human dignity, the right to the protection of personal data, freedom of thought, conscience and religion, and with the rights related to Hungarian citizenship. The Constitutional Court shall have the unrestricted right to annul the related Acts for non-compliance with the Fundamental Laws procedural requirements for the drafting and publication of such legislation (Halász 2011, p. 491).

5 It is worth noting that constitutions rarely explicitly state what a nation's budget (budget act) shall contain. Generally, the constitution only determines the form of state budgets. Nevertheless, a constitution is the proper place from which to determine what content a state budget (budget act) should contain.

6 Some constitutional lawmakers pay great attention to this issue and decide to enter it into their constitutions. As a notable exception, the Estonian constitutional lawmaker should be

38 *Grzegorz Kuca*

the rule of law and the rule of legal transactions security, which are elements of a democratic state ruled by law.

Second, government is obliged to make, and parliament must accept, necessary expenditures to operate the state bodies and institutions specified in their constitution. These are provisions that directly refer to the sphere of a state's incomes and expenditures, that is, provisions that require consideration of expenditures from entities that enjoy budgetary autonomy;[7] provisions allowing budgetary deficit (e.g., Article 135 of the Constitution of Spain, Article 220(1) of the Constitution of Poland); or provisions determining the deficit's amount by means of an act (e.g., Article 84 of the Constitution of Finland) and consideration of funds for the remuneration of specified entities (e.g., Article 135 of the Constitution of Spain, Article 220(1) of the Constitution of Poland) even in crisis situations. Without financial security, these necessary entities would be unable to operate, which would breach the constitution. Therefore, a state budget must incorporate the operations of the head of state, prime minister, governmental administrations, courts, tribunals, and organs of state control, and also provide funding for the defence of rights and administration. There should also be provisions that do not refer directly to the state's incomes and expenditures but concern finances for performing basic tasks assigned to the constitutionally required institutions. The absence or significant limitation of these funds could be considered a breach of the principle of a democratic state ruled by law.

Thus, in one way, passing a deficit budget limits the ability of the government or parliament to prepare drafts or pass laws that imply new spending or reduce taxes and other public levies. According to a well-established definition from the fields of economy and law, a budget deficit is a surplus of public expenditures over public incomes, which is planned in a state budget. Financing public needs with a budget deficit is accepted as the economic standard in most contemporary states. However, as a result of the 21st-century financial crises in the EU Member States, both deficits and public debt increased, similar to its relation to gross

---

mentioned, as § 116(2) of the Constitution of Estonia provides that parliament cannot abolish or decrease, in a budget bill or in a state budget, any expenditures that result from other acts. Another aspect of this issue is regulated by the Finnish constitutional lawmaker, as § 88 of the Constitution of Finland states that each person is entitled to levy a claim against the state for what lawfully should be granted to him or her, notwithstanding the accepted state budget.

7 Provisions regarding budgetary autonomy have two basic goals. First, they exempt the minister in charge of the budget from the obligation to develop a state budget bill within the scope of references to bodies and institutions. Consequently, the role of this minister consists of entering the proposed projects into a state budget bill. Without proper authorisation, governments should not modify these proposals. Second, the aim of such regulations is to guarantee the independency of specified entities from the government. For instance, the constitutions of Belgium, Bulgaria, Denmark, Spain, and Luxembourg contain regulations regarding the budgetary independency of specified entities. These concern the competences of the legislative powers (Bulgaria, Belgium, Spain), heads of the state (Belgium, Denmark, Spain, Luxembourg) or judicial power (Bulgaria) for determining or disposing of their own budgets.

domestic product (GDP). When a deficit budget is passed, any decrease in taxes or any new expenditures will be followed by an increase in the deficit.

In accordance with Article 126 of the Treaty on the Functioning of the European Union (TFEU), Member States must avoid excessive budget deficits, and the Commission shall monitor the development of the budgetary situation and the stock of government debt in the Member States. The Commission examines Member States' budgets based on two criteria: (1) whether the ratio of planned or actual public deficit to GDP exceeds 3% and (2) whether the ratio of public debt to GDP exceeds 60%. These rates are determined by a procedure protocol concerning excessive budget deficits, which is an attachment to the TFEU. When Member States exceed the specified ratios, EU authorities may implement deficit limiting actions and recommendations, and sanctions may be imposed on a Member State that fails to limit its deficit.

As mentioned above, the question of public debt and budget deficit has been recognised in the constitutions of certain EU Member States: Hungary (Article 37 of the Constitution of 2011); Germany (Articles 109 and 115 of the Constitution of Germany, in the wording of 29 July 2009); Poland (Articles 216(5) and 220 of the Constitution); and Spain (Article 135, as created by the act amending Article 135 of the Constitution, 27 September 2011; Ruiz Robledo 2013, p. 154). In Article 216(5) of the Constitution of Poland, the maximum allowable rate of public debt shall not exceed three-fifths of GDP. In other words, the ratio of state public debt to GDP should not exceed 60%. Similar debt limits are enforced in Spain and Germany; however, these regulations differ in that the Spanish and German constitutional lawmakers did not explicitly specify the ratio limits, instead referring to the corresponding EU acts (i.e., Article 104 of the Treaty establishing the European Economic Community and the TFEU). Thus, Germany and Spain essentially constitutionalised these acts. In Germany, according to Articles 109(3) and 115(2), public budgets must be balanced 'without revenue from credits', also known as the 'debt brake' (Schuldenbremse). This principle is satisfied when the revenue obtained from borrowing funds 'does not exceed 0.35 per cent in relation to the nominal gross domestic product' (Delledonne 2014, p. 187). The Constitution of Hungary states, in Article 37, that 'no debt or financial obligation may be assumed which allows state debt to exceed half of the Gross Domestic Product'.

Such constitutional prohibitions of excessive debt first limit the government, as the entity entitled to contract loans or give state financial guarantees (government, minister of finance, central bank), and second, the parliament, which cannot pass laws or make amendments that will cause the state to exceed its constitutional debt limit. If such limits were exceeded, the persons holding office would transgress the constitution; however, because of doubts concerning the effectiveness of constitutional liability, the actual implementation of such liability is doubtful. Another view suggests that cases in which the constitutional deficit ratios are exceeded should be followed by proceedings before the constitutional court, attempting to declare the occurrence legal (Banaszak 2012, p. 1047).

40   *Grzegorz Kuca*

It must also be considered that debt limits can be exceeded, not only as a result of actions made by proper authorities but also for objective reasons not dependent on state authorities (e.g., as a result of an economic crisis, which causes a decrease in GDP). Therefore, lawmakers should consider relativising the legal consequences of exceeding debt limits, particularly because, in certain constitutions, such prohibitions are very strict (e.g., 'one cannot' [Hungary]; 'one mustn't' [Poland]; 'it cannot be allowed' [Spain]). It seems, therefore, that exceeding debt limits, though economically harmful, should not always involve legal consequences.

Hungarian political lawmakers have acted on this suggestion, as the country now allows the debt limits to be exceeded solely during a special legal order, to the extent required for mitigating the consequences of whatever has caused the limit to be exceeded and, if there is a significant and enduring national economic recession, to the extent required to redress the state's economic balance (Article 36(6) of the Constitution of Hungary). Similarly, in Spain, thresholds of structural deficit may be exceeded during natural disasters, economic recessions, or other sudden, exceptional situations which are out of state's control and significantly harm its financial situation or social and economic sustainability (Article 135(4) of the Constitution of Spain). Exceptions from the debt rule can be also found in Germany (Article 115 of the Basic Law for the Federal Republic of Germany); they, rather like Spain's provisions, refer to deviations in the economic situation, national disasters, and extraordinary situations.

It is worth mentioning that, if there are no such regulations indicating acceptable exceptions (Poland), a threat to the state's existence is considered a boundary. Determining such boundaries is entrusted to the Constitutional Tribunal, which has pointed, in numerous judgements, to the value of counteracting excessive debt (Case K 40/02). For example, in one case, the Constitutional Tribunal did not have opportunity to determine the boundaries for applying Article 216(5) of the Constitution of Poland; however, it applied this constitutional norm to determine the boundaries of the social rights and guarantees stated in the constitution, creating a premise that could provide reasons for their limitation (Case SK 30/03). According to the Tribunal, 'in the circumstances of economic recession . . . the state may be forced to change and deteriorate effective legal regulations, adjusting the scope of social right performance to economic circumstances' (Cases K 5/99, P 9/05).

In this context, it must be added that Article 220(1) of the Constitution of Poland states that increased expenditures or decreased revenues planned by the government (Council of Ministers) cannot cause the Sejm (the lower house of Poland's parliament) to create a higher budget deficit than that proposed in the budget bill. That is the parliament cannot establish a higher budget deficit rate than the one projected by the Council of Ministers in the budget bill presented to the parliament. Thus, the parliament adopting a budget act is bound by the Council of Ministers' decision regarding the budget deficit rate (Borodo 2013, p. 14). In other words, in the light of the Constitution of Poland, the parliament has no influence on the deficit determined in a budget bill; that is, it cannot lower taxes or introduce new expenditures which would result in a deficit increase.

Economic crises and transformation 41

Because of the two 21st-century economic crises, it must be noted that the condition of a state's public finances is significantly influenced by its central bank's decisions. To eliminate the influence of political powers (parliament, government) on monetary power (central bank)—that is using central bank to finance the state's tasks—the central bank's tasks are subject to the constitutionalisation process. A Finnish constitutional lawmaker was the first to recognise this threat and, in 1919, he granted constitutional range to Finland's central bank, stating: 'The Bank of Finland shall function under the guarantee and management of Parliament and under the supervision of Governors elected by Parliament' (§ 73(1) of the Constitution of Finland of 1919). This was the first step towards establishing a precedent for determining the constitutionality of central banks' decisions, which involves a procedure of appointment and of determining the legal status of central bank authorities, its operational aims, and its independence guarantees. This process also includes prohibiting the central bank from financing the government, though such financing attempts are rare (Elster 1994, p. 68).

Thus, the role of the central banks depends on answers to three detailed questions. First, is it possible to return to classic fiscal policy, in which budget deficit and public debt are treated as real limitations to decisions made by the public authorities responsible for fiscal policy? In answering that question, it must be stated that, in the past, there were strong relationships between public debt and GDP, generally related to wars. For instance, in the UK in 1822 (after the Napoleonic Wars), the ratio of public debt to GDP equalled 194.1%. Lowering this ratio to less than 100% took 37 years. In 1945, the ratio of debt to GDP in the UK equalled 215.6%. It was reduced by one-half after ten years, and until around 1985, the ratio of public debt to GDP was less than 40%. An analysis of data concerning the nominal amount of public debt and its relationship to the GDP shows that decreases in this relationship resulted from faster economic growth, cuts in expenditures, higher taxes, debt restructuring, high inflation, and financial repressions (involving regulations underestimating interest rates or forcing financial institutions to invest in government bonds). This data suggests that even high ratios of public debt to GDP do not automatically lead to bankruptcy. It must, however, be considered that the above examples concerned the state (an economic power), and reducing the ratio of public debt to GDP does not place any real burden on the economy. However, it must be a long-term process or it will have negative economic consequences.

Second, is it possible to reduce central banks' balances to their pre-crisis rates? Any answer to this question must consider that reducing the balance sums of central banks would have to be followed by a radical decrease in public debt, as well as the sale of government securities in financial markets. The first solution is rather impossible in a shorter time horizon, as a decrease in the public debt would have to be followed by an increase in private sector debt. Similarly, the large-scale sale of government securities would have to be followed by price reductions and increased interest rates.

Third, is it possible to return to conventional monetary policy, in which inflation is a goal and the major instruments are short-term interest rates? Any answer to this question must consider that, from the late 1980s, inflation has ceased to be the world economy's major problem. There are also no undeniable arguments that low inflation results from effective central bank policies, and other points may impact this matter. Thus, interest rate policies must consider other factors (e.g., the cost of public debt service) which define the interest rate.

In sum, the macroeconomic policy, for the foreseeable future, will be determined by the necessity to maintain proper relationships between interest rates, inflation, public debt, and the value and structure of central banks' assets. From this viewpoint, it can safely be assumed that it is necessary to create new relations between monetary and fiscal powers, particularly since monetary policy, during the 21st-century crises, has been forced to respond to situations created by fiscal and economic policies (van der Sluis 2014, p. 122). It seems that, otherwise, there will be no possibility to resolve the world's major economic and social problems within several decades. One theory, the Modern Monetary Theory, which is controversial and therefore has not yet been put into practice, may be applicable to this situation. It is based on the assumption that governments and central banks must cooperate in solving major economic problems in contemporary society, presenting the opinion that the budget process and central banks must be unified (Kelton 2020).

3.4 Final remarks

This analysis shows that the budget process now applied in the political practice of EU Member States is beginning to vary from the established theoretical model. The debate over the most adequate roles for the legislative and executive powers in the budget process remains largely unresolved. More research must be conducted to compare and contrast the effectiveness of legislative oversight. Based on the above considerations, the following conclusions can be drawn.

First, it is necessary to balance the competences of governments and parliaments within the scope of budget process, particularly limiting both parties strictly to their competences as determined by their states' constitutions and acts, and also considering the role of the EU and the requirements Member States must meet. This process should not be considered as a negative phenomenon that must be eliminated; on the contrary, the iterative process has significant advantages allowing it to be gradually and carefully developed. However, it must be precisely regulated so that any potential doubts or interpretation (competence) disputes can be avoided, both between parliament and government and between Member States and the EU.

Second, the government must include some budget items in a state's budget bill, and the parliament is not allowed to change or reject those items, even when the constitution or budgetary law acts fail to directly address the items. Thus, some advice regarding the content of a state budget can reasonably be offered, even during economic crises. The absence or significant limitation of such advice in a state budget could be considered a potential breach of the principle of a democratic state ruled by law.

Economic crises and transformation 43

Third, regulating some (essential) mechanisms concerning the protection of a state's economic safety in ordinary acts is inappropriate from a legislative viewpoint, as an act concerning budgetary law is equivalent to an annual budget act, in which all essential issues may be regulated differently than in ordinary acts regarding the budget. Therefore, this significant postulate covers the basic mechanisms of constitutional regulations, or at least provides them with a legal status higher than that of a budget act (e.g., by giving them the form of an organic law). This particularly applies to budgetary rules that determine the content and structure of the budgetary process and are subject to a normative approach in budgetary law, as well as to state premises for withdrawing, during an economic crisis, from the introduced restrictions.

Fourth, constitutional courts must create jurisdictional instruments that do not result in an economic interpretation of the law. Such mechanisms could easily be taken out of the context of constitutional rules and values or even contrasted with those rules and values. The independent role of these mechanisms would be enormous, but this could restrict citizens' ability to enjoy their freedoms and rights.

Fifth, numerous doubts have been levied against fiscal control because parliament is generally not bound by SAIs' critical assessments of state budget execution. This seems to undermine the effort involved in enacting such control. This should be considered, as even when there are significant differences in the normative revenues and the states' expenditures presented in the budget act, that does not necessarily indicate refusal to discharge by the government acting alongside a stable parliamentary majority. As Santiso notes:

> The functional linkages between parliaments and audit office[s] are critical to strengthen fiscal transparency and enforce financial accountability. Improving transparency and accountability in public finances necessarily requires focusing on the overall process of fiscal control as much as on the individual organisations in charge of specific aspects of budget oversight.
>
> (Santiso 2008, p. 261)

Sixth, because of the consequences of economic crises, it is necessary to create new relationships between political powers (government, parliament) and monetary powers (central bank). Otherwise, it will be difficult to deal with the consequences of economic crises for several decades. This will require implementing effective institutional solutions and perhaps even defining a theory to serve as the intellectual ground for such solutions.

References

Armstrong, K. A. (2014). Differentiated economic governance and the reshaping of dominium law. In: Adams, M., Fabbrini, F. and Larouche, P. eds. *The Constitutionalization of European Budgetary Constraints.* Oxford and Portland, OR: Hart Publishing.

44 Grzegorz Kuca

Bałaban, A. (2007). Sześć funkcji Sejmu Rzeczypospolitej Polskiej. *Przegląd Sejmowy*, 4, pp. 127–148. Available from: http://orka.sejm.gov.pl/przeglad.nsf/0/D39230BCD AC49F33C12579370043F916/%24File/ps81.pdf [Accessed 18 November 2020].

Banaszak, B. (2012). *Konstytucja Rzeczypospolitej Polskiej. Komentarz.* Warszawa: C.H. Beck.

Borodo, A. (2013). State authorities' powers to determine the budget deficit and public debt in the light of the articles of the constitution and the law of the European Union. *Prawo Budżetowe Państwa i Samorzadu Terytorialnego*, 1(1), pp. 11–24.

Debrun, X., Hauner, D. and Kumar, M. (2009). Independent fiscal agencies. *Journal of Economic Surveys*, 23(1), pp. 44–81.

Delledonne, G. (2014). A legalization of financial constitutions in the EU? Reflections on the German, Spanish, Italian and French experiences. In: Adams, M., Fabbrini, F. and Larouche, P. eds. *The Constitutionalization of European Budgetary Constraints.* Oxford and Portland, OR: Hart Publishing.

Diamant, M. and van Emerik, M. (2014). Mandatory balanced budget in Dutch legislation following examples abroad. In: Adams, M., Fabbrini, F. and Larouche, P. eds. *The Constitutionalization of European Budgetary Constraints.* Oxford: Oxford University Press.

Ehrhart, K. M., Gardner, R., von Hagen, J. and Keser, C. (2007). Budget processes: Theory and experimental evidence. *Games and Economic Behavior*, 59(2), pp. 279–295.

Elster, J. (1994). Constitutional courts and central banks: Suicide prevention or suicide part? *East European Constitutional Review*, 3(3–4), pp. 66–71.

Gherghina, S. (2013). *Balanced Budget Rule as a Legal Principle: A Choice between Simple and Complicated?* Available from: www.fcbb.cdcip.ro/library/files/03_simona_gherghina.pdf [Accessed 22 November 2020].

Granat, M. (2017). Równowaga budżetowa jako zasada prawa (na marginesie orzecznictwa Trybunału Konstytucyjnego czasu kryzysu finansowego). *Przegląd Konstytucyjny* (3). Available from: www.przeglad.konstytucyjny.law.uj.edu.pl/article/view/117/78 [Accessed 10 November 2020].

Gustafson, R. C. (2003). *Legislatures and the Budget Process: An International Survey.* Washington: National Democratic Institute for International Affairs.

Halász, Z. (2011). Public finance. In: Csink, L., Schanda, B. and Varga, A. Z. eds. *The Basic Law of Hungary: A First Commentary.* Dublin: Clarus Press.

Jacobs, K. (2008). Budgets: An accountant's perspective. In: Stapenhurst, R., Pelizzo, R., Olson, D. M. and von Trapp, L. eds. *Legislative Oversight and Budgeting: A World Perspective.* Washington, DC: World Bank.

Kelton, S. (2020). *The Deficit Myth: Modern Monetary Theory and How to Build a Better Economy.* London: Hachette UK.

Konrath, C. and Berger, H. (2014). *The Role of the Austrian Parliament in the Budget Process*, Vienna. Available from: www.pempal.org/sites/pempal/files/attachments/4_the-role-of-parliament-in-the-budget-process.pdf [Accessed 20 November 2020].

Kopits, G. and Craig, K. (1998). Transparency in government operations. *IMF Occasional Paper 158*, International Monetary Fund, Washington, DC.

Kuca, G. (2015). Konstytucyjne limity zadłużenia w Polsce oraz w wybranych państwach UE. In: Mikuli, P., Kulig, A., Karp, J. and Kuca, G. eds. *Ustroje. Tradycje i porównania. Księga jubileuszowa dedykowana prof. dr. hab. Marianowi Grzybowskiemu w siedemdziesiątą rocznicę urodzin.* Warszawa: Wydawnictwo Sejmowe.

Kuca, G. (2018). *Procedura budżetowa we współczesnym prawie konstytucyjnym. Analiza porównawcza na przykładzie państw UE.* Warszawa: Wolters Kluwer.

Mazur, J. (2009). Główne rodzaje najwyższych organów kontroli. In: Bożyk, S. ed. *Prawo, parlament i egzekutywa we współczesnych systemach rządów. Księga poświęcona pamięci Profesora Jerzego Stembrowicza*. Białystok: Temida 2.

Posner, P. and Park, C.-K. (2007). Role of the legislature in the budget process: Recent trends and innovations. *OECD Journal on Budgeting*, 7(3), pp. 1–26. Available from: www.oecd.org/gov/budgeting/43411793.pdf [Accessed 2 December 2020].

Raundla, R. (2010). The evolution of budgetary institutions in Estonia: A path full of puzzles? *Governance*, 23(3), pp. 463–484.

Rubin, S. ed. (2015). *Public Budgeting: Policy, Process and Politics*. London and New York: Routledge.

Ruiz Robledo, A. (2013). The Spanish constitution in the turmoil of the global financial crisis. In: Contiades, X. ed. *Constitutions in the Global Financial Crisis: A Comparative Analysis*. Farnham: Routledge.

Santiso, C. (2008). Keeping a watchful eye? Parliaments and the politics of budgeting in Latin America. In: Stapenhurst, R., Pelizzo, R., Olson, D. M. and von Trapp, L. eds. *Legislative Oversight and Budgeting: A World Perspective*. Washington: World Bank.

Schick, A. (2002). Can national legislatures regain an effective voice in budget policy? *OECD Journal on Budgeting*, 1(3). pp. 1–33.

Sinkevicius, V. (2003). Budgetary competences of parliament in judgments of the constitutional court. *7th Conference of the Constitutional Tribunal of the Republic of Poland and Constitutional Court of Lithuania 26th–29th June 2002*, vol. 17, Studies and Papers, Warsaw.

Stapenhurst, R. (2008). Legislature and the budget. In: Stapenhurst, R., Pelizzo, R., Olson, D. M. and von Trapp, L. eds. *Legislative Oversight and Budgeting: A World Perspective*. Washington, DC: World Bank.

Steger, G. (2010). Austria's budget reform: How to create consensus for a decisive change of fiscal rules. *OECD Journal of Budgeting*, 1. Available from: www.oecd.org/austria/48168584.pdf [Accessed 2 December 2020].

van der Sluis, M. (2014). Economic constitutionalism, the ECB and the Bundesbank. In: Adams, M., Fabbrini, F. and Larouche, P. eds. *The Constitutionalization of European Budgetary Constraints*. Oxford and Portland, OR: Hart Publishing.

von Hagen, J. (1992). *Budgeting Procedures and Fiscal Performance in the European Communities*. Commission of the European Communities, DG ECFIN, European Economy Economic Paper No. 96, pp. 1–79.

von Hagen, J. (2007). Budgeting institutions for better fiscal performance. In: Shah, A. ed. *Budgeting and Budgetary Institutions*. Washington, DC: The World Bank.

von Hagen, J. and Harden, I. J. (1995). Budget process and commitment to fiscal discipline. *European Economic Review*, 39, pp. 771–779.

Wehner, J. (2010a). Institutional constraints on profligate politicians: The conditional effect of partisan fragmentation on budget deficits. *Comparative Political Studies*, 2(43), pp. 208–229.

Wehner, J. (2010b). *Legislature and the Budget Process: The Myth of Fiscal Control*. New York: Palgrave Macmillan.

Zubik, M. (2001). *Budżet państwa w polskim prawie konstytucyjnym*. Warsaw: Sejm Publishing House.

Zubik, M. (2015). W poszukiwaniu efektywnych mechanizmów bezpieczeństwa ekonomicznego państwa. In: Gdulewicz, E., Orłowski, W. and Patyra, S. eds. *25 lat transformacji ustrojowej w Polsce i w Europie Środkowo-Wschodniej*. Lublin: Wydawnictwo Uniwersytetu Marii Curie-Skłodowskiej.

4 Financial accountability and transparency of public sector institutions in the Republic of Serbia

Jelena Kostić and Marina Matić Bošković

4.1 Introduction

Financial accountability in the public sector implies responsible stewardship of the use of public money (Rabrenović 2009, p. 40). These funds are considered revenues that the government collects from taxes, contributions, and other duties paid by citizens in order to finance its operations, and funds are given to public sector institutions for their use in the performance of certain activities in the public interest (Watson 1997). Public funds are not only financial assets but also real estate and movable properties. It should be emphasised that financial responsibility involves three key components: planning of public revenues and expenditures, debate in the parliament and approval of the state budget, and spending and responsibility for public spending (White and Hollingsworth 1999, p. 1). These components coincide with the budget cycle phases and indicate the financial responsibility of public fund users during both the preparation of financial plans and the expenditure of allocated funds. Serbian legislation does not define financial accountability but defines managerial accountability as an obligation of managers at all levels of public fund users to perform all tasks legally, respecting the principles of economy, effectiveness, efficiency, and transparency, and to be accountable for their decisions, actions, and results to the institution that appointed them or transferred responsibility to them.[1]

Although budget regulations prescribe limits on public spending, these are often insufficient.[2] Efficient, economical, and legal public spending implies public sector institutions' actions in accordance with the provisions of various laws and bylaws. To prevent the possibility of violating these provisions, an existing system of internal financial control and external audit embodied in the State Audit Institution (SAI) comprises important mechanisms for preventing irregularities and improving financial accountability. Internal financial control

---

1 Article 2, paragraph 1, point 51(a) of the Law on Budget System of the Republic of Serbia, *Official Gazette of the Republic of Serbia*, No. 54/2009 . . . 149/2020 defines the notion of managerial accountability.
2 Budget limits for certain expenditures are defined by the Law on Budget of the Republic of Serbia and by local government budget decisions, which are adopted annually and changed depending on the needs during the fiscal year.

is ex-ante control whose primary function is to improve financial responsibility and the prevention of irregularities at the level of the institution where it is established. The existence of ex-post control of public spending is an efficient mechanism for the prevention of unintended spending and illegal actions of public sector institutions (Lončar 2011, p. 543). The SAI also controls the functioning of the system of internal financial control in the public sector. The recommendations and the suggestions for improvement of the mentioned system are contained in the SAI reports, which are publicly available. Publicised reports enable citizens to inspect the legality of public sector institutions' financial operations. This is one of the possibilities to exercise the principle of transparency of budget spending, which refers to the government's obligation to be accountable for the management of taxpayers' funds, both in parliament and to the citizens. As the main body of representative democracy, parliament has the dual duty to approve (on behalf of the citizens) the imposition of revenues and to control budget spending in order to ensure the lawful and purposeful use of public funds (Rabrenović and Ćorić Erić 2012, p. 282). The first role implies the adoption of the Law on Budget, and the second refers to the adoption of the Law on the Final Account of the budget. Both laws are published in the national official gazette, and the whole text is available to citizens, representing the practical implementation of the principle of transparency. The mentioned principle enables taxpayers to be acquainted with the volume of budget revenues and the purpose of spending in all phases of the budget cycle. This offers citizens insight into the financial activities of the state and should have a positive effect on reducing or preventing tax evasion (Anđelković 2010, p. 55). The transparency of public spending contributes to improving the financial accountability of public sector institutions. The government will act more responsibly if citizens gain insights into the manner of public spending and if they avail themselves of this possibility. The Law on Budget System of the Republic of Serbia defines the principle of transparency. According to this law, the mentioned principle implies that the tasks and the responsibilities of various state bodies, local authorities, and officials in relation to fiscal policy management are clearly defined and that the relevant up-to-date financial and non-financial information is provided and available to enable effective public scrutiny of fiscal policy and the state of public finances. The principle of transparency also implies that those responsible for publishing such information do not withhold it, unless its publication would cause significant damage to the Republic of Serbia's national security, defence, or international relations.[3]

In this chapter, the research subject is the state of unawareness in the Republic of Serbia's public sector institutions regarding the importance of internal and external financial control for improving financial accountability and the transparency of public spending. Some past studies pointed to the fact that the system of internal financial control in the Republic of Serbia's public sector was not

---

3 Article 27b, paragraph 1, point 5 of the Law on Budget System of the Republic of Serbia.

48 *Jelena Kostić and Marina Matić Bošković*

adequately accepted by public fund users.[4] Additionally, the Law on the Final Account of the Budget had not been adopted and published in the Republic of Serbia for 17 years.[5]

In this chapter, we start from the hypothesis that the system of financial responsibility has not yet been established at full capacity in the Republic of Serbia's public sector institutions and that, in practice, there is a lack of consistent application of the principle of fiscal transparency. To confirm this assumption and provide possible recommendations for improving the existing situation, in the second and third section of this chapter, we analyse the content of the audit report on the financial statements of budget fund users and the final report on the final account of the Republic of Serbia, prepared by the SAI over the last four years.[6] Before the assessment, we review the role and the legal regulation of internal financial control in the Republic of Serbia's public sector. Using the dogmatic-legal method in the fourth section of the chapter, we highlight the legal complexity of the roles of the SAI and other institutions that are important for improving financial responsibility and the transparency of public spending.

4.2 The role of internal financial control in the public sector

Internal financial control is the first level of control over public spending. The basis for its establishment was first defined by the Law on Budget System[7] that

---

4 For more information, see Šuput (2013, p. 260). The author analysed the state of internal financial control in the public sector of the Republic of Serbia, based on the analysis of SAI's Audit Reports on the Final Account of the Budget of the Republic of Serbia for the 2008, 2009, and 2010 fiscal years.

5 However, the Law on the Final Account of the Budget had been adopted retroactively in December 2019 for every year and published in the national official gazette. Bearing in mind the legal definition of the principle of fiscal transparency, the subsequent adoption of a law and its publication do not constitute a realisation of that principle.

6 Bearing in mind that our conclusions in this chapter are based on the analysis of available reports on financial statements of budget fund users and the final report on the final account of the Republic of Serbia, prepared by the SAI for the last four years, in some parts of this chapter we use the term *budget fund users* when we refer to the SAI reports. The term *public fund users* has a much broader sense than *budget fund users*. According to Article 2, paragraph 1, point 5 of the Law on Budget System of the Republic of Serbia, the term *public fund users* implies direct and indirect users of budget funds, users of funds of organisations for obligatory social insurance and public companies established by the Republic of Serbia and local authorities, legal entities established by these public enterprises, legal entities over which the Republic of Serbia or local self-government has direct or indirect control over more than 50% of the capital or more than 50% of the votes in the board of directors, other legal entities in which public funds account for more than 50% of total revenues generated in the previous business year, and public agencies and organisations that apply the regulation on public agencies.

7 Articles 81 and 82 of the Law on Budget System (*Official Gazette of the Republic of Serbia*, Nos. 54/2009, 73/2010, 101/2011, 93/2012, 62/2013, 63/2013–corrigendum, 102/2013, 142/2014, 68/2015–other law, 103/2015, 99/2016, 113/2017, 95/2018, 31/2019, and 72/2019) do not regulate financial management and control and internal audit in detail. These provisions only describe the main elements of internal financial control in the public sector and contain a legal basis for their further regulation by other legislation.

defines the elements of internal financial control in the public sector, which are regulated in more detail by the Rulebook on Joint Criteria for Organizing and Standards and Methodological Instructions for Proceeding and Reporting of Internal Audit in the Public Sector and the Rulebook on Joint Criteria and Standards for Establishing, Functioning and Reporting on the System of Financial Management and Control in the Public Sector. The adoption of these regulations was a major step forward in strengthening financial responsibility in the public sector and is the basis for the realisation of one of the economic conditions of the European Union for the admission of new members (Šuput 2012, pp. 247–248).[8] In the very beginning of the establishment of internal financial control in the public sector of the Republic of Serbia, according to the European Commission's progress report on Serbia, it was emphasised that internal audit could not reach its full potential if the financial management and control system in public sector institutions was not developed (Šuput 2012, p. 249). If we analyse the SAI's reports on the audit of the final account of the budget of the Republic of Serbia over the past four years and the reports on the audit of the financial reports of direct users of budget funds in 2019, it seems that the financial management and control system in the public sector is not fully implemented. Given the powers of internal audit and the fact that it is established among some budget fund users much earlier than financial management and control, a reasonable question arises on whether it exercises its powers in an adequate manner.[9]

Internal audit is an advisory activity that exists to improve an organisation's operations and to help the organisation accomplish its objectives by systematic and disciplined evaluations and implementations of risk management, control, and management of the organisation. Its goal is to check the adequacy and efficiency of the management and control system in relation to the operations' compliance with laws, internal acts, and contracts, as well as the reliability and completeness of financial and other information. Examining regularity and legality (by internal audit) means determining whether the laws and other regulations related to public expenditures, public revenues, and financial obligations have been complied with, and whether the regulations related to asset management and economic affairs have been applied. The findings and the opinions presented in the audit report should serve as instructions for further action of the audited entity in order to prevent further irregularities (Šuput 2012, p. 160). This is important to improve the financial management and control system at the level of each public sector institution and to establish a professional and efficient organisational unit

---

8 Analytical Report Accompanying the Document, Communication from the Commission in the European Parliament and the Council, Commission Opinion on Serbia's Application for Membership in the European Union (http://ec.auropa.eu//englargement/pdf/kez_documents/2011/prackage/sr_analytical_report_2011_en.pdf.1.10.2012).
9 According to Article 9, paragraph 1, points 5 and 6 of the Law on State Audit Institution, assessment of the functioning of internal financial control in the public sector is one of the important competencies of the SAI of the Republic of Serbia.

for internal audit. Therefore, if the financial management and control system is not established or not sufficiently developed at the level of a certain institution, the question of the expertise or efficiency of internal audit could be raised.

According to the provisions of the Rulebook governing the field of internal audit, the audit should have been established in one of the ways prescribed by the Rulebook's provisions for all public fund users. Direct users of budget funds that have indirect users, ministries, and users that have over 250 employees, in accordance with the provisions of national regulations, should establish an independent organisational unit for internal audit.[10] In the case of indirect users, they establish an internal audit by organising a special, functionally independent organisational unit or by forming a joint unit on the proposal of two or more users of budget funds, with the consent of the Central Harmonization Unit.[11] If the internal audit of indirect users of budget funds has not been established in any of the above-mentioned ways, the internal audit function for them is performed via the internal audit of their direct users.[12]

4.3 Assessment of the financial management and control system according to the reports of the State Audit Institution

Having in mind the SAI's reports on the audit of the final account of the Republic of Serbia's budget for the period 2015–2019, there seems to be a need to increase the public sector's awareness of the necessity to establish a system of internal financial control, despite the fact that it should have been established in 2007.

According to the SAI's Audit Report on the Final Account of the Budget of the Republic of Serbia for 2016, internal audit had been established in all ministries but had not been established for most indirect users of budget funds in the manner prescribed by the Rulebook. Even with those for whom the internal audit system had been established, it was assessed that it did not function in the manner prescribed by the Law on Budget System and the Rulebook, which regulated its work with 16 audit entities.[13] Financial management and control system in the observed period was not fully established in 19 audit entities, while in three it was not established at all.[14]

The Audit Report on the Final Account of the Budget for 2017 contained almost the same findings as those of the 2016 audit. Similar statements were made regarding the functioning of financial management and control. The report

---

10 Articles 4, paragraphs 1 and 2 of the Rulebook on Joint Criteria for Organizing and Standards and Methodological Instructions for Proceeding and Reporting of Internal Audit in the Public Sector.
11 Article 3 of the Rulebook.
12 Article 5, paragraph 2 of the Rulebook.
13 SAI's Audit Report on the Final Account of the Budget of the Republic of Serbia for 2016, No. 400–534/2017.03/31, the State Audit Institution of the Republic of Serbia, Belgrade, 29 December 2017, p. 11.
14 *Ibid.*, p. 63.

stated that they had not been fully established in accordance with the relevant regulations and that this prevented the realisation of the goal for which the system of internal financial control had been established among budget fund users.[15]

According to the SAI's Audit Report on the Final Account of the Budget of the Republic of Serbia for 2018, internal audit had not been established and organised by budget fund users in a way that would ensure full application of regulations, rules, and procedures, as well as the achievement of other goals, in line with the Law on Budget System and the Rulebook on Joint Criteria for Organizing and Standards and Methodological Instructions for Proceeding and Reporting of Internal Audit in the Public Sector, as established with budget fund users.[16] Although the report stated that the establishment of internal audit of indirect budget users would depend on the real possibilities of financing—that is on the volume of funds at their disposal and the limitation of the possibility of increasing the number of employees—we could not agree with that statement. The obligation to establish internal audit among public fund users was introduced in 2007, when the Rulebook regulating this area was adopted, and the validity of the ban on employment in the public sector took effect in 2013, when the decree on the procedure for obtaining consent for new and additional employment of public fund users was adopted.[17] If it is a newly established institution, where it really is an obstacle due to the ban on employment, it is also possible to establish internal audit at the level of the institution, and for indirect users, internal audit could be performed by the organisational unit for internal audit of their direct user.[18]

Additionally, in 2018, the SAI's Audit Report on the Final Account of the Budget of the Republic of Serbia recorded an inadequate financial management and control system for most budget fund users.[19] Although the obligation to

---

15 Audit Report on the Final Account of the Budget of the Republic of Serbia for 2017, No. 400–575/2018–03/36, the State Audit Institution of the Republic of Serbia, Belgrade, 14 December 2018, pp. 23 and 43.

16 That has been prescribed by Article 82 of the Law on Budget System of the Republic of Serbia (quoted according to the Audit Report on the Final Account of the Budget of the Republic of Serbia for 2018, No. 400–200/2019–03/16, Belgrade, 20 September 2019, p. 13).

17 Decree on the Procedure for Obtaining Consent for New Employment and Additional Employment in the Public Sector Institutions, *Official Gazette of the Republic of Serbia*, Nos. 113/2013, 21/2014, 66/2014, 118/2014, 22/2015, 59/2015, 62/2019, and 50/2020.

18 Article 3, paragraph 1, point 2 of the Rulebook on Joint Criteria and Standards for Establishing, Functioning and Reporting on the System of Financial Management and Control in the Public Sector prescribes that internal audit can also be established by organising a joint internal audit unit on the proposal of two or more users of public funds, with the prior consent of the Central Harmonization Unit of the Ministry of Finance. According to the same article, paragraph 2, if there are no conditions for organising an internal audit unit, internal audit activities may also be performed by an internal auditor employed by public fund users. Article 3, paragraph 1, point 2 of the above-mentioned Rulebook also prescribes the possibility for the internal audit of the indirect user of budget funds, to be performed by the unit for internal audit of the direct user of budget funds.

19 Audit Report on the Final Account of the Budget of the Republic of Serbia for 2017, No. 400–575/2018–03/36, the State Audit Institution of the Republic of Serbia, Belgrade, 14 December 2018, p. 37.

52 Jelena Kostić and Marina Matić Bošković

establish financial management and control system has been enforced since 2007, it is unusual that even after so many years, it is recommended that the Ministry of Finance should continue to familiarise managers and employees in budgetary institutions with the internal financial control system in the public sector. This also indicates that the internal financial control system in the public sector has not taken root in the Republic of Serbia, even after 13 years.

Somewhat more detailed insight into the shortcomings concerning the functioning of the internal financial control system in the public sector can be gained from the analysis of the content of the SAI's audit reports on budget fund users' financial statements. The mentioned reports show that some direct users of budget funds have not yet established internal audit although, according to the provisions of the Rulebook that guarantees its functioning, they have been obliged to establish a fully functionally independent internal audit unit since 2007.[20]

The obligation to establish internal audit for some budget fund users seems to be understood as a formality than a necessity. This is evidenced by the fact that in some internal audit units, the position of internal auditor was systematised for one year but was filled only two years later.[21]

The financial management and control system in the Republic of Serbia is not established according to legislation.[22] The existing procedures have not been updated, and there is no business risk assessment. Additionally, in some institutions, the manager for financial management and control has been appointed only recently, which means that internal financial control in the public sector institution is still in the beginning of establishing the process.[23]

For some budget fund users, although part of the business processes is regulated by internal acts, there are no written procedures to verify the legality and the documentation of transactions, and there is neither any reporting at the internal level nor a mechanism for monitoring financial management and control.[24] Based on the Audit Report on the Final Account of the Budget of the Republic of Serbia for the last five years and the Report on the Audit of Financial Statements and Regularity of Business Operations of direct users of budget funds

---

20 Report on the Audit of Financial Report and Regularity of Business Operations in the Ministry of Youth and Sport of the Republic of Serbia for 2018, No. 400–213/2019–03/12, Belgrade, 2 December 2019, p. 29.

21 Report on the Audit of Financial Report and Regularity of Business Operations in the Anti-Corruption Agency of the Republic of Serbia for 2017, No. 400–658/2018–03/29, Belgrade, 27 August 2018, p. 10 and Report on the Audit of Parts of the Financial Report and Regularity of Business Operations in the Ministry of Labour, Employment and Social Affairs of the Republic of Serbia for 2016, No. 400–2033/2017–03/26, 21 December 2017, p. 21.

22 Article 3 of the Rulebook on Joint Criteria and Standards for Establishing, Functioning and Reporting of the System of Financial Management and Control in the Public Sector.

23 Report on the Audit of Financial Report of the Ministry of Defence, No. 400–2015/2019–03/13, Belgrade, 19 August 2019, p. 19.

24 Report on the Audit of Financial Report and Regularity of Business Operations in the Ministry of Youth and Sport of the Republic of Serbia for 2018, No. 400–213/2019–03/12, 2 December 2019, p. 28.

of the Republic of Serbia for 2019, it can be concluded that internal audit has been established, but financial management and control system is only in the beginning of establishing its process. However, the question of the effectiveness of the internal audit established among the budget fund users can also be reasonably raised.

According to the provisions of the Rulebook on Joint Criteria for Organizing and Standards and Methodological Instructions for Proceeding and Reporting of Internal Audit in the Public Sector, the basic task of internal audit is to assess financial management and control systems in relation to risk identification; risk assessment and risk management by managers at all levels of an institution; assessment of business operations' compliance with laws; internal acts and contracts; reliability and completeness of financial and other information; efficiency; effectiveness and economy of business operations; protection of funds and data (information); and execution of tasks and achievement of goals.[25] Therefore, the question of whether internal audit performed its tasks in accordance with the Rulebook, which regulates its operations, can also be raised. Additionally, it is noticeable that financial management and control seems to be understood more as a formality than a real need. Perhaps such an attitude stems from the fact that the regulations governing the functioning of internal audit and financial management and control in the public sector do not explicitly state that public fund users are 'obliged' to establish such systems. The regulations only prescribe they be 'established'. Probably, the legislators thought that in practice, it would be recognised that the systems' establishment would be in the interest of employees and managers in public sector institutions as well as in the public interest. Therefore, the national regulation should enforce public fund users' obligation to establish internal financial control and should impose adequate sanctions in case they fail to do so.

4.4 The role of the State Audit Institution and Budget Inspection

The executive branch of the government's accountability to parliament for spending budget funds is a key element of modern democratic systems (Rabrenović and Ćorić Erić 2012, p. 282). This control is exercised by parliament through the SAI.

External audit of budget funds performed by the SAIs, such as the SAI of the Republic of Serbia, is an important mechanism for controlling public spending. In accordance with international standards, these institutions are independent bodies that audit the legality and purposefulness of public spending and form an indispensable part of the institutional control of public spending in all modern democracies (Rabrenović and Ćorić Erić 2012, p. 282; Šuput 2015, p. 322).[26]

---

25 Article 10 of the Rulebook.
26 International standards refer to the INTOSAI standards issued by the International Organization of the State Audit Institution.

In the Republic of Serbia, the SAI belongs to a constitutional category. The provisions of the Constitution of the Republic of Serbia define it as the highest state body for the audit of public funds in the Republic of Serbia and as an independent institution subject to the supervision of the National Assembly, to which it is responsible for its work.[27] The SAI's objective is 'to help the nation spend wisely' (Dobre 2012, p. 698), which means that it should ensure that deliveries of public goods and services maintain proper accounts (Norton and Smith 2018, p. 924).

To enable the independence of the SAI's institution, according to the law governing its work, the acts by which it exercises its competence may not be contested before courts and other state bodies.[28] According to the same provision, the SAI of the Republic of Serbia may provide expert assistance to the National Assembly, the Government of the Republic of Serbia, and other state bodies on certain significant measures and important projects in a way that does not diminish its independence; and the SAI may offer advice and opinions to public fund users on issues in the field of public finances.

According to the Constitution of the Republic of Serbia, the National Assembly, on the proposal of the government, adopts the final account of the Republic of Serbia by a special law.[29] The external audit report on the revision of the annual report on budget execution is an obligatory part of the above-mentioned law.[30] Bearing this in mind, a legal scholar may ask why the SAI of the Republic of Serbia has not pointed out the problem related to the non-submission of the draft Law on the Final Account of the Budget to the National Assembly for its adoption or non-adoption. Although it should be adopted each year, the Law on the Final Account of the Budget has not been adopted over the period 2002–2019. This means that the provisions of the Law on Budget System have been violated for 17 years by the key state institutions and that none of the independent institutions that should handle transparent and legal spending of public funds has shown a timely reaction.[31] Therefore, we argue that the SAI should be able to react in such situations and warn the representatives of the highest executive and legislative institutions about the illegality and irregularity of their actions. Furthermore, according to INTOSAI standards, the state audit institution of each country should be responsible for public sector monitoring, which also entails providing information that highlights both good government and inefficient administrative structures (González et al. 2008, p. 503).

Public spending is mainly financed by public revenues collected from taxes and other duties paid by citizens. Therefore, it is in the citizens' interest to gain

---

27 Article 96 of the Constitution of the Republic of Serbia, *Official Gazette*, No. 98/2006.
28 Article 3, paragraph 4 of the Law on the State Audit Institution.
29 Article 99, paragraph 1, point 11 of the Constitution of the Republic of Serbia.
30 Article 79 of the Law on Budget System.
31 The Final Accounts of the Republic of Serbia have been adopted by the Law on the Financial Account of the Budget for each year and published in the *Official Gazette of the Republic of Serbia*, No. 95/2019.

insights into the manner and scope of public spending. In addition, public institutions are obliged to enable citizens to exercise their right to access information.

The possibility of exercising control over the legality of budget execution by means of an independent audit for each state is one of the essential issues of fiscal policy. Establishing a good and efficient mechanism of subsequent control over the spending of budget funds is the best method of preventive action by the most responsible officials (Lončar 2011, p. 543). If there is any doubt about the independence of the SAI, the question arises regarding its ability to perform its specified function. Therefore, the employees and the management of the SAI should contribute to strengthening public trust in its work.

In addition to the external control embodied in the SAI of the Republic of Serbia, the traditional concept of control by the Budget Inspection has been retained. This form of control in the Republic of Serbia dates back to the 19th century (or more precisely, 1 July 1829), when the Law on Main Control was passed, which regulated the issue of state budget control and several bylaws that accompanied the implementation of the said law. Until 1869, the Main Control was responsible to the State Council, which was the supreme legislative committee, but it also included certain judicial functions. From 1868 it was under the patronage of the government, and the members of that body were appointed like other state officials (Tošović 2013, p. 55).[32] There is no difference in relation to the present solution. The Budget Inspection remains under the patronage of the executive power (i.e., the government), considering that it is part of the Ministry of Finance, while at the level of autonomous territories and local self-government units, it is responsible to the executive body for its work. Today, budget control implies a set of control measures and methods applied to provide protection against illegal and irrational spending of budget funds, that is, to harmonise budget spending with the adopted budget policy and economic policy goals. To prevent a budget deficit and achieve financial stability, public revenues must be spent efficiently and rationally in accordance with the adopted budget, and control over public expenditures must be independent (An elković 2010, p. 88).

However, regarding the Budget Inspection, it is not possible to assess a greater degree of independence, bearing in mind that it comprises civil servants employed in the Ministry of Finance or civil servants employed in the autonomous territories and local self-government units. The works of the Budget Inspection and the SAI differ. After the completion of the inspection, the Budget Inspection compiles a report on the inspection control and proposes measures for eliminating the established illegalities and irregularities in budget fund expenditures. By a decision, it orders the subject of the budget control to take measures for eliminating such irregularities and returning illegal payments to the budget fund,

---

32 Article 16 of the Law on the General Control, *Serbian Gazette*, No. 103, 10 May 1892. Article 1 of the aforementioned law specified that the body was the State Accounting Court and that it was empowered to review and audit all state accounts and other accounts that were under the state supervision. Article 15 stated that the body was authorised to audit, review, and liquidate general administrative accounts and other chief accounts of the State Treasury.

56 Jelena Kostić and Marina Matić Bošković

and an administrative dispute may be initiated against that decision.[33] As can be concluded, the Budget Inspection has administrative and legal powers, which the SAI lacks. Since it is an administrative body, it cannot impose penalties but only order the undertaking of certain activities at the level of the subject of inspection. The SAI prepares an audit report that contains opinions and recommendations for eliminating illegalities and irregularities.

Although there is a high possibility that in the procedure of controlling business books, reports, records, and other documentation prepared by public fund users, the SAI and the Budget Inspection will find evidence indicating the commission of a certain criminal act, the Decree on Labour, Authorizations and Budget Inspection does not prescribe the obligation to report criminal acts. The manner of filing a criminal report is provided by the Criminal Procedure Code. In accordance with it, state bodies, other bodies, and legal and natural persons should report criminal acts whose perpetrators are prosecuted ex officio and which have been committed or discovered in another way, under the conditions provided by law or other regulation.[34] Therefore, state bodies are obliged to report criminal acts, which are prosecuted ex officio, and which they have found out while exercising their powers.[35] However, there is no information that any of these institutions has acted in accordance with Article 281 of the Criminal Procedure Code.

The SAI of the Republic of Serbia and the Budget Inspection were established to ensure financial discipline in the public sector. Detecting criminal offences is not the primary focus of their activities. However, combating crime in accordance with the current trends in the field of criminal policy requires a joint action of society as a whole, not only the police and judicial authorities (Matić Bošković and Kostić 2019, pp. 255–279).[36] With their knowledge, they can contribute not only to the detection of criminal acts but also the acquisition of the evidence necessary for the initiation of criminal proceedings and the issuance of the final judgement (Matić 2013, pp. 123–154; Šuput 2014, pp. 331–346).

4.5 Conclusion

In this chapter, we have started from the hypotheses that the system of financial responsibility has not yet been established at full capacity in the public sector institutions of the Republic of Serbia and that in practice, it lacks a consistent

---

33 Article 87 of the Law on Budget System.
34 Article 10 of the Regulations on the Work, Authorizations and Characteristics of the Budget Inspection, *Official Gazette of the Republic of Serbia*, No. 93/2017.
35 Article 281 of the Criminal Procedural Code, *The Official Gazette of the Republic of Serbia*, Nos. 72/2011, 101/2011, 121/2012, 32/2013, 45/2013, 55/2014, and 35/2019.
36 The State Audit Institution can encourage input from citizens and civil organisations as well. For example, fraud hotlines are used by the UK National Audit Office to encourage the public and whistle-blowers to provide information on suspected irregularities in the management of public funds (van Zyl et al. 2009, p. 23). Such a mechanism also exists in the US and South Korea.

application of the principle of fiscal transparency. Both hypotheses have been confirmed.

According to the reports of the SAI of the Republic of Serbia, which have been reviewed in this chapter, it seems that some budget users have just started to establish financial management and control and that most users have established internal audit. However, the concern is raised on whether the concept of internal financial control has been accepted according to its purpose, bearing in mind that one of the main internal audit activities is to check the financial management and control system's adequacy and efficiency in relation to the compliance of public sector institutions and their operations with laws, internal acts, and contracts as well as the reliability and completeness of financial and other information. We could not identify that legislation has been implemented in practice according to the definition. It could mean that the role of internal audit has not been adequately understood.

Bearing in mind that internal financial control has not yet been established at full capacity in the Republic of Serbia, the question should be considered whether there is a need for amendments of the legislation to ensure consistency and mitigate legal gaps. Instead of two Rulebooks, the organisation and functioning of internal audit and financial management and control could be regulated by a law which could prescribe the sanctions for its non-establishment. The proposed approach will lead to the improvement of the legality, efficiency, and effectiveness of business operations among public fund users.

The state institutions are accountable to both parliament and the citizens for the management of taxpayers' funds. Transparency is a very important part of such accountability, bearing in mind that citizens contribute to public revenues. The SAI's role is highly relevant for strengthening the transparency of financial operations. Considering the SAI's lack of reaction when the Final Account of the Republic of Serbia has not been adopted for 17 years, the SAI should be encouraged to react in such a situation. This will contribute to increasing the citizens' confidence in the work of public sector institutions. It is one of the main tasks of the SAI, which the SAI failed to implement.

In addition to the establishment of the SAI of the Republic of Serbia, the traditional concept of public spending control embodied in the Budget Inspection has been retained. However, the SAI has a greater degree of independence than the Budget Inspection, which is accountable to the government or the executive body of the autonomous territory and local self-government units for its work. In contrast to the Budget Inspection, the SAI is not authorised to issue decisions that require certain behaviours of public fund users but is authorised to file misdemeanour and criminal charges in case the business operations of public fund users fail to comply with relevant national legislation.

Despite the three parallel systems of financial control in Serbia, further actions should be taken to improve financial accountability and transparency in the public sector. The Republic of Serbia should improve the system of training of managers and employees in the public sector to increase their awareness of the importance and the role of financial responsibility and raise their existing level

58 Jelena Kostić and Marina Matić Bošković

of knowledge about their own responsibility for efficient, economical, and legal financial management and use of public funds. In contrast to the Budget Inspection, which also represents a form of external financial control, the SAI has a higher level of independence in its actions. According to its role, the SAI should act for the benefit and on behalf of the citizens. Although the SAI is responsible to parliament for its activities, the highest state institutions should be warned in cases of regulation violations. Its advisory role should be in the service of all citizens (taxpayers) but not in the service of state institutions. To raise awareness of the SAI's role, not only additional training programmes should be organised but also conferences and round table discussions with representatives of other state institutions and the non-governmental sector.

References

Analytical Report Accompanying the Document, Communication from the Commission in the European Parliament and the Council, Commission Opinion on Serbia's Application for Membership in the European Union. (2011). [Online]. 1 October 2012. Available from: http://ec.auropa.eu//englargement/pdf/kez_documents/2011/prackage/sr_analytical_report_2011_en.pdf. [Accessed 20 April 2020].

Anđelković, M. (2010). *Budget Law.* [*Budžetsko pravo*]. Niš: Faculty of Law, University of Niš.

Audit Report on the Final Account of the Budget of the Republic of Serbia for 2016. (2017, 29 December). Belgrade: The State Audit Institution of the Republic of Serbia. No. 400-534/2017.03/31.

Audit Report on the Final Account of the Budget of the Republic of Serbia for 2017. (2018, 14 December). Belgrade: The State Audit Institution of the Republic of Serbia. No. 400-575/2018-03/36.

Audit Report on the Final Account of the Budget of the Republic of Serbia for 2018. (2019, 20 September). Belgrade: The State Audit Institution of the Republic of Serbia. No. 400-200/2019-03/16.

Dobre, C. (2012). Great Britain and Germany Supreme Audit Institutions. *Annals of Faculty of Economics, University of Oradea*, 1, pp. 695–701.

González, B., López, A. and Garcia, R. (2008). How do Supreme Audit Institutions measure the impact of their work? In: Jorge, S. ed. *Implementing Reforms in Public Sector Accounting.* Coimbra: Coimbra University Press, pp. 503–517.

Lončar, Z. (2011). Legal issues of state budget audit procedures. [Pravna pitanja postupaka revizije državnog budžeta]. In: *Aktuelna pitanja savremenog zakonodavstva.* Belgrade: Association of Lawyers of Serbia and Republika Srpska, pp. 529–544.

Matić, M. (2013). Supreme Audit Institution and the fight against corruption. [Vrhovne revizorske institucije i borba protiv korupcije]. In: Ćirić, J. ed. *Borba protiv korupcije—iskustva i poređenja.* Belgrade: Institute of Comparative Law, pp. 123–154.

Matić Bošković, M. and Kostić, J. (2019). Specialization of state authorities in combating financial crime and corruption. [Specijalizacija državnih organa u suzbijanju finansijskog kriminaliteta i korupcije]. *Srpska politička Misao* [Online], 3, pp. 255–279. https://doi.org/10.22182/spm.6532019.11.

Norton, D. S. and Smith, L. M. (2018). Contrast and foundation of the public oversight roles of the US Government Accountability office and the UK national audit office. *Public Administration Review*, 68(5), pp. 921–931.

Rabrenović, A. (2009). *Financial Accountability as a Condition for EU Membership.* Belgrade: Institute of Comparative Law.

Rabrenović, A. and Ćorić Erić, V. (2012). The role of the National Assembly in the application of the external audit recommendations. [Uloga Narodne skupštine u primeni preporuka eksterne revizije]. In: Rabrenović, A. and Ćeranić, J. eds. *Usklađivanje prava Republike Srbije sa pravnim tekovinama EU, prioriteti, problemi, perspektive.* Belgrade: Institute of Comparative Law, pp. 282–299.

The Report on the Audit of Financial Report and Regularity of Business Operations in the Anti-Corruption Agency of the Republic of Serbia for 2017. (2018, 27 August). Belgrade. No. 400-658/2018-03/29.

The Report on the Audit of Financial Report and Regularity of Business Operations in the Ministry of Youth and Sport of the Republic of Serbia for 2018. (2019, 2 December). Belgrade. No. 400-213/2019-03/12.

The Report on the Audit of Financial Report of the Ministry of Defence. (2019, 19 August). Belgrade. No. 400-2015/2019-03/13.

The Report on the Audit of Parts of the Financial Report and Regularity of Business Operations in the Ministry of Labour, Employment and Social Affairs of the Republic of Serbia for 2016. (2017, 21 December). No. 400-2033/2017-03/26.

Šuput, J. (2012). Internal financial control in the prevention of the criminal offence misappropriation of budget funds. [Interna finansijska kontrola u prevenciji krivičnog dela nenamenskog trošenja budžetskih sredstava]. *Nauka, bezbednost, policija*, 1, pp. 153–163.

Šuput, J. (2013). Internal financial control in public sector. [Interna finansijska kontrola u javnom sektoru]. In: Rabrenović, A. and Ćeranić, J. eds. *Usklađivanje prava Republike Srbije sa pravnim tekovinama Evropske unije: prioriteti, problemi, perspective.* Belgrade: Institute of Comparative Law, pp. 247–261.

Šuput, J. (2014). The role of the State Audit Institution in prevention of the white-collar crime in the public sector. [Državna revizorska institucija i prevencija kriminaliteta belog okovratnika u javnom sektoru]. *Collection of Papers, Faculty of Law, University of Niš*, 67, pp. 331–346.

Šuput, J. (2015). *Fiscal Offences.* [*Fiskalna krivična dela*]. Doctoral dissertation. Niš: Faculty of Law, University of Niš.

Tošović, N. (2013). *Budget Control.* [*Budžetska kontrola*]. Belgrade: Faculty of Law of the University of Belgrade.

Van Zyl, A., Ramkumar, V. and De Renzio, P. (2009). *Responding to Challenges of Supreme Audit Institutions: Can Legislatures and Civil Society Help?* Bergen: U4 Anti-Corruption Resource Centre, Chr Michelsen Institute.

Watson, S. (1997). What should count as public expenditure. In: Corry, D. ed. *Public Expenditure, Effective Management and Control.* London: The Dryden Press/ Institute for Public Policy Research, pp. 41–62.

White, F. and Hollingsworth, K. (1999). *Audit, Accountability and Government.* Oxford: Clarendon Press.

Part II
Fairness and rights

5 Disciplinary liability of judges
The Polish case

Piotr Mikuli and Maciej Pach

5.1 Introduction

This chapter focuses on those normative solutions in the Polish law that relate to the procedures applied to hold judges accountable under the concept of disciplinary liability. First of all, it discusses the measures practised in Poland after several legal modifications that the Law and Justice Party (PiS) introduced during the years 2015–2020. It is argued that the new measures concerning judges' disciplinary liability fail to achieve greater judicial transparency and are actually inconsistent with the national constitution and European Union (EU) and international standards. Under the guise of formulating more just rules for individual judicial accountability, Polish authorities aim to subjugate the entire judicial system, which must be perceived in light of the systematic breach of the rule of law (Sadurski 2019).

Referring to the introduction to this volume, it must be emphasised that the concept of accountability may be perceived very broadly (in relation to the judiciary, see Shetreet 2013; Tushnet 2013; Piana 2010; Yusulf 2010). Disciplinary responsibility is one of the various mechanisms to keep the judiciary accountable. Obviously, the notion of accountability when referring to the judicial power also comprises several mechanisms, not only relating to judges as such (internal and external assessment [evaluation] and periodic reporting by the judiciary) but also to functions of institutions beyond the scope of the dispensation of justice (e.g., courts reporting on financial issues). In this context, E. Meyer and T. Bustamante denote judicial accountability as 'the set of mechanisms aimed at making judges and courts personally or institutionally responsible for behaviours and decisions contrary to constitutional or legal standards' (Meyer and Bustamante 2020).

The titular disciplinary liability, in turn, means the use of certain measures to hold judges accountable for unlawful acts (that are not common offences) or to judicial ethics that are not subject to appeal in judiciary due course. At the same time, enforcing accountability may result in certain sanctions and penalties, including removal from office.

Regardless of which system of government is adopted in a contemporary democratic state ruled by law, in both parliamentary and presidential regimes, the separation of the judiciary from the legislative and the executive powers is necessary to implement the rule of law. Today's democratic states have developed a number of safeguards to guarantee both the judiciary's independence and the high level of competence of those who have to exercise judicial power. Such guarantees are stipulated not only by the provisions of the constitution and of judicial procedures but also by the political elite and society's legal and political culture as a whole. In this context, both the Venice Commission's opinions and the jurisprudence of international courts show the adoption of two different standards in terms of the legal requirements for judicial appointments and precisely the issue of judges' responsibility. Generally, in this approach, regulations that are formally insufficient to ensure an objective assessment of the functioning of political power and those concerning the influence of political power on the formation of the judiciary's personal substrate are accepted in the so-called countries of old democracies. It is so because of the extra-legal and political standards that sanction the judiciary's separation. In contrast, in the so-called countries of young democracies, importance is attached to several legal safeguards for this separation due to the inadequate legal culture that has to be developed over generations. Of course, this approach is understandable to a certain extent, but it has many disadvantages. Apart from the very criterion of the division into stabilised/old and new democracies, the problem is that in Western countries that attach importance to the standards of the rule of law, a significant increase in populist sentiment can also be observed in recent years. In countries where an erosion of democracy is witnessed, such as in Poland and Hungary, the existing standards protecting the judiciary's independence have been disregarded relatively easily. Therefore, an issue of concern is that in countries with no formal safeguards, it will be so much easier to bring about a pathological politicisation of the judiciary without making a 'jump on the courts'. In this context, the importance of formal safeguards is appreciated, and they can certainly make it significantly more difficult for populist politicians to take over the courts in a hostile manner. Legal solutions that have been in place for many years also contribute to developing appropriate attitudes of respect for the law and a suitable political culture. Regardless of this finding, there is no doubt that to maintain the courts' principles of independence, democracy, and separation of powers, social-political consensus on these fundamental values is important. Without this, any legal and formal solutions may fall apart like a house of cards due to a populist revolution.

The disciplinary liability of judges is one of those institutions that can be used exceptionally easily to undermine the essence of the judiciary's independence and to provoke repressions, the 'chilling effect' violating the right to a fair trial.

However, there is not the slightest doubt that the rules for holding judges liable to disciplinary action, as well as the question of waiving judicial immunity, must be extremely precise and structured in such a way as to eliminate, as far as possible, any irregularities and pathologies that may arise in practice (see Kosař 2016). Therefore, many models of judges' accountability can be imagined, including the broad aspect of the notion of disciplinary liability as such. However, the basic premise of these mechanisms is to strive for objectivity in the assessment of a judge's disciplinary misconduct, as well as to ensure impartiality in the procedures (procedural fairness) and to safeguard, as much as possible, against the discretionary treatment of a judge's misconduct so that the institution of disciplinary responsibility does not develop into a mechanism that tramples on judicial independence. In the latter context, it is necessary to create such a definition of the tort and disciplinary misconduct, which cannot interfere with the judgement sphere under any circumstances. Of course, the latter may be assessed directly by a higher court in the event of an appeal/revocation by the parties, or indirectly when the assessment system for the promotion of judges takes account of the number of judgements, handed down by the candidate concerned, that were amended or overturned by higher courts.

5.2 Models of disciplinary liability of judges and the Polish solutions

It is challenging to make a simple classification of the models of disciplinary responsibility because various legal solutions in this respect may overlap with other types of personal responsibility of judges (e.g., involving complaints lodged by the public or the parties to the proceedings) and may also be strictly connected to separate procedures aimed at the judges' removal from office (see Kosař and Spáč 2018). It should also be emphasised that the understanding and treatment of the institution of disciplinary responsibility may vary. For example, in the Polish tradition, disciplinary responsibility is explained not only by defining the material scope of this responsibility (as done at the outset of this chapter) but also by referring to individuals entitled to assess a person's guilt in committing a disciplinary tort. The point is that these individuals must be engaged in the same profession as the guilty person. In this way, the disciplinary accountability is internal: a certain 'court of equals'. In the case of public trust professions, the internal disciplinary responsibility is the rule (the responsibility of teachers, professors, officials, attorneys), with the possibility of challenging the final decision in court. In the case of judges' disciplinary responsibility, the problem is that from beginning to end, the disciplinary delicacy in this regard should be decided by judges, without external control, which may be subject to some criticism. Of course, the disadvantages of such a solution can be countered here by ensuring the judiciary's necessary independence.

Referring to different models of holding judges liable for disciplinary action, in general terms, it may be pointed out that the bodies competent to decide in such cases may comprise certain types of disciplinary courts, often created as a composition of the ordinary courts (e.g., in the Federal Republic of Germany and in Austria). Another solution is to entrust these tasks to the high councils of the judiciary or their internal bodies. The model based on the judicial council concept seems to be quite attractive, especially in the council's diverse membership. In such a system, it is possible to imagine creating a mechanism where lay members (i.e., people who do not come directly from the judicial community alone) can be involved in handing down the guilty verdict on disciplinary responsibility. It is also worth noting that the judges' responsibility may also comprise various

66 *Piotr Mikuli and Maciej Pach*

procedures regarding complaints against courts. In this regard, a particular role may be played by special offices linked to judicial authorities (e.g., in England and Wales) or ombudsmen (in Sweden and Finland).

5.3 Scope of disciplinary liability of judges and disciplinary penalties in Poland after the changes provided under the PiS administration

As stated above, the principles of independence of courts and judges create an indispensable standard of each democratic state ruled by law. The 1997 Polish Constitution expresses both in Article 173 and Article 178, para. 1, and includes numerous provisions guaranteeing respect thereof. However, it does not mean that judges remain unpunished in the exercise of their office. To ensure the correct functioning of the judiciary and an appropriate social image of judges, the Act of 27 July 2001–Law on Common Courts Organisation (Journal of Laws of 2020, item 365, as amended; hereinafter LCCO), since its very beginning, included provisions enforcing criminal responsibility (by regulating the procedure of immunity waiving) and disciplinary liability for misconduct in office. According to the LCCO:

> A judge is liable to disciplinary actions for misconduct, including an obvious and gross violation of legal provisions and impairment of the authority of the office (disciplinary misconduct).
>
> (Art. 107, § 1)

> A judge is also liable to disciplinary actions for their conduct before the accession to the post if, due to such conduct, they failed to fulfil their respective duties at the state office held at that time or appeared to be unworthy of holding a judicial post.
>
> (Art. 107, § 2)

In the literature, disciplinary misconduct is also conceptualised by a notion of a disciplinary tort, defined as follows: 'A disciplinary tort is an illegal act for which fault can be attributed to a perpetrator, of more than a negligible social harmfulness' (Laskowski 2019, p. 168). It is worth stressing that the above-quoted general provisions of the LCCO have not been amended in the course of almost two decades. It seems justified to notice that an excessively detailed legal definition of disciplinary misconduct may improperly correspond to disciplinary liability aims. Instead, general, unclear provisions could raise judges' fears that disciplinary proceedings can be initiated against them, and such fears could weaken their independence in adjudicating. However, a sufficient means to counteract this threat was provided by the case law of the Supreme Court (SC), interpreting the statutory wordings (e.g., the notion of 'an obvious and gross violation of legal provisions') uniformly and strictly (see Sawiński 2013; LEX, thesis no. 25 and the SC judgement of 29 October 2003, SNO 48/03). Knowing this case law,

Disciplinary liability of judges   67

judges could have predicted what kinds of actions may be qualified as grounds for disciplinary liability.

The initial wording of Article 107 of the LCCO had been in force from 1 October 2001 to 14 February 2020; § 1 was amended only by the Act of 20 December 2019 amending the Act–Law on the Common Courts[1] Organisation, the Act on the Supreme Court, and certain other acts (Journal of Laws of 2020, item 190). Currently, this provision is much more detailed, stating:

> A judge is liable to disciplinary actions for disciplinary misconducts, including 1) an apparent and gross violation of legal provisions, 2) actions or abandonments that can disable or relevantly obstruct the functioning of a judiciary organ/body, 3) actions that question the office status of a judge, the effectiveness of the appointment of a judge or the legitimacy of the constitutional organ of the Republic of Poland, 4) public activities incompatible with the principles of independence of the courts and judges, 5) impairment of the authority of the office.

Points 1 and 5 repeat the previous statutory regulation. Point 4 is identical to Article 178, para. 3 of the Polish Constitution, which forbids judges from performing public activities incompatible with the principles of independence of courts and judges. Nevertheless, taking into account the uninterrupted smear campaign against the judiciary, led by PiS since 2015, points 3 and 4 of the amended § 1 raise crucial doubts. One of the decisive stages of this campaign was changing the system of electing the members of the National Council of Judiciary (NCJ).

The Act of 8 December 2017 amending the Act on the National Council of Judiciary and certain other acts (Journal of Laws of 2018, item 3) abolished the model established in 1990, according to which the judicial self-government elected 15 judge-members of the NCJ[2] (Śledzińska-Simon 2018). Currently, they are elected by the Sejm (first chamber of the parliament). This kind of solution must be assessed as incompatible with Article 187, para. 1 of the Polish Constitution, which in this provision limits the Sejm's appointment function to the election of four deputies of the NCJ, and inconsistent with Article 186 para. 1, which states that the NCJ 'shall safeguard the independence of courts and judges' (see Mikuli 2017). Although Article 187, para. 1, point 2 literally does not regulate who elects judges of the NCJ, Article 186, para. 1 must be taken into consideration in its interpretation. If the politicians directly nominate the majority of the NCJ members, the NCJ's function of safeguarding the judiciary's

---

1 Common courts refer to courts of general jurisdiction and comprise district courts (*sądy rejonowe*), provincial courts (*sądy okręgowe*), and appellate courts (*sądy apelacyjne*). These courts decide (among other things) cases concerning criminal, civil, family, and juvenile law; commercial law; and labour and social security laws—except for cases vested in other special courts.

2 The NCJ comprises 25 members.

68   *Piotr Mikuli and Maciej Pach*

independence may easily be questioned. Meanwhile, the NCJ is the only authority with the power to submit to the President of the Republic of Poland a motion aiming at a judge's appointment (Art. 179). The discussed changes of the NCJ model were introduced with a violation of the constitutional four-year term of office of the previous judicial members of the NCJ. For this reason (and many others), the Act amending the Act on the NCJ is perceived as unconstitutional by the majority of scholars. However, in the judgement of 25 March 2019 (file reference: K 12/18), the Constitutional Tribunal did not share this point of view. It must be mentioned that, at this time, it had already been captured by PiS (Koncewicz 2019; Sadurski 2019), and a person who was illegally elected to the tribunal (Justyn Piskorski) was the 'judge-rapporteur' in this case.

The status of judges appointed by the President of the Republic on the motion of the 'new' NCJ was a subject of many preliminary references directed to the Court of Justice of the European Union (see, e.g., the SC's three decisions of 30 August 2018; file references III PO 7/18, III PO 8/18, III PO 9/18). Just after the discussed 2019 amendments to the LCCO were passed and before they entered into force, on the motion of the first president of the SC of that time, a resolution of the Civil, Criminal, and Labour and Social Security Chambers of the Supreme Court of 23 January 2020 (file reference: BSA I-4110–1/20) was adopted. It aimed to solve the issue raised on the grounds of the interpretation of the provisions of the Code of Civil Procedure and the Code of Criminal Procedure concerning the unlawful bench composition. According to this resolution:

> A court formation is unduly appointed within the meaning of Article 439(1) (2) of the Code of Criminal Procedure or a court formation is unlawful within the meaning of Article 379(4) of the Code of Civil Procedure also where the court formation includes a person appointed to the office of a judge of the Supreme Court on the application of the National Council for the Judiciary formed following the Act of 8 December 2017 amending the Act on the National Council for the Judiciary and certain other Acts (Journal of Laws of 2018, item 3).

This resolution was later quashed by the Constitutional Tribunal (see the judgement of 20 April 2020, file reference: U 2/20), although the majority of academia argued that the tribunal acted beyond its competence, as it cannot assess the constitutionality of the SC's resolutions. It is also worth noting that the intellectual justification for this judgement, which remains at an extremely low level, was based on a caricatured reading of both the principles of the Polish Constitution and the EU law, which may be perceived as a further degradation of the Polish system of constitutional review.

The Polish judges' long-lasting resistance against the so-called reform of the judiciary, which in fact means unconstitutional legislative changes, violating the EU law at the same time, resulted in an expansion of the disciplinary liability conditions mentioned in Article 107, § 1 of the LCCO. Such clauses as 'actions or abandonments that can disable or relevantly obstruct the functioning of a judiciary organ/body' and 'actions that question the office status of a judge, the effectiveness of the appointment of a judge or the legitimacy of the constitutional organ of the Republic of Poland' were added to the statutory catalogue. It would seem that these regulations were supposed to create a chilling effect on the judges to discourage them from taking advantage of legal procedures to verify the status of judges appointed on the motion of the 'new' NCJ (Laskowski 2019, pp. 178–180). For instance, currently, a preliminary reference to the Court of Justice of the European Union (CJEU), suggesting some legal drawbacks of an act of appointment of a judge, can be treated as 'an action that can relevantly obstruct the functioning of a judiciary organ' (e.g., because of the length of time between the preliminary reference and the preliminary ruling of the CJEU) or as 'an action that questions the effectiveness of the appointment of a judge' and trigger disciplinary liability or at least, an investigation to be conducted by the disciplinary commissioner. The disciplinary commissioner for common court judges and two deputy disciplinary commissioners for common court judges, appointed by the minister of justice, are now equipped with a specific statutory basis for taking steps of that kind. Moreover, according to the mentioned Act of 20 December 2019 that amended the LCCO, a judgement of a disciplinary court stating an act of commission of a disciplinary tort in one of the two new forms obliges the court to punish the judge with the most severe penalties, that is, a transfer to another place of service or dismissal from the office of a judge.

Furthermore, the evolution of the LCCO provisions pertaining to the disciplinary penalties in the time of the PiS administration should be assessed in the aggregate context of political power activities towards the judiciary after 2015 and the critical reaction of the judicial self-government. For more than 15 years, the statutory catalogue of disciplinary penalties has encompassed the following:

- an admonition,
- a reprimand,
- deprivation from the function held,
- a transfer to another place of service,
- a dismissal from the office of a judge.

(Art. 109, § 1 of the LCCO)

The Act of 30 November 2016 amending the Act–Law on the Common Courts Organisation and certain other acts (Journal of Laws of 2016, item 2103) added a new sort of penalty: 'lowering the basic salary of a judge by five to twenty per cent for a period from six months up to two years' (new Art. 109, § 1, Point 2a of the LCCO). The Act of 8 December 2017 on the Supreme Court (Journal of Laws of 2018, item 5; hereinafter the 2017 Act on the SC) increased the upper limit of the allowed reduction to 50%. Another change was provided by the mentioned Act of 20 December 2019 amending the LCCO. A new penalty appeared in the LCCO: a financial penalty in the amount of one month's income increased by judicial income extras. Both of these new penalties can be adjudicated for all kinds of disciplinary torts, in principle, except for the two new categories of torts linked with questioning the judicial nominations. It is said to be 'in principle' because for the new kinds of disciplinary torts, these penalties can also come into play but only in less grave cases (the new § 1a in Art. 109 of the LCCO).

In light of the current legal status, after the changes provided under the PiS administration, the catalogue of disciplinary torts and the disciplinary penalties concerning the SC judges are almost identical as in the case of judges of common courts (see Art. 72, § 1 and Art. 75, § 1 of the 2017 Act on the SC). The only and minor difference is that there is no such penalty as a transfer to another seat of service in the SC judges' case. Furthermore, for 'actions or abandonments that can disable or relevantly obstruct the functioning of a judiciary organ/body', 'actions questioning the status of a judge, the effectiveness of the appointment of a judge or the legitimacy of the constitutional organ of the Republic of Poland', or 'public activities incompatible with the principles of independence of the courts and judges', the only penalty that can be imposed on an SC judge is dismissal from office. In contrast, an alternative penalty in the form of a transfer to another place of service is imposed on common court judges. An exception to this rule is made for less grave cases, which allows the disciplinary court to adjudicate the reduction of income, financial penalty, or dismissal from the function held.

Due to the lack of different regulations on the matter of disciplinary torts and disciplinary penalties in the Act of 25 July 2002–Law on the Administrative Courts Organisation (Journal of Law of 2019, item 2167, as amended; hereinafter LACO), the provisions regarding the SC and the common courts shall also apply to the Supreme Administrative Court (SAC) judges and to the Voivodship Administrative Court (VAC)[3] judges, as appropriate (Art. 49, § 1 and Art. 29, § 1 of the LACO). Therefore, the above remarks pertain to both the VAC judges and the SAC judges.

The discussed Act of 20 December 2019 that amended the LCCO and the Act on the SC established disciplinary torts referring to military judges—the same as referring to common court judges—concerning questioning judges' status (see Art. 37, § 2 of the Act of 21 August 1997–the Law on the Military Courts Organisation [Journal of Laws of 2019, item 2216, as amended]; hereinafter LMCO). Similarly, new disciplinary penalties for military judges, added after 2015, are identical (see Art. 39, § 1, Points 2a and 2b of the LMCO), with a minor difference—allowing the reduction in a judge's basic salary by 5% to 20%, not 50%.

To sum up, the changes in the provisions that regulate the subject of disciplinary liability and disciplinary penalties are illustrations of coercive legislation against judges (Kardas 2020). If this analysis is limited to the new provisions' wording, perhaps it would not entitle the authors to make such alarming remarks. However, a proper interpretation of these provisions must be put in the context of the current situation of the Polish judiciary, which, after 2015, involves permanent attacks on judges from the side of the legislative and the executive

---

3 Administrative courts in Poland comprise 16 VACs and one nationwide SAC.

Disciplinary liability of judges 71

branches. Piotr Kardas rightly argues that disciplinary proceedings against judges 'have become an important aspect of the conflict about the rule of law and the primacy of law over politics' (Kardas 2020, p. 152). The new mechanisms must be perceived as part of a package of legal changes to the judiciary; the system was created to ensure that judges would be subservient to the political will of the authorities (Gajda-Roszczynialska and Markiewicz 2020). It must be noted that in recent years, the Disciplinary Commissioner for Common Court Judges and two Deputy Disciplinary Commissioners initiated investigations, in many cases linked to the activities of judges in judicial associations and even worse, sometimes also concerning decisions made by judges during the courts' proceedings (Mikuli 2019). Gajda-Roszczynialska and Markiewicz (2020) are right in stating that although disciplinary proceedings are by no means the only forms of repression that affect judges, they may create an instrument for breaking the rule of law in Poland.

5.4 Current jurisdiction of disciplinary courts and of disciplinary commissioners

The crucial element of the 'reform' of disciplinary proceedings introduced by the PiS parliamentary majority was the establishment of a new chamber in the SC, namely the Disciplinary Chamber (DC). In the overwhelming opinion of academia, the new chamber is perceived as a bogus court, as it has a special systemic and independent status within the SC,[4] which is not envisaged by the constitution; moreover, it is fully composed of judges appointed by the politically captured NCJ (Zoll and Wortham 2019, p. 895). For these and many other reasons, at the end of 2019, the SC adjudicated that the DC was not a court in light of Article 47 of the Charter of Fundamental Rights of the EU, Article 6 of the European Convention on Human Rights and Article 45 of the Polish Constitution (see the SC judgement of 5 December 2019, III PO 7/18). In this judgement, the SC took into account the judgement of 19 November 2019. Replying to preliminary references regarding the independence of judges of its DC,[5] the CJEU ruled that the Polish SC, as the referring court, should assess whether the DC was in fact independent. In its judgement, the CJEU set the criteria for this assessment, also quoting its previous case law (see Krajewski and Ziółkowski 2019). Furthermore, on 8 April 2020, when the European Commission–initiated infringement procedure against Poland was underway (C-791/19), the CJEU ordered an interim measure obliging Poland

---

4 The chamber is in fact an extraordinary, separate court only formally linked to the rest of the SC. The judges in this chamber are paid a 40% higher salary, and proceedings benches (apart from judges) comprise lay judges elected by the Senate.
5 These refer to the joined cases C-585/18, C-624/18, and C-625/18. See InfoCuria 'Judgement of the Court (Grand Chamber)' (19 November 2019) <http://curia.europa.eu/juris/document/document.jsf?docid=220770&text=&dir=&doclang=EN&part=1&occ=first&mode=DOC&pageIndex=0&cid=611315> [Accessed 20 November 2020].

to immediately suspend the application of the national provisions on the powers of the DC of the SC concerning judicial disciplinary cases.[6]

As far as the jurisdiction in the SC judges' disciplinary cases is concerned, according to Article 73, § 1 of the 2017 Act, in the first instance, the SC adjudicates by a bench composed of two judges of the DC and one lay judge of the SC. In turn, in the second instance, the SC adjudicates by a bench consisting of three judges of the DC and two lay judges of the SC. In light of the previous statutory provisions, in the first instance, the SC adjudicated by a bench comprising three judges of the SC, and in the second instance, by a bench consisting of seven judges of the SC. The new act maintains previously existing regulations regarding the disciplinary commissioner of the SC and his/her deputy. Both are still elected for a four-year term by the board of the SC (Art. 74 of the 2017 Act on the SC). However, compared with the 2002 Act, the new provisions have a different regulation on the issue of the authorities entitled to request the disciplinary commissioner of the SC to initiate an investigation. The competences of the first president of the SC, the board of the SC, and the disciplinary commissioner of the SC's own initiative, remain intact. Nevertheless, currently, the list of entitled authorities is expanded, as it also comprises the president of the DC of the SC, the public prosecutor general, and the national public prosecutor. Considering that the public prosecutor general is at the same time the minister of justice and that the national public prosecutor is the deputy minister, the evolution of the provisions cannot be perceived in other way than permitting the executive's pressure on the judicial power.

After conducting an investigation, the disciplinary commissioner of the SC may either initiate disciplinary proceedings against the SC judge or refuse to do so if there are no grounds for such an action (Art. 76, §§ 2 and 4 of the 2017 Act on the SC). The disciplinary commissioner has to inform the President of the Republic of Poland and all the authorities entitled to request the launch of the investigation about the refusal in initiating disciplinary proceedings. These authorities may appeal to the first instance's disciplinary court (Art. 76, § 4 in fine). They can take advantage of the same competence when the disciplinary commissioner of the SC discontinues the disciplinary proceedings due to the lack of grounds for submitting a case for examination. Once again, it should be emphasised that the disciplinary court of the first instance is currently the DC of the SC, created from scratch under the PiS administration, with judges having strong personal ties with Minister of Justice Zbigniew Ziobro. Moreover, if the disciplinary court quashes the decision of the disciplinary commissioner of the SC, the guidelines provided by this court are binding for the commissioner (Art. 76, § 6).

---

6 At the time of writing, the CJEU judgement of April 2020 has been obeyed only partially, as the DC still operates in judicial immunity cases. Apart from its role in disciplinary procedures, this organ is also entitled to waive judicial immunity. Discretional waiving of the immunity also plays an important role in persecuting judges who dare to criticise the governmental actions that intimidate the judiciary.

Disciplinary liability of judges   73

According to Article 110, § 1 of the LCCO, disciplinary cases against judges of common courts shall be heard in two instances. In the first instance, adjudication is generally handled by disciplinary courts at appeal courts by a bench of three judges. In exceptional situations enumerated in the provision, the SC adjudicates by a bench of two judges of the DC and one lay judge of the SC.[7] In the second instance, the jurisdiction belongs to the SC acting as a bench of two judges of the DC and one lay judge of the SC. Thus, the final judgement in disciplinary cases against judges is supposed to be adopted by the chamber of the SC, which was created from scratch under the PiS government and is accused of strong politicisation, shaped entirely on the motion of the 'new' NCJ.

Another sign of the politicisation of disciplinary proceedings against judges can be observed on the grounds of the new Article 110a, § 1 of the LCCO, added by the 2017 Act on the SC. According to this provision, the minister of justice has the competence to entrust the duties of a disciplinary court judge in an appeal court, for a six-year term of office (Art. 110a, § 3), to a common court judge with at least ten years of experience as a judge. Thus, in disciplinary cases in appeal courts, only judges entrusted by a politician (a minister) may handle disciplinary cases. The obligatory consultation with the NCJ has not changed much because, as noted above, the NCJ has been packed with the politicians' nominees. Moreover, the NCJ's opinion does not bind the minister of justice in any way. Another factor that raises doubts from the perspective of the court's independence is that the presidents of disciplinary courts are appointed by the president of the DC of the SC (Art. 110b, § 1).

The crucial new authorities, introduced to the LCCO by the 2017 Act on the SC, are the disciplinary commissioner for common court judges and two deputy disciplinary commissioners for common court judges, appointed by the minister of justice for a four-year term of office (Art. 112, § 3 of the LCCO). They act as prosecutors before disciplinary courts (Kardas 2020, pp. 93–102). Apart from them, prosecutors in disciplinary cases against judges can also serve as deputy disciplinary commissioners at appeal courts and deputy disciplinary commissioners at regional courts (Art. 112, § 1). According to Article 112, § 2:

> In cases of appeal court judges and presidents and vice-presidents of appeal courts and regional courts, the following persons may act as prosecutors before disciplinary courts: the Disciplinary Commissioner for Common Court Judges and Deputy Disciplinary Commissioners for Common Court Judges. In cases of other regional court judges and presidents and vice-presidents of district courts, the person authorised to act as a prosecutor shall be a deputy disciplinary commissioner at an appeal court, and in cases of other district court judges and trainee judges, this shall be a deputy disciplinary commissioner at a regional court.

---

7 Before the 2017 Act on the SC entered into force, also amending Art. 110 of the LCCO, the jurisdiction in disciplinary cases against judges belonged in the first instance to appeal courts and in the second instance to bench of SC judges.

However, the 'central' commissioners are allowed to 'take over the case conducted by a deputy disciplinary commissioner' operating at a regional court or at an appeal court and to 'hand over the case to that commissioner' (Art. 112a, §§ 1a and 3). A deputy disciplinary commissioner at an appeal court and a deputy disciplinary commissioner at a regional court are appointed by the disciplinary commissioner for common court judges (Art. 112, §§ 6 and 7).

After the Act of 20 December 2019 amending the LCCO entered into force, general assemblies of judges of appeal court areas and court circuits, as appropriate, have been deprived of their powers to submit to the 'central' commissioner candidatures for the office of a deputy commissioner at an appeal court and at a regional court. It proves that the powers of the central commissioner, who is nominated by the minister of justice, have been strengthened at the expense of judicial self-government bodies. Furthermore, the establishment of the institutions of the disciplinary commissioner for common court judges and both deputies already manifests centralisation and politicisation of the disciplinary commissioner function. Although the institution of the central disciplinary commissioner was established earlier, the commissioner was appointed by the NCJ among candidatures submitted by the general assemblies of judges of appeal court areas. In turn, deputies of the central commissioner were elected by judicial self-government representation in appeal court areas and court circuits. Currently, the central commissioner (and his/her deputies) is (are) discretionally appointed by the minister of justice, and in turn, the central commissioner freely nominates deputy disciplinary commissioners at appeal courts and regional courts.

It should be emphasised that the central disciplinary commissioner (currently Justice Piotr Schab), as well as both of his deputies (Justices Michał Lasota and Przemysław Radzik)—owing their nominations to Minister of Justice Ziobro—are extraordinarily diligent in launching disciplinary proceedings against judges who have criticised the controversial changes in the judiciary field. According to the latest report of the Association of Polish Judges (Iustitia), describing the period from 2015 to the end of 2019, the disciplinary commissioners initiated investigations or disciplinary proceedings in cases against 31 judges (see Ko cierzy ski 2020, pp. 11–74). Sometimes, the disciplinary commissioners violated the provisions in their jurisdictions. These occurred when they initiated investigations independently, ignoring the fact that the initial jurisdiction belonged to the deputy disciplinary commissioner at the appeal court or the regional court. The LCCO provisions allow the central disciplinary commissioners to take over a case but only under the condition that the 'local' disciplinary commissioner initiated it, thus not from the beginning. One example of such violations was the case of three judges who referred to the CJEU for a preliminary ruling, citing the so-called judiciary reform's nonconformity with EU law (see Mazur 2019, pp. 46–49).

Another proof of the politicisation of disciplinary proceedings in Poland is provided by Article 112b of the LCCO, introduced by the 2017 Act on SC. It allows the minister of justice to appoint 'the Disciplinary Commissioner of the Minister of Justice to conduct a specific case relating to a judge'. If the minister of justice decides to do so, actions in the case taken by any other commissioner are excluded (§ 1). Such a disciplinary commissioner ad hoc is appointed from among common court judges or the SC judges; in some cases, it is also possible to appoint a prosecutor for this office (§ 2). The commissioner 'may initiate proceedings upon the request of the Minister of Justice or join pending proceedings' (§ 3). The commissioner's appointment 'shall be equivalent to a request for initiating investigation proceedings or disciplinary proceedings' (§ 4). According to Article 112b, § 5, the minister is entitled to reappoint a commissioner ad hoc even if the previous appointment has expired, since 'a ruling refusing to initiate disciplinary proceedings, discontinuing disciplinary proceedings or closing disciplinary proceedings becomes final'. This provision has not been applied until now, but it can easily be used as a tool to create a chilling effect among judges, as they have to take into account the fact that the minister of justice can even appoint a commissioner ad hoc several times in a row, to resume investigations and disciplinary proceedings against independent judges who contest the unconstitutional 'judiciary reform', for instance. By any means, the LCCO does not limit the will of the minister, whose political interest may often contradict the interest of the independent judiciary.

The 2017 Act on the SC inducted the disciplinary commissioner of the minister of justice in the LMCO with powers similar to those known from the LCCO's analogous offices of disciplinary commissioners, who were introduced ad hoc into the SC. The disposition of Article 76, §§ 8–11 of the 2017 Act on the SC entitles the President of the Republic of Poland or the minister of justice (if the president did not appoint a disciplinary commissioner) to appoint the extraordinary disciplinary commissioner to handle a specific case relating to a judge of the SC. Such an appointment means that the disciplinary commissioner of the SC and deputies are excluded from taking action in this specific case. After the Act of 20 December 2019 amending the LCCO and other acts entered into force, the President of the Republic of Poland is now allowed to appoint an extraordinary disciplinary commissioner also in cases of administrative court judges (the new § 5 in Art. 48 of the LACO). These are blatant expressions of politicisation of disciplinary proceedings against the SC judges and administrative court judges.

In light of Article 114, § 1, sentence 1 of the LCCO, the authorities entitled to request the disciplinary commissioner to initiate an investigation include the minister of justice, the president of the appeal court or the president of the regional court, the board of the appeal court or the board of the regional court, and the NCJ. The commissioners can also act on their own initiative. A statutory condition that must be fulfilled to initiate an investigation is 'establishing the circumstances necessary to state that the criteria of disciplinary misconduct were satisfied'. After the investigation, if there are grounds for disciplinary proceedings, the disciplinary commissioner is entitled to initiate such proceedings and to 'draw up the disciplinary charges in writing' (§ 3). According to § 7, sentence 1, 'When serving charges, the disciplinary commissioner shall request that the President of the Supreme Court heading the Disciplinary Chamber designate a disciplinary court to examine the case at first instance'. If there are no grounds for disciplinary proceedings, 'the disciplinary commissioner shall issue a decision refusing to initiate proceedings'. However, the minister of justice 'may file an objection within 30 days. Filing an objection shall be equivalent to an obligation to initiate disciplinary proceedings and any instructions of the Minister of Justice regarding further proceedings shall be binding on the disciplinary commissioner' (§ 9). These new powers of the minister were established in the LCCO by the amendment introduced by the 2017 Act on the SC and constitute another example of a potentially coercive regulation against judges who criticise the controversial changes in the judiciary. A government official has an opportunity to oblige the disciplinary commissioner to initiate disciplinary proceedings even if the commissioner does not find it justified.

In the current legal status, the disciplinary jurisdiction for military judges is shaped analogous to that for common court judges. According to Article 39a of the LMCO, in the first instance, disciplinary cases are adjudicated by a bench of three judges at regional military courts. In cases strictly enumerated in the LMCO, the disciplinary jurisdiction belongs to the SC sitting as a bench of two judges of the DC and one lay judge of the SC (and in some cases specific to the SC, as a bench of one judge of the DC). In the second instance, disciplinary cases are adjudicated, in principle, by the SC as a bench of two judges of the DC and one lay judge of the SC (in exceptional cases—the SC by a bench of three judges of the SC).

The 2017 Act on the SC added Article 39b to the LMCO, which stipulates that the minister of justice, having consulted the NCJ, 'shall entrust the duties of a disciplinary court judge at a regional military court to a judge with at least 10 years of experience as a judge' (§ 1). Such a position has a six-year term of office (§ 3). Thus, in this area, a full analogy to the LCCO regulations exists.

The LMCO's regulation on the disciplinary commissioner position is not as complicated as that of the LCCO. The deputies of the disciplinary commissioner, acting at regional military courts, are not established. The only commissioners are the disciplinary commissioner for military court judges and the deputy disciplinary commissioners for military court judges, who are prosecutors before disciplinary courts. The amendment to LMCO introduced by the 2017 Act on the SC also politicised these offices. Currently, the disciplinary commissioner for military court judges and the commissioner's deputy are appointed for a four-year term of office by the minister of justice, after consultation with the minister of national defence and the NCJ (Art. 40, § 2 of the LMCO). According to the previous legal status, they were appointed by the NCJ from among the candidates submitted by the Assembly of Military Court Judges—an organ of judicial self-government.

Until now, disciplinary proceedings in administrative court cases seem to be the most immune to politicisation. The jurisdiction in these cases belongs entirely to the SAC (Art. 48, § 1 of the LACO). In the first instance, the SAC adjudicates by a bench of three judges, and in the second instance by a bench of seven judges. The prosecutors' role is played by the disciplinary commissioner of the SAC and the commissioner's deputy, elected by the board of the SAC for a four-year term of office (Art. 48, § 4). However, it is worth keeping in mind the President of

Disciplinary liability of judges   77

the Republic of Poland's new powers to appoint the extraordinary disciplinary commissioner, which results in excluding the jurisdiction of the disciplinary commissioners acting within the SAC.

5.5 Final remarks

To sum up the preceding discussion and after a review of the arrangements for disciplinary liability, the following findings are presented:

1   The provisions amending the laws relating to the judiciary, specifically the principles and the scope of judges' disciplinary responsibility, in the intention of politicians, aimed at politicising the courts, undermining the principle of separation of powers. In light of political practice and the PiS politicians' statements, there can be no doubt about the ruling party's intentions in this regard.
2   The legal solutions discussed in this text must be considered against the background of other reforms and changes that involve taking political control over independent institutions and bodies. Thus, the PiS majority's measures must be perceived as symptoms of the law system's decay. The law becomes a tool of political repression. As known, one of the most important phenomena of the current form of authoritarianism is that legal institutions or procedures are not abolished but abused, transformed as bodies/organs ready to rubberstamp decisions already made by those who gained political power (Ginsburg and Moustafa 2008).
3   Any legal solution must be assessed against its operation's general context, including political practice (this is a general statement about any constitutional system). Without this, a pure assessment of textual provisions will lead to wrong conclusions. The assessment of the solutions presented without taking 'law in action' (i.e., political practice) would not be so negative. Entrusting the SC with the power to decide on judges' disciplinary matters would finally fall under the judicial concept, referring to autonomy accountability issues. Some may even argue that it may be undesirable, not because of the threat of politicisation but because all judicial disciplinary matters have been closed within 'the judicial bubble'. Meanwhile, in Poland's case, the creation of the DC of the SC, staffed in violation of the constitution by lawyers connected with the ruling party, was nothing else than establishing an external, political machine of harassment and intimidation.

References

Gajda-Roszczynialska, K. and Markiewicz, K. (2020). Disciplinary proceedings as an instrument for breaking the rule of law in Poland. *Hague Journal on the Rule Law.* https://doi.org/10.1007/s40803-020-00146-y.

Ginsburg, T. and Moustafa, T. (2008). Introduction: The functions of courts in authoritarian politics. In: Ginsburg, T. and Moustafa, T. eds. *Rule by Law: The*

78 Piotr Mikuli and Maciej Pach

Politics of Courts in Authoritarian Regimes. Cambridge: Cambridge University Press, pp. 1–22.

Kardas, P. (2020). *Dyscyplinowanie sędziów.* Kraków: Krakowski Isntytut Prawa Karnego.

Koncewicz, T. T. (2019, 27 February). From constitutional to political justice: The tragic trajectories of the Polish Constitutional Court. *VerfBlog* [Online]. Available from: https://verfassungsblog.de/from-constitutional-to-political-justice-the-tragic-trajectories-of-the-polish-constitutional-court/ [Accessed 14 November 2020].

Kosař, D. (2016). *Perils of Judicial Self-Government in Transitional Societies.* Cambridge: Cambridge University Press.

Kosař, D. and Spáč, S. (2018). Conceptualization(s) of judicial independence and judicial accountability by the European network of councils for the judiciary: Two steps forward, one step back. *International Journal for Court Administration*, 9(3), pp. 37–46.

Kościerzyński, J. eds. (2020). *Justice under pressure – repressions as a means of attempting to take control over the judiciary and the prosecution in Poland. Years 2015–2019*, pp. 11-71 [Online]. Avaiable from https://www.iustitia.pl/images/pliki/raport2020/Raport_EN.pdf

Krajewski, M. and Ziółkowski, M. (2019, 26 November). *The Power of 'Appearances' VerfBlog* [Online]. Available from: https://verfassungsblog.de/the-power-of-appearances/. https://doi.org/10.17176/20191126-122149-0.

Laskowski, M. (2019). *Uchybienie Godności Urzędu sędziego jako podstawa odpowiedzialności dyscyplinarnej.* Warszawa: Wolters Kluwer.

Mazur, D. (2019, 5 March). *Judges under Special Supervision, That Is 'The Great Reform' of the Polish Justice System* [Online]. Themis Association of Judges. Available from: http://themis-sedziowie.eu/wp-content/uploads/2019/03/Judges_under_special_supervision_-first-publication-pdf.pdf.

Meyer, E. and Bustamante, T. (2020). Judicial accountability. In: Grote, R., Lachenmann, F. and Wolfrum, R. eds. *Max Planck Encyclopedia of Comparative Constitutional Law.* Oxford: Oxford University Press [Online]. Available from: https://oxcon.ouplaw.com/view/10.1093/law-mpeccol/law-mpeccol-e329.

Mikuli, P. (2017, 23 February). An explicit constitutional change by means of an ordinary statute? On a bill concerning the reform of the National Council of the Judiciary in Poland. *Int'l J. Const. L. Blog* [Online]. Available from: www.iconnectblog.com/2017/02/an-explicit-constitutional-change-by-means-of-an-ordinary-statute-on-a-bill-concerning-the-reform-of-the-national-council-of-the-judiciary-in-poland.

Mikuli, P. (2019, 9 April). Attacking judicial independence through new 'disciplinary' procedures in Poland. *Int'l J. Const. L. Blog* [Online]. Available from: www.iconnectblog.com/2019/04/attacking-judicial-independence-through-new-disciplinary-procedures-in-poland/.

Piana, D. (2010). *Judicial Accountabilities in New Europe: From Rule of Law to Quality of Justice.* Abingdon, Oxon: Routledge.

Sadurski, W. (2019). *Poland's Constitutional Breakdown.* Oxford: Oxford University Press.

Sawiński, J. (2013). Komentarz do Art. 107. In: Górski, A. ed. *Prawo o ustroju sądów powszechnych. Komentarz.* Warszawa: Lex, p. 107.

Shetreet, S. (2013). *Judges on Trial: The Independence and Accountability of the English Judiciary.* Cambridge: Cambridge University Press.

Śledzińska-Simon, A. (2018). The rise and fall of judicial self-government in Poland: On judicial reform reversing democratic transition. *German Law Journal*, 19(7), pp. 1839–1870.

Tushnet, M. (2013). Judicial accountability in comparative perspective. In: Bamforth, N. and Leyland, P. eds. *Accountability in the Contemporary Constitution*. Oxford: Oxford University Press, pp. 57–76.

Yusulf, H. O. (2010). *Transitional Justice, Judicial Accountability and the Rule of Law*. Abingdon, Oxon: Routledge.

Zoll, F. and Wortham, L. (2019). Judicial independence and accountability: Withstanding political stress in Poland. *Fordham International Law Journal*, 42(3), pp. 875–948.

6 Transparency and accountability versus secrecy in intelligence operations
An Italian case study*

Arianna Vedaschi

6.1 Introduction

Transparency is a key principle of democracies. A system in which citizens are not informed promptly and correctly about public authorities' decisions and actions cannot be defined as democratic (Bobbio 1984). Besides, the principle of accountability is closely dependent on transparency; only if transparency is ensured can those who committed crimes (or any other kind of unlawful act)—including public officials—be held accountable for their conduct.

The concepts of transparency and accountability, as currently understood, became known through the works of Rousseau, Bentham, and Kant. For Rousseau (1762), transparency had to be considered a way to prevent public servants from committing fraud and other wrongdoings against the state. Along the same line, Bentham (1791) argued (even more openly than Rousseau) that if the Government and its officials were not obliged to be transparent regarding their choices and activities, they would very likely become influenced by external forces—or worse, corrupted—rather than driven by the intent to enhance the public good. Kant (1795) even conceived the idea of transparency (as opposed to secrecy) as one of the main mechanisms to ensure accountability of governmental bodies and to stave off war and anarchy.

These theories contributed to shaping the contemporary concepts of transparency and accountability, to the point that they can be said to be two mutually reinforcing principles (Bobbio 1984). Only together, as two faces of the same coin, can they enable citizens to be *aware* of what public powers do and to *have a voice* about their actions, influencing decision-making and having the opportunity to hold decision makers to account. Due to transparency, public powers become 'visible' (Cassese 2018) to all citizens, emerging from 'obscurity' (Sandulli 2007). At the same time, transparency and accountability are two tools from which public powers themselves draw their legitimisation in society (Habermas 1962). In fact, transparency and accountability allow the public sector to earn and maintain public trust.

However, even a democracy has some grey areas where full transparency cannot be guaranteed, for the sake of competing values or public interests that also deserve protection, of which national security is the most important. Citizens

---

* The author thanks Chiara Graziani for her research assistance.

Transparency, accountability, secrecy 81

expect their governments to keep them safe from threats to their security; to do so, in some cases, governments may need to hide some information (Schoenfeld 2010). Therefore, to protect *salus rei publicae*, democracies can legitimately resort to secrecy. Nonetheless, to avoid (possible) abuses perpetrated behind the cloak of secrecy, strict guarantees must be provided, despite any exceptional circumstances. In other words, to be consistent with basic democratic values, any legal system must deem transparency as the rule and secrecy (or more generally, lack of transparency) as a limited exception (Vedaschi 2018a).

Intelligence activities exemplify the challenging balance between transparency (and, consequently, accountability) and the need to not reveal classified information, whose disclosure may jeopardise national security.

This chapter discusses the tricky relation between transparency and secrecy, focusing on the Italian intelligence services. The first section takes a diachronic perspective and analyses the evolution of intelligence from ancient times to the contemporary age, particularly dwelling on the history of Italian intelligence. The section explains how intelligence services are organised in Italy, after the entry into force of Law no. 124/2007, which—as modified by subsequent acts—currently regulates the Italian intelligence system. The chapter then addresses the relationship between Italian intelligence agencies and state powers (legislative, executive, and judiciary). Particular attention is paid to the mechanisms (as oversight of state secret privilege) that trigger significant tensions between transparency and accountability on the one hand, and secret agencies' need to work covertly to safeguard national security on the other. The next section examines how the intelligence system and the corresponding oversight mechanisms work in practice when major threats, such as international terrorism, must be tackled. Some brief concluding remarks follow.

6.2 The history of intelligence: a brief overview

The concept of intelligence refers to activities aimed at obtaining useful information to defend state security. Given the fact that such information needs to be shielded, insofar as its disclosure to potential enemies could harm security (Steele 2002, p. 129), intelligence activity has a strong link to secrecy.

There are at least two dimensions of security: internal and external. They are two sides of the same coin (i.e., national security).[1] Ensuring internal security means that threats *within* the state (e.g., domestic terrorism) must be monitored and prevented. In contrast, external security is safeguarded by operations seeking to contain threats from outside (e.g., war, international terrorism).

A brief historical overview is useful to show that protecting state security by obtaining information about (potential) enemies is a key goal that has been

---

1 Regarding the Italian Constitution, some scholars argue that there are two distinct constitutional foundations to legitimise the action of secret services in internal and external security (Massera 1990, p. 336). According to this theory, Art. 54 of the Italian Constitution, enshrining the duty of Italian citizens to be loyal to the Republic, grounds internal security activities, while Art. 52, the duty to defend the country, is the basis for external action.

82 Arianna Vedaschi

pursued by public authorities since ancient times, long before the modern state came into existence (Mosca et al. 2008, p. 20).[2]

6.2.1 Intelligence from early history to the Restoration: a comparative perspective

In the 18th century BC, Hammurabi, the most famous king of the first Babylonian dynasty, used to ask some of his subjects to sneak among the soldiers of his enemies' armies in order to obtain information about their war strategies. Starting from the 16th century BC, the Egyptians took the same approach.[3] These tactics can be called proto-espionage.

The Persians brought in an innovation, in the form of a better organised informative apparatus, to be exploited during hostilities, while the Greeks elaborated on the first theories of military intelligence and tactics.

It is well known that espionage as a pivotal war element was promoted by the Chinese general Sun Tzu, who lived between 600 and 500 BC. Espionage techniques were also widely used by the Carthaginian general Hannibal, who led the First Punic War against the Roman Republic (Sheldon 1986, p. 53). Furthermore, the idea of *salus rei publicae*, which must prevail over any individual needs if endangered by any internal or external threat, owes its existence to Ancient Rome. In his work *De Legibus* (IV), written in 52 BC, Cicero argued that '*salus rei publicae suprema lex esto*'.

Going ahead through history, the Middle Ages did not grant espionage and informative activities the same importance as they had in the past, since conflicts were often characterised by the lack of information about the enemy's strategies (Vedaschi 2007, p. 13).

In the 13th century ad, when Genghis Khan launched the Mongol invasion and conquered many territories of Eurasia, he spread the use of espionage and, at the same time, exploited fake information to gain advantage over his enemies. Genghis Khan and his empire contributed to boosting information-sharing as a tool to build political alliances; he forged a close relationship with the Republic of Venice, and the exchange of information between the two parties was crucial for destroying the military bases of other maritime Republics, particularly Genoa. The Republic of Venice quickly implemented the techniques learned from its relations with the Mongol Empire. In subsequent years, Venice created a proto-intelligence, assigning espionage tasks to several officials. This approach was replicated by other states of the Italian peninsula.

Against this background, intelligence gained momentum, and several works began to discuss this topic, including Machiavelli's *The Art of War* (1519). Consequently, an increasing number of officials became interested in this matter,

---

2 The formal date for the birth of the modern state is 1648, when the peace of Westphalia put an end to the Thirty Years' War.

3 Even the Holy Bible refers to spies sent by Moses to Canaan in order to assess whether there were potential enemies.

Transparency, accountability, secrecy   83

gathering sensitive information for security purposes and improving their expertise in internal and external security. For example, Sir Walsingham, an English diplomat during the reign of Elizabeth I, laid the basis for developing cryptography (Archer 1993, p. 41). Some years later, in France, Cardinal Richelieu contributed to the establishment of a well-functioning spy service (Mosca et al. 2008, p. 21).

In England, the first intelligence department was created in 1653 by Sir Thurloe, Cromwell's secretary of state in the Commonwealth (Peacock 2020, p. 8). To improve the work of this department, which played a key role in discovering plots against Cromwell and his regime, Sir Thurloe hired an expert in cryptology to be in charge of breaking secret codes.[4]

During the Restoration, secret services evolved further, attributed to General von Clausewitz, who considered them an essential part of any war strategy, so the attention was mainly focused on military intelligence.

6.2.2 Intelligence from the 19th century onwards: focus on Italy

Starting from the 19th century, the UK and the US established full-fledged intelligence branches, that is, bodies with their own autonomous standing but whose activities are performed within the institutional framework. These were quickly followed by other countries in the comparative scenario, one of which is Italy, the focus of this chapter.

In Italy, intelligence activities started in the 1850s. At that time, some provisions governed them, but these rules were really fragmented and heterogeneous. Additionally, the regulation of intelligence was often left to secondary sources of law issued by the executive (if not to the orders of the Ministry of Defence).

The first secret agency[5] was created in 1854, when Italy had not been unified yet under the reign of the Savoy dynasty. It was established within the Ministry of Foreign Affairs and had no autonomy from it. A year later, another body was set up, performing informative functions within the military forces.

These bodies were still operational when the First World War broke out in 1914. By the time Italy joined the war in 1915, it was immediately evident that the informative system needed to be strengthened and improved. Therefore, a special investigative body dedicated to counterespionage activities was rapidly put in place.

During the Fascist regime (1922–1943), the military intelligence service was further enhanced. In particular, Servizio Informazioni Militari (SIM, or the Military Information Service) was organised in several departments and special units. SIM was an integrated service operating for land, air, and naval armed forces.

In 1939, at the outbreak of the Second World War, SIM was split into two branches: Servizio Informazioni (SI, or the Information Service), working for the Italian armed forces, and Servizio Informazioni Difensive (SID, or the Defensive

---

4 They dismantled the Sealed Knot (i.e., a royalist secret society) due to this information.
5 In this chapter, 'agency' and 'service' are used as synonyms to identify bodies dealing with intelligence activity.

84 *Arianna Vedaschi*

Information Service), the informative body of the Italian Social Republic (the so-called Repubblica di Salò).[6]

At the end of the war in 1945, SI was replaced by Servizio Informazioni delle Forze Armate (SIFAR, or the Information Service of the Italian Armed Forces), whereas SID was still operating. Additionally, Servizio Informazioni Operative e Situazioni (SIOS, or the Service for Operative Information and Situations) was created, tasked with acquiring information about foreign countries that were considered potential enemies. They all answered directly to the Capo di Stato Maggiore della Difesa (Chief of Defence), the chief general officer of the Italian armed forces, who reported to the Ministry of Defence.

No amendments to the organisation of the Italian intelligence services were made in the immediate aftermath of 1948, when the Republican Constitution entered into force.[7] Only in 1965 did the Decree of the President of the Republic no. 1477/1965[8] merge SIFAR and SID, under the name of SID, carrying out functions that earlier pertained to both. This new body reported to the minister of defence.

Since SIOS coexisted with the 'new' SID, many of their activities were duplicated, causing uncertainty and inefficiency. A reform in this field, aimed at unifying the existing bodies and simplifying such intricate regulation, emerged as an imperative need. This scenario was exactly the rationale behind the adoption of Law no. 801/1977 by the Italian Parliament. Importantly, this law is the first primary source regulating intelligence services in Italy, overriding previous secondary regulations.

In addition to the above-mentioned necessity to have a comprehensive legislative reform enacted as early as possible, due to the complexity of the earlier intelligence framework, some other reasons, entirely political in nature, led to the enactment of Law no. 801/1977. Specifically, during the 1960s, some Italian intelligence agents became embroiled in the so-called *Solo* plan scandal.[9] At that time, Italy was under

---

6 Repubblica di Salò was named after the small town (Salò, in Northern Italy) where Benito Mussolini—following the armistice of 8 September 1943—established the headquarters of a Fascist state, comprising some of the Italian territories that were still under the Nazi military occupation. The Italian Social Republic was de facto controlled by the Germans, to the point that it was commonly identified as a 'puppet state'.

7 The only relevant innovation regarding secret services and intelligence matters was that in 1948, Divisione Affari Generali and Riservati (Division for General and Confidential Affairs) was established within the Interior Ministry; in 1974, it was dissolved and replaced by an Anti-Terrorism Inspectorate.

8 In the Italian legal system, although this act is formally issued by the President of the Republic, its substantive content is determined by the executive branch, and within the hierarchy of sources, it has secondary rank (see Art. 87 of the Italian Constitution). Therefore, these changes were substantively enacted by the Government, which, by its own act, decided that secret services answered to one of its ministers.

9 The *Solo* plan refers to a planned military coup, led by Giovanni De Lorenzo, commander-in-chief of the Carabinieri and previously of the SIFAR. It was based on assessments, made by De Lorenzo and other former SIFAR officials, regarding the subversive nature of some political opponents. The attempt failed, and De Lorenzo was immediately removed from his position.

the threat of political terrorism,[10] while on the international scene, the Cold War caused a situation of persisting tension. All these factors—and the related political debate—contributed to pushing the Italian legislature towards a new regulation of intelligence, which tried to take democratic principles, including transparency and accountability, into greater consideration (Anzon 1991, p. 1).

The main feature of Law no. 801/1977 is the key role of the Italian President of the Council of Ministers (PCM).[11] According to Article 1, the PCM was 'responsible overall'[12] for security intelligence policies and had to coordinate the activities. In particular, the 1977 Law established two secret agencies: Servizio per le Informazioni e la Sicurezza Militare (SISMI, or the Service for Military Information and Security)[13] and Servizio per le Informazioni e la Sicurezza Democratica (SISDE, or the Service for Democratic Information and Security).[14] The former dealt with military issues and reported to the minister of defence,[15] while the latter, answering to the interior minister, addressed all those situations that threatened the democratic order of the state and its institutions.[16] In both cases, the minister of defence (with regard to SISMI) and the interior minister (with regard to SISDE) acted on the basis of (detailed) guidelines issued by the PCM (Labriola 1978, p. 46).[17]

Within this framework, the PCM was supported in his or her activities by a body named Comitato Esecutivo per i Servizi di Informazione e di Sicurezza (CESIS, or the Executive Committee for Information and Security Services).[18] It had to provide the PCM with all useful elements to coordinate the secret services, and it was tasked with processing and analysing all the information retrieved by SISMI and SISDE. Additionally, it coordinated the relationship with foreign intelligence agencies. CESIS was chaired by the PCM, who appointed its members.[19]

---

10 In Italy, the 1970s are known as the 'leaden years'. The country was characterised by outbursts of political violence from both left-wing and right-wing extremist groups.

11 The PCM is the head of the Italian Government. In Italy, the executive power is vested in the PCM and the Council of Ministers (Art. 95, Italian Constitution). In giving the PCM a pivotal role in the intelligence system, Law no. 801/1977 implemented two judgements of the Italian Constitutional Court (nos. 82/1976 and 86/1977), pointing out the PCM's primary responsibility for national security matters, due to the PCM's institutional status.

12 The translation from Italian to English is made by the author.

13 Art. 4 of Law no. 801/1977.

14 Art. 6 of Law no. 801/1977.

15 The minister of defence had to appoint the SISMI director and other high officials.

16 The interior minister was vested with the power to appoint the SISDE director and other high officials. Both the interior minister (for SISDE) and the minister of defence (for SISMI) had to ask for the preventive opinion of the Interministerial Committee for Information and Security.

17 In this regard, this Italian scholar argued that the activity of the two ministers was hierarchically subordinated to the PCM.

18 Art. 3 of Law no. 801/1977.

19 The composition of CESIS could vary, being determined by the PCM. Anyway, pursuant to Art. 3 of Law no. 801/1977, it was mandatory to include the heads of SISMI and SISDE among the members of CESIS.

86 *Arianna Vedaschi*

Another crucial body was Comitato Interministeriale per le Informazioni e la Sicurezza (CIIS, or the Interministerial Committee for Information and Security).[20] Comprising several ministers of the Italian Republic,[21] it had the primary function of counselling the PCM regarding general goals to be pursued through the activity of the intelligence system. Similar to CESIS, CIIS was headed by the PCM. Formally, CESIS and CIIS were separate bodies with unambiguously different tasks, and both answered to the PCM.

Finally, political oversight of Italian intelligence activities was carried out by Comitato Parlamentare di Controllo (COPACO, or the Parliamentary Oversight Committee).[22] It consisted of eight members of the Houses of the Italian Parliament,[23] four deputies and four senators, who elected the chair among themselves. They were appointed by the presidents of the two Houses 'based on proportionality requirements'.[24] COPACO had to monitor the intelligence system and check that all bodies acted in compliance with Law no. 801/1977. Furthermore, it was empowered to request the PCM and CIIS for information about intelligence activities, submit proposals about the forthcoming actions of secret services and make observations on matters dealing with intelligence. However, when COPACO required information from the PCM, the latter, invoking state secrecy, could reject the request, even based on a flimsy explanation of the reasons on which secrecy was grounded.

From a more general perspective, the PCM played a critical role regarding state secrecy. Although the PCM was not the only authority empowered to assert it— since high officials of intelligence agencies could do so as well—he or she was the only one who could confirm the existence of a state secret, in case the privilege was invoked by a public official acting as a defendant or a witness during criminal proceedings.[25] Nonetheless, among other limits, secrecy could never shield acts against the 'constitutional order'.[26] Such a limit would then be reiterated by the current legislation and, as Section 6.5 will show, was at the core of the *Abu Omar* case (Pace 2014, p. 7; Vedaschi 2013a, p. 163).

---

20 Art. 2 of Law no. 801/1977.
21 These included the minister for foreign affairs, the interior minister, the minister of justice, the minister of defence, and the minister of economics and finance. Other ministers who are not included in this list—as well as the heads of SISMI and SISDE, several public authorities and intelligence experts—could occasionally join CIIS meetings, but they did not enjoy voting rights.
22 Art. 11 of Law no. 801/1977.
23 Italy has a bicameral Parliament, comprising two Houses (the Chamber of Deputies and the Senate of the Republic).
24 Art. 11, para. 2 of Law no. 801/1977. The translation from Italian to English was made by the author.
25 When a witness or a defendant invoked state secrecy to shield any information requested during criminal proceedings, the judge was obliged to suspend the process and ask the PCM whether (or not) he or she confirmed secrecy. The PCM had 60 days to answer.
26 Art. 12 of Law no. 801/1977. The same prohibition was reiterated by Art. 39 of Law no. 124/2004 (see Section 6.4.2). According to some scholars, this is a logical (rather than a legal) limitation to the use of secrecy (e.g., Giupponi 2007, p. 384).

6.3 The current intelligence legal framework

The described legal framework, provided by Law no. 801/1977, was reformed in 2007, when the 1977 legislation was repealed by Law no. 124/2007,[27] addressing intelligence agencies and the use of state secrecy. This law remains in force, as amended in 2012.[28] Specifically, Law no. 133/2012 enhanced the use of technology in information-gathering techniques and, above all, strengthened the oversight of intelligence operations performed by Comitato Parlamentare per la Sicurezza della Repubblica (COPASIR, or the Parliamentary Committee for the Security of the Republic, discussed below), which replaced COPACO (Franchini 2014, p. 1).

The 2007 legislative reform occurred for many reasons (Giupponi and Fabbrini 2010, p. 443). First, a change in the international scenario, after the 9/11 terrorist attacks, progressively entailed the need for a stronger role of secret services and a quicker exchange of secret information (Pisano 2003, p. 263). Second, from 2003 onwards, Italian SISMI officials became involved in the *Abu Omar* case,[29] joining an extraordinary rendition operation coordinated by the US Central Intelligence Agency (CIA); consequently, some judicial investigations were conducted, bringing criminal proceedings concerning unlawful actions allegedly committed by them. These events pushed forward the demands for better oversight and the consequent accountability of secret agencies, as well as an independent review of the use of state secrecy. Third, between 1977 and 2007, the Italian Constitutional Court had addressed the issue of state secrecy in several judgements (Vedaschi 2013b, p. 98), always emphasising the PCM's role in secrecy issues and, more generally, his or her 'leadership' in secret services.[30]

6.3.1 Law no. 124/2007: main features

The 2007 legislative reform enhanced the PCM's status as the head of the Italian intelligence system and created the Comitato Interministeriale per la Sicurezza della Repubblica (CISR, or the Interministerial Committee for the Security of the Republic)[31] to provide advice to other bodies, make proposals, and set priorities in the field of security. Among other relevant novelties, the following can be listed: a set of functional guarantees granted to intelligence agents,[32] the consolidation

---

27 Indeed, several reform projects had already been presented from 1977 onwards. Among them, it is worth mentioning the one presented in 1993 by the then PCM, Carlo Azeglio Ciampi, to merge the two secret services into one agency divided into two branches (one dealing with internal threats and the other with external threats). This project was dropped because it came at the end of the parliamentary term. From 1993 to 2007, at least 60 further projects were presented, but they never succeeded.

28 See Section 6.4.1.

29 See Section 6.5.2.

30 See Judgement no. 110/1998 and Ord. no. 404/2005.

31 A security committee within the executive branch.

32 This means that they can be exempted from criminal conviction for some unlawful activities committed when performing their duties.

88 Arianna Vedaschi

and improvement of oversight mechanisms on intelligence operations, and some procedural rules regarding the use of secrecy in criminal proceedings.

However, the so-called double track system has been preserved, insofar as external and internal intelligence agencies are still separate but with their names changed; they are now called Agenzia Informazioni e Sicurezza Interna (AISI, or the Agency for Internal Information and Security) and Agenzia Informazioni e Sicurezza Esterna (AISE, or the Agency for External Information and Security). While AISI addresses internal threats, AISE is focused on external ones, and Article 7, para. 4 of Law no. 124/2007 prevents them from interfering with each other's activities. Thus, it seems that a merely 'geographical' criterion distinguishes between AISI's and AISE's tasks, yet scholars (e.g., Bonetti 2008, p. 264) note that this territorial differentiation entails functional implications, since AISI is more inclined to address terrorism and domestic criminalities, whereas AISE specialises in military issues. Nevertheless, with the outbreak of international terrorism, along with the evolution of the traditional concept of war (Vedaschi 2007), it is difficult to keep a strict distinction based on the territorial reach of the threat or on its nature.

It is useful to separately examine each of the mentioned new features brought by Law no. 124/2007. The PCM's role was emphasised by the reform. Indisputably, the head of the Italian Government already held a key position within the intelligence system. At any rate, the 2007 law stipulates that the PCM is vested with the 'oversight of and overall responsibility for security intelligence policy in the interests and defence of the Republic and its underlying democratic institutions as established by the Constitution'.[33] Furthermore, the PCM decides on the budget of secret services and issues regulations on matters regarding them. As for state secrecy, the PCM is in charge of applying and confirming the state secret privilege in criminal proceedings, being the only one empowered to do so. The PCM also appoints a number of high officials of the secret services. Notably, the PCM can delegate his or her functions to the delegated authority, whose appointment is not mandatory, but the PCM can only designate ministers without a portfolio[34] or undersecretaries of state.[35] When the PCM appoints a delegated authority,[36] the opinion of the Council of Ministers is not required.[37]

---

33 Art. 1, para. 1(a) of Law no. 124/2007. The official English translation of Law no. 124/2007 is available at www.sicurezzanazionale.gov.it/sisr.nsf/english/law-no-124-2007.html.

34 In the Italian legal system, they are ministers of the Italian Government with no spending power.

35 In Italy, undersecretaries of state are appointed by a decree of the President of the Republic, on the PCM's proposal, in agreement with the concerned minister.

36 After Law no. 124/2007 took effect, six PCMs decided to appoint delegated authorities, as follows: Silvio Berlusconi appointed Gianni Letta; Mario Monti appointed Gianni De Gennaro; Enrico Letta appointed Marco Minniti, who was appointed again during the administration led by Matteo Renzi; Paolo Gentiloni appointed Luciano Pizzetti; Giuseppe Conte, in both the administrations he led, has decided not to appoint a delegated authority. The current PCM, Mario Draghi, appointed Franco Gabrielli.

37 This provision derogates from the general rules established by Art. 9, para. 2 of Law no. 400/1988.

The PCM (or the delegated authority) is supported by the Dipartimento delle Informazioni per la Sicurezza (DIS, or the Security Intelligence Department), whose head he or she appoints.[38] DIS coordinates the activities of AISE and AISI, reports the information gathered by the two agencies to the PCM, and promotes meetings between AISE and AISI to ensure the exchange of information between them. Hence, DIS has relevant connecting functions, acting as a link between the PCM and secret services on one hand, and between AISE and AISI on the other.

As mentioned, Law no. 124/2007 set up another body, still within the Presidency of the Council of Ministers but outside DIS: CISR, headed by the PCM and comprising the delegated authority (if appointed) and several ministers.[39] CISR performs a number of tasks, including to 'advise, make proposals and take decisions regarding the lines and general goals of security intelligence policy'.[40]

Another relevant new feature of the 2007 legislative reform is embodied by functional guarantees. According to Article 17 of Law no. 124/2007, in some narrowly tailored circumstances, members of AISE and AISI[41] are exempted from judicial investigation and prosecution for their conduct in the performance of their duties when their actions would qualify as crimes pursuant to the law (Pisa 2007, p. 1431). In other words, functional guarantees are very limited exceptions to the general rule of accountability before criminal courts and de facto provide secret agents with partial immunity from ordinary jurisdiction (Praduroux 2015, p. 282).

Functional guarantees aim at balancing two competing interests. On one hand, intelligence services need room to discharge their duties; on the other hand, it must be ensured that intelligence agents carry out their activities within the bounds of the law and are accountable for their actions. To apply functional guarantees, four (cumulative) requirements must be met. First, unlawful acts must have been authorised by the PCM. Importantly, generic authorisations to commit criminal offences do not justify them, since ad hoc authorisation is requested.[42] Second, the commission of crimes must be 'indispensable' to accomplish an operation and proportionate to the goal pursued.[43] Third, the conduct must result from a careful and objective 'weighing of the public and private interest

---

38 The PCM also has to appoint the heads of AISE and AISI.
39 Specifically, the ministers of foreign affairs, the interior, defence, finance, and economic development.
40 Art. 5, para. 1 of Law no. 124/2007.
41 They can also apply to citizens who are not involved in intelligence agencies if they are cooperating with intelligence agents and their cooperation is essential for attaining the pursued goal.
42 In ordinary circumstances, the authorisation is granted by the PCM or when appointed, by the delegated authority. However, in extraordinary cases of 'absolute urgency', it can be provided by the director of AISE or AISI, but the PCM (or the delegated authority) has to ratify it within 10 days (otherwise, they have to inform the judicial authority without delay). Art. 18, paras. 4–6 of Law no. 124/2007.
43 In other words, there must be no room for any alternative.

90 *Arianna Vedaschi*

involved'. Fourth, criminal acts must 'cause the minimum damage possible to affected interests'.[44]

When all the above-mentioned conditions occur, functional guarantees can be invoked by persons under investigation and defendants at any stage of criminal proceedings, from preliminary investigations up to the trial. The judge (or the public prosecutor) has to ask the PCM whether he or she confirms the existence of an ad hoc authorisation. On one hand, if the PCM confirms that the operation has been authorised and all other requirements are fulfilled, the judicial process (or the investigation) must be dismissed. On the other hand, if the PCM says that there has been no authorisation or that the conduct by the intelligence official(s) has exceeded the limits set by the authorisation, the criminal proceedings go ahead. If the judiciary and the PCM disagree on the authorisation—and hence on the existence of functional guarantees—the Constitutional Court can be called on to adjudicate the dispute,[45] referred to as 'conflict of allocation of powers'.[46]

Nevertheless, Law no. 124/2007 prescribes that functional guarantees cannot be applied to some serious offences (Marenghi et al. 2007, p. 716). These include 'crimes endangering or injuring the life, physical integrity, personal dignity, personal freedom, moral freedom, health or safety of one or more persons';[47] crimes against state institutions or against political rights of citizens or against the administration of justice; and terrorism and Mafia-style crimes. These limits aim to ensure that constitutional principles and rights guarantees are not breached, even where 'special rules' govern a highly sensitive activity (as intelligence is).

Regarding oversight functions, according to Law no. 124/2007, there are two mechanisms.[48] On one hand, political oversight of secret services' activities is handled (at least at the first stage) by COPASIR, which replaced COPACO (as mentioned). On the other hand, the Constitutional Court rules on disputes that may arise between the PCM and the judiciary when secrecy is invoked in criminal proceedings (judicial oversight). It must be borne in mind that no other Italian judge is empowered to scrutinise these matters.

---

44 Art. 17, para. 6 of Law no. 124/2006.
45 Art. 19, para. 8 of Law no. 124/2007.
46 The tasks of the Constitutional Court are listed by Art. 134 of the Italian Constitution, according to which it can rule on:
  '– controversies on the constitutional legitimacy of laws and enactments having force of law issued by the State and Regions;
  – conflicts arising from allocation of powers of the State and those powers allocated to State and Regions, and between Regions;
  charges brought against the President of the Republic, according to the provisions of the Constitution' (translation by the Italian Senate).
47 Art. 17, para. 2 of Law no. 124/2007.
48 A couple of scholars (Giupponi and Fabbrini 2010, p. 454) also include internal administrative review as one of the oversight mechanisms. These tasks are carried out by the Inspection Office, set up within DIS. This office has to check that 'security intelligence activities comply with Acts of Parliament and with governmental Regulations, as well as with the directives and Provisions issued by the President of the Council of Ministers' (Art. 4, para. 3(i) of Law no. 124/2007).

Both oversight mechanisms (on the activity of intelligence services and the use of state secrecy in criminal cases) are examined in detail in the next section, as they shed light on the challenging relation between the intelligence system and state powers. Section 6.5 then discusses how intelligence agencies work and state secrecy is resorted to in times of international terrorism.

6.4 The Italian intelligence system and its interactions with state powers

In the current framework, Italian intelligence services interact—in varying degrees and at different stages—with the legislative, executive, and judicial branches. These interactions form the focal point of oversight mechanisms, political and judicial. In particular, political oversight focuses on the relation between intelligence and the legislative power. In contrast, judicial oversight may be triggered when state secrecy is resorted to in criminal proceedings to shield intelligence activities. This perspective shows how secrecy may work as an element of tension between intelligence services and the judiciary on one hand, and the latter and the PCM on the other hand. Acting as the sole reviewer of state secrets, the Constitutional Court[49] is called on to resolve these disputes.

6.4.1 Political oversight of secret services' activities

Political oversight is handled by a parliamentary committee, that is, COPASIR. Pursuant to Article 30 of Law no. 124/2007, this body consists of five deputies and five senators, appointed by the president of each House of Parliament within 20 days of the opening of every Parliament. The committee's composition is proportional to the number of parliamentary groups,[50] so equal representation of both majority and opposition groups should be ensured. It is chaired by a member of the political opposition.[51]

COPASIR's general function is to 'constantly and systematically verify that the Security Intelligence System's activities are carried out in observance both of the Constitution and of the law and in the defence and exclusive interests of the Republic and its institutions'.[52] To discharge its duties, it can resort to several tools. First, it examines the report on the intelligence services' activities that the PCM has to submit every six months. Second, COPASIR has to be informed within 30 days when intelligence agencies have performed operations

---

49 In the Italian legal system, the Constitutional Court is not part of the judiciary, given its constitutional adjudication functions.
50 In Italy, parliamentary groups can be defined as the transposition of political parties within the Parliament.
51 The president is elected by absolute majority and secret ballot. If no candidate attains the absolute majority at the first ballot, a second will be held between the two candidates who have obtained the highest number of votes. The president of the COPASIR represents the whole body and convenes its meeting.
52 Art. 30 of Law no. 124/2007.

92 *Arianna Vedaschi*

in which unlawful actions have been authorised by the PCM (see Section 6.3.1). The PCM is also obliged to keep COPASIR informed when asked to confirm state secrecy in criminal proceedings, and must also disclose his or her final decision (i.e., whether to confirm secrecy). Third, COPASIR can require copies of sensitive documents from the PCM, who can refuse to disclose them by resorting to state secrecy. However, if COPASIR does not agree on the invocation of secrecy, it can bring the matter before the Houses of Parliament, which may pass a motion of no confidence in the PCM and its Government. At any rate, in the event of a vote of no confidence, classified documents will still not be disclosed ex post. Hence, the PCM remains the sole keeper of state secrecy (Vedaschi 2018a, p. 910), even when he or she and the Government are forced to resign. Fourth, COPASIR can decide to hold hearings, asking the PCM, other ministers, heads of intelligence agencies, and individuals who are not involved in the intelligence system to provide information that might be useful for its oversight.

Along with the listed tools, and closely related to its oversight role, COPASIR has further tasks (i.e., advisory, reporting, and warning functions). As for COPASIR's advisory role, the PCM has to ask for its opinion before adopting any regulations dealing with the organisation of intelligence and prior to appointing the heads of DIS, AISI, and AISE. However, its opinion is not legally binding.

Regarding its reporting duties, COPASIR has to present an annual report to the Houses of Parliament to keep them informed of the activities carried out by the intelligence services in that period. COPASIR also plays a warning role; in performing its other functions, when it discovers irregular conduct by any of the bodies of the intelligence system, it should inform the PCM and the presidents of the Chamber of Deputies and of the Senate. After the reform enacted through Law no. 133/2012, its power in this regard has been strengthened, as it can ask the PCM not only to consider the matter but also to order internal inquiries, whose findings have to be transmitted to COPASIR itself. Finally, it can review the budget related to the operations of the intelligence agencies by accessing the DIS archives.

This overview shows that the primary raison d'être of this parliamentary committee is to create a link between intelligence activities and the Parliament (and ultimately, citizens the Parliament represents). Given that most intelligence activities are secret by nature, it would be unacceptable in a democratic country to carry them out entirely outside of democratic institutions. Therefore, COPASIR's functions are vital to ensure transparency and political accountability. The former is sought by provisions requiring that intelligence operations be disclosed to COPASIR, and even if not in detail, they may be reported to the Parliament. The latter should be guaranteed as COPASIR may refer issues to the Houses of Parliament, which may pass a motion of no confidence. From a political perspective, irregular conduct of intelligence bodies may lead to broken confidence between the Parliament (rather, its majority) and the Government.

At least in theory, COPASIR is essential to keep democracy alive in the sensitive field of intelligence, necessarily characterised by covert operations and confidential (where not classified) information.

6.4.2 *Judicial oversight and the use of state secrecy in criminal proceedings*

The other oversight mechanism may be performed by the Italian Constitutional Court. According to the Italian Code of Criminal Procedure (c.c.p.)[53] and Law no. 124/2007,[54] public officials[55] taking part in criminal proceedings as defendants or witnesses are obliged not to answer questions by the public prosecutor (during investigations) or by the judge (during the process) about facts or information shielded by state secrecy. Nevertheless, when a defendant or a witness invokes state secret privilege to avoid answering questions, the public prosecutor or the judge (depending on the stage of the criminal proceedings) cannot take this claim for granted. However, they must suspend any activity aimed at obtaining such information and ask the PCM to confirm whether (or not) the matter of concern is really a state secret.

At that point, the situation is in the hands of the PCM (not of the Government as a whole), who has 30 days to examine the issue and decide whether (or not) state secrecy should be confirmed. If the PCM does not give any answer within this period (or provides an explicitly negative answer), the defendant or the witness is obliged to refer the matter to judicial authorities, since no secrecy is considered to exist. Within 30 days, if the PCM confirms the existence of the state secret privilege, the PCM must submit a document to the judge (or the prosecutor), explaining the reasons behind his or her decision, so the public prosecutor or the judge are prevented from obtaining and using, directly or indirectly, the information shielded by the privilege. Hence, there are two alternatives. First, if this material is essential to the criminal investigation (or process), the case must be dismissed 'due to the existence of a state secret'.[56] Second, if there are distinct and autonomous elements that are in no way related to the classified material, the criminal trial can move forward by relying on them.[57]

This overview of the approach to secrecy in the Italian legal system—in particular, during criminal proceedings—highlights the central position of the executive branch, specifically of the PCM, in secrecy matters. However, in some cases, the judge or the prosecutor does not agree with the PCM on the invocation of secrecy; for example, arguing that the PCM has not confirmed secrecy in compliance with the law. In other circumstances, the PCM does not agree with the judge or the prosecutor, claiming that they are using the materials

---

53 Art. 202.
54 Art. 41.
55 Members of secret agencies qualify as public officials in the meaning of Art. 357 of the Italian Criminal Code (c.c.).
56 Art. 41, para. 3 of Law no. 124/2007.
57 In this regard, the Constitutional Court states that 'the assertion of the state secrecy' by the PCM may not 'forbid prosecutors from investigating crimes relating to the reported crime' but may only 'prevent the prosecutors from acquiring and using any elements or evidence shielded by secrecy'. Nonetheless, in practice, this is often very difficult for judges and prosecutors. See the Constitutional Court judgement of 10 April 1998, no. 110 (translated by the author).

94 *Arianna Vedaschi*

that are supposed to be classified as evidence. The Italian Constitutional Court is called on to decide on these disputes (called conflicts of allocation of powers).[58] Since Law no. 124/2007 states that no state secret can be invoked against the Constitutional Court,[59] this court has a very important role, being the only one empowered to scrutinise the assertion of secrecy from a substantive point of view.

When the Constitutional Court assesses the legitimacy of secrecy invocation, it must take into account the limits of secrecy. The most important one is enshrined in Article 39, para. 11 of Law no. 124/2007. According to this provision, under no circumstance can acts endangering the 'constitutional order' or other serious crimes[60] be concealed by secrecy. In other words, defendants and witnesses cannot invoke state secrecy in criminal proceedings to hide the fact that they committed crimes against the constitutional order. Ideally, if any defendant or witness does so, the PCM should not confirm secrecy; ultimately, should the PCM confirm secrecy to shield these acts, the Constitutional Court should declare his or her assertion unlawful, since Article 39, para. 11 of Law no. 124/2007 is breached.

In cases where the Constitutional Court decides that secrecy has been neither correctly invoked nor confirmed by the PCM, its judgement allows the judge or the prosecutor to use the concerned material as evidence. Therefore, the prosecutor can investigate, and the judge can base his or her decision on this information. In the opposite circumstance—that is, when the Constitutional Court ascertains that secrecy has been correctly resorted to—its word is final. Judges and prosecutors must abstain from any further inquiry or evaluation on that material, and the criminal proceedings can continue only if there are further pieces of evidence.

In this legal framework, the Constitutional Court is vested with significant powers. Although its oversight role is performed only when a conflict of allocation of powers arises between the PCM and the judiciary, it can be considered the 'last bulwark' of transparency and accountability of intelligence services. To what extent this role is effectively performed in practice will be clearer through the analysis in the next section of a recent Italian case dealing with secrecy, intelligence, and national security threats.

6.5 Intelligence agencies 'in action' in times of international terrorism

The examined legal framework, governing intelligence agencies and the use of state secrecy in Italy, needs to be viewed from a practical perspective. How do intelligence services operate in times of international terrorism? Do oversight mechanisms work in practice? Is the tension between secrecy on one hand, and transparency and accountability on the other hand, increased by jihadist terrorism? The *Abu Omar* case, concerning the extraordinary rendition of a suspected

---

58 See note 46.

59 Art. 40, para. 8.

60 Ravaging (Art. 285 c.c.), Mafia-related crimes (Arts. 416-bis, 413-ter c.c.), and slaughter (Art. 422 c.c.).

terrorist, sheds light on these questions, and its analysis is essential for investigating intelligence services from an 'operative' viewpoint. Before addressing it, some contextual information on the 'new' terrorist threat is needed.

6.5.1 International terrorism and the metamorphosis of security threats

As mentioned, the outbreak of international terrorism in 2001 and attacks perpetrated in Europe in the following years (Madrid in 2004 and London in 2005)[61] were among the factors contributing to the emphasis on the need for a legislative reform of intelligence services. International terrorism since 2001 is different from that which occurred before (Walker 2011, p. 5), but one of the main features of this new phenomenon is its ongoing metamorphosis.

The terrorism that many European countries had already experienced before 2001 (e.g., Rote Armee Fraktion in Germany, political terrorism in Italy, Euskadi Ta Askatasuna in Spain, Irish Republican Army in the UK) had some traits that differentiated it from international terrorism. For example, 'old' terrorism was prevalently domestic because it lacked a transnational reach and it had a political, or at least an ideological, purpose (e.g., independence). In contrast, international terrorism aims at destruction (at least apparently and at the first stage) without a well-defined goal. It can unleash its violence at any moment, in whatever place, against anybody, and without a clear reason.

However, international terrorism itself evolved over the years. In the aftermath of the 9/11 attacks, it was essentially identified with Al-Qaeda (and other related terrorist cells). It worked as an extremist group whose main targets were the US and the Western world in general (Baines and O'Shaughnessy 2016, p. 172). Al-Qaeda primarily involved its members in its activities, and it did not seek to include people who were geographically and culturally distant from Islamic extremism, nor was its goal to build a state (Vedaschi 2020, p. 302). The situation changed in 2014, when Al-Adnani delivered a speech self-proclaiming the Islamic Caliphate a state, led by Al-Baghdadi (Vedaschi 2016a, p. 1). Radicalisation efforts—also exploiting new technologies—increased in order to attract as many people as possible from other countries, religions, and cultures to embrace extremist ideologies. Afterwards, the Islamic State was militarily defeated and lost all of its territories, so its state ambitions were disrupted; nonetheless, recruiting strategies are still being implemented as the terrorists hope to 'come back' by keeping the allegiance of its 'citizens' alive.

Against this background, from 2001 to the present, security threats have been dramatically transformed; consequently, approaches to tackling them have changed too. A number of measures have been enacted, limiting—where not breaching—human rights that constitutions and supranational tools guarantee

---

61 This 'escalation of violence' continued in the following years in Paris (2015), Berlin (2016), Nice (2016), and Strasbourg (2018), among others, and is still ongoing.

96 *Arianna Vedaschi*

(Roach et al. 2005). Some of them, namely targeted killings and extraordinary renditions, violate the right to life and the right not to be tortured (Vedaschi 2018b, p. 89). The former practice consists of killing suspected terrorists, targeted overseas, usually by means of airstrikes (O'Connell 2012, p. 263). The latter involves the abduction of individuals suspected of having links with terrorism in order to bring them to territories where they are tortured to induce them to reveal useful information to fight terrorism (Satterthwaite 2013, p. 589). In both cases, targets are identified by relying on secret intelligence files, and covert operations are carried out, with the cooperation of the intelligence services of multiple countries.[62]

6.5.2 *Extraordinary renditions, state secrecy, and the Italian Constitutional Court*

The *Abu Omar* case, involving extraordinary rendition, is well known. Nasr Osama Mustafa Hassan (aka Abu Omar) was an Egyptian-born imam with refugee status in Italy. In 2003, while he was under investigation due to alleged ties to a terrorist cell, he was abducted in Milan by CIA and SISMI agents and rendered to Egypt, where he was detained incommunicado and tortured (Amnesty International 2006).

After an investigation led by the Public Prosecutor of Milan, in 2009, the Tribunal of Milan (Judgement no. 12428/2009) convicted 23 US officials in absentia for Abu Omar's kidnapping (the other three US citizens were acquitted because of diplomatic immunity). Five Italian intelligence agents invoked the state secret privilege, and the PCM confirmed it, so the tribunal was forced to dismiss charges against them (Vedaschi 2013b, p. 95).

A long and complex judiciary path began (Vedaschi 2017, p. 166), in which the PCM's decision to confirm state secrecy—shielding actions of SISMI officers—was repeatedly challenged by Italian judicial and prosecuting authorities at different stages of the criminal proceedings, giving rise to conflicts of allocation of powers before the Constitutional Court.[63] However, the latter always decided in the PCM's favour. As a result, a 'curtain of secrecy'[64] was dropped on the events. Due to the Constitutional Court's approach, even the Court of Cassation (i.e., the court of last instance in the Italian legal system) was forced to acquit Italian agents due to the existence of the state secret (Judgement no. 20447/2014).

The Constitutional Court issued two decisions (Judgements nos. 106/2009 and 24/2014) in which it argued in favour of the head of the executive branch.

---

62 Both targeted killings and extraordinary renditions are led by the US (Scheppele 2005, p. 285), but other democratic countries cooperate with them.

63 See note 46.

64 This was evocatively stated by the Court of Appeals of Milan, when in 2010 (Judgement no. 3688/2010), after the first ruling of the Constitutional Court, it was forced to dismiss charges against Italian agents, upholding the decision of the Tribunal of Milan.

In its 2009 ruling, the Constitutional Court recalled its previous case law, dating back to the 1970s,[65] where it emphasised the link between state secrecy and *salus rei publicae*. Although the court remarked on its own role as the sole reviewer of state secrecy, it stressed the PCM's significant powers in this domain, paving the way for the following steps of its reasoning, based on a restrictive interpretation of the concept of constitutional order, to allow a wide use of state secrecy. As mentioned, the state secret privilege cannot be claimed on acts against the constitutional order. The Constitutional Court affirmed that this concept identified the acts aimed to 'overthrow the democratic system or the institutions of the Italian Republic' and to dismantle 'the overall democratic structure of the institutions'. Although SISMI officers cooperated with the US in an operation—Abu Omar's rendition—whose outcome was the kidnapping aimed to torture the target, definitely infringing human rights and, ultimately, the fundamental value of human dignity, they did not try to subvert state institutions; therefore, in the court's view, their acts did not breach the constitutional order.

This reading of constitutional order is far too narrow. In the Italian constitutional framework, constitutional order is a wider concept, embracing all those rights and values on which democracy rests. Hence, this concept includes (but is not limited to) the restrictive meaning given by the court, which pertains to the idea of the constitutional system, referring to state institutions and their reciprocal relation (i.e., the form of Government). By conflating the constitutional order with the constitutional system, the court de facto avoided ruling on the issue, showing self-restraint and deference to the PCM.

The arguments in favour of transparency and accountability for human right violations fared no better in 2014, when a further conflict of allocation of powers arose between the PCM and the judiciary. In its Decision no. 24/2014, the Constitutional Court followed three main steps. First, it reiterated its 2009 reasoning, holding that the exclusive power to decide on secrecy issues was vested in the PCM. Second, it addressed a point raised by the Court of Cassation, which had called on the Constitutional Court to resolve the dispute. The Court of Cassation claimed that secrecy had been invoked too late; the defendants resorted to it only after the investigative stage of the criminal proceedings ended. Moreover, the facts were already known by civil society.[66] According to the Constitutional Court, these elements were irrelevant and did not affect the lawfulness of the PCM's decision. Third, the Constitutional Court reacted to a further argument of the Court of Cassation. The latter maintained that the Italian officials' actions had been performed outside of their official capacity; thus, they could not be shielded by the state secret privilege. The Constitutional Court argued that this hypothesis was not realistic because if the agents had acted in their personal

---

65 Judgements nos. 82/1976 and 86/1977.

66 This was due to reports on extraordinary renditions, widely circulated by institutions and non-governmental organisations (Open Society Foundation 2013; European Parliament 2007).

98 *Arianna Vedaschi*

capacity, the PCM would have taken measures against them, but nothing like that happened (Vedaschi 2013a, p. 163).

With its 2014 judgement, the Constitutional Court put an end to the *Abu Omar* case at the national level.[67] The only form of relief for Abu Omar and his wife came in 2016 from the European Court of Human Rights, which, of course, could only grant them compensation, being unable to effectively punish the Italian agents (Vedaschi 2016b).

By showing self-restraint and limiting its scrutiny to a mere formal and procedural assessment, the Constitutional Court gave up its role as the reviewer of state secrecy, leaving it to the PCM's high-handedness (potentially leading to abuses). This stance might ultimately trigger the erosion of basic principles of democracy, such as transparency and accountability, and lead to unpunished violations of human rights.

Moreover, in *Abu Omar*, political oversight was not initiated, since COPASIR did not bring the matter before the Parliament. Indeed, this oversight mechanism, when triggered, is weak in practice. In fact, in a parliamentary system such as Italy's, there is a political continuum between the majority of the Parliament and the executive branch (and its head), so the former will hardly vote against the latter on national security matters. Additionally, in the unlikely event of a vote of no confidence, the PCM's decision to keep the material classified cannot be changed. Furthermore, national security is a field where political forces (the majority and the opposition) traditionally share the same positions, so the bipartisan composition of COPASIR[68] might not be enough to ensure effective checks.

6.6 Concluding remarks

This chapter has examined Italian intelligence agencies' history, current framework, and practical issues in times of international terrorism. A few relevant points arise from the analysis.

The overview of the historical development of Italian intelligence services shows that the Italian legislature, from the origins of the regulation of intelligence up to 2012 (when the 2007 law was slightly amended), has been striving to enhance transparency and accountability in this sensitive field. This effort stems from at least two features. First, from 1977 onwards, intelligence services and their activities have been regulated by legislative acts, which means that many more guarantees are ensured, compared with secondary sources, which governed these issues before 1977. Second, due to the 2007 legislative reform, at least in principle, oversight is now better framed. In particular, the Constitutional Court is endowed with significant review powers.

However, some flaws persist in this framework. As explained, the political oversight performed by COPASIR is weak in practice. The Constitutional Court,

---

67 The Court of Cassation was forced to dismiss the case against the Italian agents.
68 See Section 6.4.1.

called on to decide on the use of secrecy in a case of extraordinary rendition, took a deferential approach and blatantly limited its scrutiny to formal and procedural issues.

These drawbacks can hardly be overcome by means of further legislative reforms. On one side, the weaknesses of the COPASIR oversight function depend on the intrinsic nature of the Italian parliamentary system (i.e., the political continuum between the executive branch and the majority of the Parliament) and on political dynamics (i.e., the above-mentioned alignment, at least traditionally, between the majority and the opposition parties on national security matters). On the other side, the Constitutional Court has chosen to embrace a self-restrained attitude, albeit it has highly significant review powers (pursuant to the legal framework). Therefore, two contrasting trends can be detected: the 2007 legislative reform's commitment to better safeguarding of transparency and accountability when intelligence is in action, opposed by the self-restraint of the Constitutional Court when called on to resolve disputes on the assertion of state secret privilege.

Nonetheless, this court's stance must be interpreted in the light of the historical-political context of the world under ongoing terrorist threats. In this scenario, many sensitive interests need protection. Specifically, relations with foreign secret services are crucial, and perhaps the need to preserve them was part of the rationale that led the Constitutional Court to decide in favour of the PCM. However, it must not be forgotten that human dignity, the right to life, and the right not to be tortured stand on the other side. They are at the core of democracy and should thus prevail over national security, which should not overstep transparency and accountability when the above-mentioned values and rights are concerned.

References

Amnesty International. (2006). *Below the Radar: Secret Flights to Torture and 'Disappearance'* [Online]. Available from: www.amnesty.org/en/documents/AMR51/051/2006/en/ [Accessed 25 March 2020].

Anzon, A. (1991). Servizi segreti. In: AA.VV. *Enciclopedia Giuridica*. Roma: Treccani, pp. 1–6.

Archer, J. M. (1993). *Sovereignty and Intelligence: Spying and Court Culture in the English Renaissance*. Stanford: Stanford University Press.

Baines, P. R. and O'Shaughnessy, N. J. (2016). Al-Qaeda messaging evolution and positioning, 1998–2008: Propaganda analysis revisited. *Public Relations Inquiry*, 3(2), pp. 163–191.

Bentham, J. (1791 [1962]). Panopticon; or the inspection house. In: Bowring, J. ed. *The Works of Jeremy Bentham (1838–1843)*. New York: Russel & Russel, pp. 65–123.

Bobbio, N. (1984). *Il Futuro della Democrazia*. Torino: Einaudi.

Bonetti, P. (2008). Aspetti costituzionali del nuovo sistema di informazione per la sicurezza della Repubblica. *Diritto e Società*, 2, pp. 251–312.

Cassese, S. (2018). Evoluzione della normativa sulla trasparenza. *Sinappsi*, 8(1), pp. 5–7.

European Parliament, Rapporteur Giovanni Claudio Fava, Temporary Committee on the Alleged Use of European Countries by the CIA for the Transportation and Illegal Detention of Prisoners. (2007). *Report on the Alleged Use of European Countries by the C.I.A. for the Transportation and Illegal Detention of Prisoners.* 2006/220 (INI).

Franchini, M. (2014). Alcune considerazioni sulle nuove competenze del comitato parlamentare per la sicurezza della repubblica. *Rivista AIC* (1), pp. 1–12.

Giupponi, T. F. (2007). Il conflitto tra governo e procura di Milano nel caso Abu Omar. *Quaderni Costituzionali*, 2, pp. 384–387.

Giupponi, T. F. and Fabbrini, F. (2010). Intelligence agencies and the state secret privilege: The Italian experience. *International Constitutional Law Journal*, 4(3), pp. 443–466.

Habermas, J. (1962 [2002]). *Storia e Critica dell'Opinione Pubblica.* Eds. Illuminati, A., et al. Rome and Bari: Laterza.

Kant, I. (1795 [2015]). *Perpetual Peace.* Ed. Orend, B. and Trans. Hastie, W. Peterborough: Broadview Press.

Labriola, S. (1978). *Le Informazioni per la Sicurezza dello Stato.* Milano: Giuffrè.

Machiavelli, N. (1519 [2003]). *The Art of War.* Trans. Lynch, C. Chicago: Chicago University Press.

Marenghi, F., et al. (2007). Artt. 17, 18, 19-L. 3.8.2007 n. 124-Sistema di informazione per la sicurezza della repubblica e nuova disciplina del segreto di stato. *Legislazione Penale*, 3, pp. 716–724.

Massera, A. (1990). I servizi di informazione e sicurezza. In: AA.VV. *Enciclopedia del Diritto.* Milano: Giuffrè, pp. 396–397.

Mosca, C., et al. (2008). *I Servizi di Informazione e il Segreto di Stato.* Milano: Giuffrè.

O'Connell, M. E. (2012). Adhering to law and values against terrorism. *Notre Dame Journal of International and Comparative Law*, 2(2), pp. 289–304.

Open Society Foundation. (2013). *Globalizing Torture: CIA Secret Detention and Extraordinary Rendition* [Online]. Available from: www.justiceinitiative.org/publications/globalizing-torture-cia-secret-detention-and-extraordinary-rendition [Accessed 25 March 2020].

Pace, A. (2014). La Corte di Cassazione e i 'fatti eversivi dell'ordine costituzionale'. *Giurisprudenza Costituzionale*, 59(1), pp. 582–586.

Peacock, T. N. (2020). Cromwell's 'spymaster'? John Thurloe and rethinking early modern intelligence. *The Seventeenth Century*, 35(1), pp. 3–30.

Pisa, P. (2007). Le garanzie funzionali per gli appartenenti ai servizi segreti. *Diritto Penale Processuale*, 11, pp. 1428–1435.

Pisano, V. (2003). The Italian intelligence establishment: A time for reform. *Penn State International Law Review*, 21(2), pp. 263–292.

Praduroux, S. (2015). Italy. In: Roach, K. ed. *Comparative Counter-Terrorism Law.* Cambridge: Cambridge University Press, pp. 269–296.

Roach, K., et al. eds. (2005). *Global Anti-Terrorism Law and Policy.* Cambridge: Cambridge University Press.

Rousseau, J. J. (1762 [2008]). *The Social Contract.* Trans. Cranston, M. London: Penguin Books Ltd.

Sandulli, A. (2007). La casa dai vetri oscurati: I nuovi ostacoli all'accesso ai documenti. *Giornale di Diritto Amministrativo*, 13(6), pp. 669–672.

Satterthwaite, M. (2013). The legal regime governing transfer of persons in the fight against terrorism. In: van den Herik, L. and Schrijver, N. eds. *Counter-Terrorism and International Law: Meeting the Challenges.* New York: Foundation Press, pp. 589–638.

Scheppele, K. L. (2005). Hypothetical torture in the 'war on terrorism'. *Journal of National Security Law and Policy*, 1(1), pp. 285–340.

Schoenfeld, G. (2010). *Necessary Secrets: National Security, the Media, and the Rule of Law*. New York and London: Norton.

Sheldon, R. M. (1986). Hannibal's spies. *International Journal of Intelligence and Counterintelligence*, 1(3), pp. 53–70.

Steele, D. (2002). *Intelligence. Spie e Segreti in un Mondo Aperto*. Soveria Mannelli: Rubettino.

Vedaschi, A. (2007). *À la Guerre Comme à la Guerre? La Disciplina della Guerra nel Diritto Costituzionale Comparato*. Torino: Giappichelli.

Vedaschi, A. (2013a). La Cassazione solleva il 'sipario nero' calato dalla consulta: Il caso Abu Omar si riapre. *Percorsi Costituzionali*, 1, pp. 163–193.

Vedaschi, A. (2013b). *Arcana imperii* and *salus rei publicae*: State secrets privilege and the Italian legal framework. In: Cole, D., Fabbrini, F. and Vedaschi, A. eds. *Secrecy, National Security and the Vindication of Constitutional Law*. Cheltenham and Northampton: Elgar, pp. 95–111.

Vedaschi, A. (2016a). Da al-Qā'ida all'IS: Il terrorismo internazionale si è fatto stato? *Rivista Trimestrale di Diritto Pubblico*, 66(1), pp. 41–80.

Vedaschi, A. (2016b). Cronaca di una condanna annunciata: Abu Omar a Strasburgo, l'ultimo atto. *DPCE Online*, 1, pp. 265–280.

Vedaschi, A. (2017). State secret privilege versus human rights: Lessons from the European Court of Human Rights ruling on the Abu Omar case. *European Constitutional Law Review*, 13(1), pp. 166–181.

Vedaschi, A. (2018a). The dark side of counter-terrorism: *Arcana imperii* and *salus rei publicae*. *American Journal of Comparative Law*, 66(4), pp. 877–926.

Vedaschi, A. (2018b). Extraordinary renditions: A practice beyond traditional justice. In: Bigo, D., et al. eds. *Extraordinary Renditions: Addressing the Challenges of Accountability*. London and New York: Routledge, pp. 89–121.

Vedaschi, A. (2020). Humiliation of terrorism victims: Is human dignity becoming a 'national security tool'? In: Paulussen, C. and Scheinin, M. eds. *Human Dignity and Human Security in Times of Terrorism*. The Hague: T.M.C. Asser Press/Springer Verlag, pp. 299–331.

Walker, C. (2011). *Terrorism and the Law*. Oxford and New York: Oxford University Press.

7 Non-judicial legal accountability

The case of the Chilean comptroller-general

Guillermo Jiménez

7.1 Introduction

This chapter provides a formal description of structure and functions of the Chilean Office of the Comptroller-General as an institution of non-judicial legal accountability that mediates between the demands of legality and the need for expeditious and expert administration in Latin America. Since the emergence of the administrative state, there has been contention about the desirability of imposing legal, and particularly judicial, constraints on public bureaucracies. To an important extent, the debate has politically revolved around whether commentators display enthusiasm or distrust with respect to ever-expanding administrative powers. The debate is also linked with conflicting preferences for legal or political forms of accountability of the executive branch.

Going beyond traditional court-centred approaches, this debate on the interactions between law and administration has been recently enriched by a growing interest in mapping and researching a broader range of accountability bodies, encompassing a continuously expanding accountability landscape. Remarkably, this literature includes a number of non-judicial institutions of legal accountability and administrative justice (Gellhorn 1966a; Cane 2010; Adler 2010; Tushnet 2020). These studies, which cover a variety of institutions of administrative justice, have enabled researchers to engage fruitfully in comparative institutional analysis of judicial and non-judicial forms of accountability in order to assess their influence on the administrative process (Hertogh 2001; King 2012, ch. 3; Doyle and O'Brien 2020; Asimow et al. 2020). Furthermore, some recent studies have focused on the development of practices, measures, and processes of legal accountability within administrative agencies, which could be labelled as internal administrative law (Mashaw 1983; Parrillo 2017). Arguably, these institutional arrangements and practices could offer additional channels to promote traditional legal values, such as consistency, predictability, and reasoned argument in administrative decision-making (Metzger and Stack 2017). Departing from the exclusive emphasis on external control of bureaucracies, these studies argue that robust democratic governments in modern societies require a mix of outside-in and inside-out accountability arrangements (Shapiro and Wright 2011). Certainly, courts have been key components in the enterprise of enquiring into the sources of legitimation for the growth of the modern administrative state. However, it is sometimes overlooked that this task has been complemented by a combination of further internal and external institutional arrangements (Vermeule 2017).

This debate somehow echoes Guillermo O'Donnell's distinction between vertical and horizontal accountability in the Latin American context. Since the return to democracy in the 1990s, the Latin American debate on accountability institutions has been largely influenced by O'Donnell's work on horizontal accountability. What is important for this study is his emphasis on the relevance of nonjudicial institutions of accountability, which should operate alongside traditional branches of government. O'Donnell argues that horizontal accountability comprises traditional bodies such as courts, legislatures, and executive bodies, yet it also particularly extends to an array of monitoring individuals and agencies, such as, ombudspersons, accounting offices, comptrollers, Conseils d' Etat (Councils of State), *fiscalías* (prosecutors), and the like (O'Donnell 1999, p. 39; 2013, p. 45). Interestingly, O'Donnell asserts that the latter institutions might perform better than the traditional machinery in relation to the accountability needs of Latin American countries. In fact, he claims that 'these agencies, unlike the older ones, were invented not so much having in mind overall balances of power but rather specific, but still quite general, risks of encroachment and/or corruption' (O'Donnell 2013, p. 45). In terms of process, traditional branches act reactively and intermittently, whereas mandated agencies proceed in a proactive and continuous manner. Additionally, the former's interventions are costly and trigger highly visible conflicts, while specialised accountability bodies focus largely on prevention and deterrence. In terms of expertise, moreover, traditional branches are seen as partisan in political conflicts and appear to be a deficient accountability device, whereas new accountability agencies act upon professional criteria and possess 'capabilities to examine complex issues of policy' (O'Donnell 2013). In sum, O'Donnell states that benefits can be expected from the operation of agencies of horizontal accountability since they work in a more flexible, efficient, and expert manner.

In O'Donnell's view, specialised accountability agencies are not necessarily court substitutes. They should operate within a broad network of agencies that oversee executive action at different levels and with different purposes. Some agencies, for instance, should aim to collect and disseminate information, while other bodies can use that information and take action against agencies that have contravened legal boundaries. O'Donnell claims that effective horizontal accountability requires 'a whole network of state agencies, culminating in high courts, committed to preserving and eventually enforcing horizontal accountability, if necessary against the highest powers of the state' (O'Donnell 2013, p. 47). As a result, designers of non-judicial legal accountability frameworks need to pay special attention to coordination issues in order to avoid excessive overlap and unforeseen loopholes.

The importance of O'Donnell's ideas lies in his emphasis on non-traditional institutions of accountability in the Latin American context rather than in his originality. He detected the absence of discussion on such agencies in the region, provided a definition for them, and pointed out some contributions that they could make to democratic governance and the rule of law. His insights coincided with the broader phenomenon of new interest in legal accountability institutions once democracy had returned to most of the countries of the region. Yet, not enough attention has been paid at either the theoretical or descriptive level to the nonjudicial agencies of accountability (Ackerman 2011). Given the explicit stress placed on these agencies by the influential work of O'Donnell, this may appear surprising. Moreover, these agencies also seem significant at the institutional design level. Indeed, as David Landau has stated while discussing the Colombian case, 'The proliferation of an array of institutions and actors other than courts and designed to temper or improve democracy may be one of the most important recent developments in constitutional design' (Landau 2013).

In this chapter, I argue that the Chilean comptroller-general is an illuminating case of non-judicial legal accountability. Mark Bovens' narrow notion of accountability as a specific social relation will guide the following discussion. He defines accountability as 'a relationship between an actor and a forum, in which the actor has an obligation to explain and to justify his or her conduct, the forum can pose questions and pass judgement, and the actor may face consequences' (Bovens 2007). Paraphrasing Boven's concept of accountability, I understand non-judicial legal accountability as a form of accountability in which executive officers have an obligation to explain and justify their conduct according to broadly legal standards to a non-judicial forum that can pose questions and pass judgements.

Drawing on the previous brief conceptual discussion, this chapter examines the current distinctive institutional features and the role played by the Office of the Comptroller-General as a non-judicial institutional agent for legal accountability in Chile. The Office of the Comptroller-General is a relatively opaque and unknown institution, even for contemporary Chilean legal and political commentators. Political and legal observers often overlook bureaucratic or administrative institutions and processes, tending to focus on more visible institutions such as legislatures, presidents, or high courts. Moreover, the sui generis character of the comptroller-general conspires against making insightful comparisons with counterpart bodies elsewhere. Through a detailed formal account, the core of this chapter reveals a hierarchical and monocratic institution whose institutional features are secured by quite rigid rules; it is an organisation with a high degree of formal independence and a variety of accountability powers. Additionally, the office's distinctive legal powers are explained in this chapter. These powers comprise an ex-ante, internal legality review of administrative decision-making and a dispute resolution power consisting of the issuance of binding legal opinions interpreting administrative legality. Such legal powers may illustrate the flexibility, informality, executive-oriented interpretation, and internal and non-adversarial nature that characterise non-judicial forms of legality.

This chapter is divided into two main sections. The first section offers an overview of the constitutional and legal sources that govern the Office of the Comptroller-General. These show strong protection against unilateral reform by political actors.

This section describes the organisational structure of the office, emphasising its single-headed and hierarchical structure and the dominant role of the office head, and highlights the importance and the reputation of its main internal bureaucracy. The second and core section points out the hybrid nature of this office as it combines financial oversight and legal accountability functions. It also examines the main features of the two central legal powers of this non-judicial institution: its distinctive and prominent ex-ante legality review power and its softer power to issue interpretive statements on the legality of administrative actions.

7.2 Constitutional and legal framework

7.2.1 Constitutional regulation

The basic provisions governing the Office of the Comptroller-General are enshrined in the Chilean Constitution. In contrast to other non-judicial accountability agencies in Latin America, this is not a recent feature of Chilean constitutional law.[1] Indeed, the agency was granted its constitutional status in 1943, 15 years after it was founded in 1927. The current constitution, enacted in 1980, introduced a new, complete chapter governing the Office of the Comptroller-General. These provisions regulate the main tasks of the institution, the appointment and prerogatives of the office head, and the procedure of ex-ante legality review of administrative action (*toma de razón* procedure).

The constitution also mentions the Office of the Comptroller-General elsewhere, such as in the provisions regulating the impeachment procedure against the office holder (Arts. 52[2c], 53), the review of secondary legislation enacted by the president (called 'decrees with force of law', Art. 64), and the review of unauthorised payment or expenditure decrees in cases of emergency (Art. 32 n. 20). Finally, the constitution establishes that any further detailed regulation of the internal organisation, procedures and powers of the agency requires a supermajority law (Art. 99[4]). This means that legislation regarding the agency should be approved by a majority of four-sevenths of the elected senators and deputies, respectively (Art. 66[2]). Furthermore, to make changes to the legal framework of the office, the Constitutional Tribunal shall conduct a mandatory ex-ante review (Art. 93 n.1). As can be expected, it is rather cumbersome to pass new legislation in this area.

7.2.2 Organisational structure

7.2.2.1 Hierarchical arrangements

The office is a single-headed institution presided by the comptroller-general of the republic (Art. 2 Organic Law). In this sense, it is comparable to some

---

1 For instance, the influential Brazilian Public Prosecution was created in 1934 as an auditing and oversight institution but was only granted constitutional status in 1988. See Sadek and Cavalcanti 2003, p. 203.

ombudspersons and comptroller-general offices elsewhere. It departs from the collegiate model of institutions, such as the French Conseil d'Etat. Below the office holder, the institution's arrangements follow a hierarchical pattern. The second highest authority in the office is the deputy comptroller-general, who is a subordinate official appointed by the comptroller-general and must replace the latter during his or her absence (Arts. 2, 4, 27). The law requires both authorities to hold a law degree (Art. 2), and the comptroller-general particularly needs legal experience of at least ten years (Art. 98 Constitution). Moreover, under the office's Organic Law, both authorities are entitled to the rights and the tenure secured for judges by the laws of the country (Art. 4). In other words, the two highest officers of the institution are isolated against political pressure from the other branches of government.

The single-headed character of the office entails a strong reliance on the personal traits of its chief authority. This organisational feature is usually associated with the need for institutional energy and increased levels of activity.[2] This assumedly 'active virtue' of the institution, shared by the tribune model of ombudspersons, seems to suggest a more vigorous approach to the office's supervisory functions. However, it may also invite administrative lethargy and, even worse, personalism or a personality cult (Gellhorn 1966b, pp. 48–50).

Various specialised departments have been established under the comptroller-general and his or her deputy. These units are subordinate to the comptroller-general, as the law defines them as dependent on the latter (Art. 2.6), and their holders and all employees of the office remain in their posts as long as they have the exclusive confidence of the comptroller-general (Art. 3.2). In other words, the office head has the power to appoint, promote, or remove any officer within the institution, with independence from any external authority. This feature imprints in the organisation its characteristic hierarchical nature. Although some departments are mentioned in the Organic Law, the comptroller-general has the broad discretion to create new units, rearrange the existing ones, and define their tasks and operative conditions (Arts. 2.2, 2.7 and 5.4).

Additionally, the operation of the office is geographically decentralised through local offices in every region of the country. Currently, 17 regional offices exist. These have no autonomy and must strictly follow the precedents set at the central level. If any novel question of law arises, they should refer it to the relevant department at the central level. Regional comptrollers are not required to have legal training. Thus, although most of them currently hold law degrees, some have other professional backgrounds, such as public management or accountancy.[3]

A two-tier Court of Accounts is also embedded in the office. The deputy comptroller-general heads the Court of Accounts of First Instance and hears indictments against public functionaries who have misused public funds

---

2 The classical locus is Federalist 70. See Hamilton et al. (2009).
3 Information as of January 2020.

Non-judicial legal accountability 107

(Art. 107). A department head or a regional office head acts as the prosecutor (Art. 107 bis). The affected party can appeal first-instance decisions to the Court of Accounts of Second Instance, composed of the comptroller-general and two external ad hoc judges.[4] Despite being within the Office of the Comptroller-General, this two-tier tribunal is viewed by commentators as pertaining to the judiciary and subordinate to the Supreme Court (Silva Bascuñán 1997, p. 215). The main reason for this is characteristically formalist, as it is argued that the institution performs a typically adjudicatory function.

The number of employees in the institution reached 2,103 in 2018 (1,992 in 2016), with 68.2% holding a professional degree. Although the institution possesses a characteristic multidisciplinary nature, lawyers constitute almost a quarter of the office's professional staff. In 2014, the office had 1,375 professional staff, of which 23% were lawyers (321 officers). Public managers constituted the second largest group at 17.5%, while business managers followed in third place with 7.7% (Comptroller General Annual Report 2015). Other professions represented in the office include architects, civil engineers, and accountants. The distribution of these professions varies according to the different departments and subdepartments in the institution.

7.2.2.2 The office head

Both the executive and the legislative branches of the government participate in the appointment of the comptroller-general as the office head. According to Article 99 of the constitution, the President of the Republic appoints the office head, with agreement from the Senate if supported by three-fifths of its active members. A constitutional amendment in 2005 increased the quorum for this decision, which used to require only a simple majority. The current provision forces the president to seek inter-party and inter-branch agreement before appointing the comptroller-general. It has recently been the case that the office is presided by a candidate favoured by the opposition parties.

Until recently, it was suggested that a political convention stipulated that the appointment of the comptroller-general should be based on seniority (Silva Bascuñán 1997, p. 196). Between 1952 and 1997, comptrollers-general were largely appointed according to this convention. In fact, with the exception of Sergio Fernández's appointment for three months in 1978 during the Pinochet dictatorship, all office holders during this period were serving as deputy comptrollers-general when appointed as office heads.[5] The rule was broken in 2002, when the president decided not to appoint a deputy comptroller-general but the head of the Legality Review Department, Gustavo Sciolla. Thus, even in this case, a senior officer was promoted to the highest post in the office. Nonetheless, the

---

4 The ad hoc judges are recommended by the comptroller-general and appointed by the President of the Republic for a four-year term (Art. 118).

5 They include five comptrollers-general: Enrique Bahamonde (1952), Enrique Silva Cimma (1959), Hector Humeres (1967), Osvaldo Iturriaga (1978), and Arturo Aylwin (1997).

108 *Guillermo Jiménez*

convention has been totally discarded for the last two appointments, as outsiders have been selected to lead the institution.

The 2005 Constitutional Reform also reduced the office holder's tenure to a non-renewable eight-year period. Before the amendment, the comptroller-general served until he or she reached 75 years of age. However, the current time frame is in line with the historical record, which shows that office holders have generally remained in the post for approximately eight years each. The eight-year period is also apparently designed to detach the comptroller-general's tenure from the presidential period, which spans four years without the right to run for re-election.

According to the constitution, the comptroller-general is required to have held a law degree for at least ten years. Since the establishment of the office, most of the office holders have been lawyers and more specifically, administrative law experts. Indeed, several have pursued careers as scholars as well as attorneys. Although some have attempted to pursue political careers after their service in the office, comptrollers-general have been viewed generally as apolitical, bureaucratic authorities. The constitution also states that to be appointed as the office head, the candidate should be over 40 years old and hold the right to vote.

The constitution stipulates strict removal rules. The office holder can be removed only by impeachment, commenced in the Chamber of Deputies for notorious dereliction of duties (Art. 52.2.c) and decided by the majority of the active members of the Senate (Art. 53.1). These provisions that regulate proceedings and charges are the same ones that apply to the members of the superior courts of justice, including Supreme Court justices. At the inception of the office, the president had the power to remove the comptroller-general as the latter was regarded as a dependent officer. However, the protections favouring this officer were strengthened in 1943 when the institution was granted constitutional status. Impeachment proceedings against a comptroller-general have taken place only once, resulting in Agustín Vigorena's removal in 1945 (Faúndez 2007a, ch. 5; De la Cruz 2019, pp. 40–43).[6] This exceptional case suggests that these provisions have secured strong protection against attacks from the political branches of the government.

Therefore, the comptroller-general enjoys a high degree of independence from the president and the congress. The constitution also provides functional mechanisms to resolve disputes between the comptroller-general's office and the judiciary. According to current rules, it is for the Senate to resolve jurisdictional disputes between the office and the higher court of justice (Art. 53.3), while disputes between the office and the lower courts have to be adjudicated by the Constitutional Tribunal (Art. 93 n. 12). In the few cases that have arisen thus far, the position of the comptroller-general has always been upheld by either the Senate or the Constitutional Tribunal (Ferrada 2018, p. 329).

---

6 Impeachment proceedings against judges have been exceptional as well. There have been fewer than a dozen cases, and only once was a judge eventually removed from office, in 1992.

Current constitutional and legal provisions do not secure budget independence for the office. This means that the executive and the legislature have to set the budget allocated to the office every year. However, between 1959 and 1977, the comptroller-general enjoyed a budget protected by law. These rules ensured the office a budget of 0.42% of the Annual National Expenditures Budget. These protections were eliminated by the Pinochet government amid neoliberal reforms, reducing the size of the state and following a series of clashes with the office.

7.3 Mandate and powers

7.3.1 Multitasking

Generally, the comptroller-general's offices operate in a number of jurisdictions, performing auditing tasks (Daintith and Page 1999, pp. 194–195; Prosser 2014, pp. 51–57). They are usually members of the commonwealth model of financial oversight institutions, as opposed to the court model (Santiso 2009). Their main aim is to ensure financial regularity in governmental activities. Operating within political accountability networks, these institutions also channel information to the legislature in order to facilitate political scrutiny of executive actions. However, as will be seen, the Chilean Office of the Comptroller-General departs from this model, since it is entrusted with the additional mission of ensuring the administrative agencies' compliance with legal standards (a similar case is found in Israel's State Comptroller; Navot 2014, pp. 175–180). In other words, in contrast to its counterparts elsewhere, the Chilean agency is not only a supreme audit institution but also a legal accountability body.

7.3.2 Ex-ante legality review

7.3.2.1 Basic provisions

The legality review (*toma de razón*) is the most characteristic power of the Chilean comptroller-general. This is the only power of the office that is regulated in some detail in the constitution. It is a process of scrutinising executive rules or decisions based on abstract legality before their promulgation. Here, abstract means that the scrutiny does not depend on concrete litigation or controversy involving the administrative action at stake (I adapt the terminology of Stone Sweet 1992, p. 226). It is currently enshrined in Article 99 of the constitution, which provides that in exercising its function of legal control, the Office of the Comptroller-General will check on decrees and administrative resolutions in the cases provided by legislation.

In brief, the formal mechanics of this checking procedure are as follows. Once an administrative department has adopted a written decision, the relevant authority should submit it to the Office of the Comptroller-General for legal review. Within a 15-day period (unless an extension is given), the checking institution

110 *Guillermo Jiménez*

should review and approve (or reject) the proposed executive action. If the comptroller-general considers it compliant with the law, he or she will uphold the decree or the resolution and return the accompanying file to the relevant agency, enabling it to officially promulgate the rule or the decision. However, if the comptroller-general concludes that the rule is unlawful, he or she will turn it down, and the administrative agency will be unable to promulgate the decision under review. In the latter scenario, the administrative procedure will simply conclude at that point.

However, under Article 99 of the constitution, the president is allowed to state his or her disagreement with the comptroller-general's judgement and insist on the approval of the decree or the resolution.[7] In this case, the procedure will continue, but the final outcome will depend on further considerations. At this point, two situations have to be distinguished. If the decree or the resolution was originally rejected on legality grounds (that is, violation of statutes), the executive will prevail with finality. In this case, the comptroller-general ought to uphold the decision, but the office must refer the entire file to the Chamber of Deputies, which in turn can scrutinise the action on policy grounds. However, if the measure was rejected on constitutionality grounds, the president is not allowed to insist on its approval, and only the Constitutional Tribunal can make the final decision. In this latter case, the president can react to the comptroller-general's adverse determination by referring the dispute to the Constitutional Tribunal, which will have the last word on the matter.

7.3.2.2 *Types of administrative actions under review*

The constitutional provisions that govern this procedure indicate the kinds of administrative actions that the comptroller-general must review. The most important group includes 'decrees and resolutions that, according to the law, shall be handled by the Comptroller-General' (Article 99). These are different forms of secondary or subordinated legislation. The distinction between decrees and resolutions refers to decisions adopted by the President of the Republic or on his or her behalf (decrees) and decisions adopted by executive agencies (resolutions), respectively. Decisions of both individual and general effects are included in the review procedure. A typical example of a decision that has to be submitted for this review is a regulation (*reglamento*) that implements the provisions of a statute.

However, a number of exceptions exist (Silva Cimma 1996, pp. 194ff.; Cordero 2007). In fact, the constitution does not itself establish which decrees and resolutions should be reviewed by the comptroller-general. The constitution merely states that the Organic Law governing the institution regulates this matter. As a result, the specific definition of the rules to be submitted to the comptroller-general for examination is determined by legislation. The office's Organic Law

---

7 See more details below in section 7.3.2.5.

Non-judicial legal accountability   111

defines the first important filter. Article 10.5 declares that the comptroller-general may exempt from review any decree and resolution that he or she perceives as 'not essential'. In practice, for efficiency reasons, since the 1960s the comptroller-general has exercised this power for the purpose of exempting the majority of administrative decisions from review, excluding those related to topics explicitly singled out by the office. This entails that only the most important decisions adopted by administrative agencies have to undergo the comptroller-general's legal scrutiny. Nonetheless, it has been estimated that over 50% of administrative regulations and orders are not exempted from this checking mechanism (Garcés and Rajevic 2009, p. 618).

The second group of exemptions regarding specific administrative agencies derives from statutes that exclude the comptroller-general's review (Carmona 2005, p. 1). A case in point is the significant exclusion of municipalities from this review mechanism (Art. 53 Organic Law of Municipalities). It is not easy for the executive to pass legislation ousting this legality check. In fact, according to the Constitutional Tribunal, a statute excluding a decree or a resolution from the comptroller-general's review should be approved by a four-sevenths supermajority.[8]

The third group does not consist of actual exclusions but of exceptions to the preventive character of the comptroller-general's check. In fact, the congress (again by a supermajority vote) may postpone a legality review, enabling the administrative authority to enact (with immediate effect) an administrative order in case of an emergency. This is the case with the so-called urgency decrees, whose promulgation does not prevent the comptroller-general's check but only entails delayed scrutiny, as the review will take place after the administrative decision at stake is entered into force (Silva Cimma 1996, pp. 230–233).

The discussion so far has concerned administrative actions, that is, individual orders or general regulations whose effects are subordinated to statutory law. However, the comptroller-general can also examine presidential regulations that have the 'force of statutory law'; that is, those that can exceptionally regulate matters falling within the legislature's domain.[9] The particularity of these so-called decrees with force of law is that they have the same legal force as that of regulations passed by the congress (Bermúdez 2011, pp. 47–48). They can actually repeal or modify congressional legislation.[10] The power to enact this sort of legislation is entrenched in Article 32 n. 3 and Article 64 of the constitution.[11]

---

8 See Constitutional Tribunal Decision (1987) Rol 45; Constitutional Tribunal Decision (1988) Rol 63; Constitutional Tribunal Decision (2003) Rol 384.
9 For an examination of this kind of power, see Carey and Shugart 1998, p. 9. They define *decree* as 'the authority of the executive to establish law in lieu of action by the assembly'.
10 These powers to make 'decrees with force of law' are comparable to the Henry VIII powers in Britain, but in Chile there is no parliamentary scrutiny regarding the exercise of these powers. Even closer to Chilean arrangements are the French *ordonnances*. See Elliott et al. 2006, pp. 72–73; Brown and Bell 1998, pp. 12–13.
11 The current constitution explicitly authorises the congress to delegate to the president the power to enact decrees 'with force of law', but this was not the case before 1980. At that

112 *Guillermo Jiménez*

Although there is no congressional scrutiny of the decrees enacted under these delegated powers, under Article 99 of the constitution, the comptroller-general must examine these decrees, rejecting them if they exceed or contravene the legislative delegation or infringe the constitution (Silva Bascuñán 2000, pp. 84–85). There is no presidential power of insistence if the comptroller-general turns down a decree with force of law. If the president disagrees with the adverse determination, he or she has to refer the dispute to the Constitutional Tribunal (Art. 93 n. 4). However, if the decree was unlawfully upheld by the comptroller-general, members of the congress could also bring the case to the Constitutional Tribunal for determination.

In short, the comptroller-general's legality review concentrates on major pieces of secondary legislation. Executive decrees regulating matters of legislative domain are also included in the jurisdiction of the office. In this sense, this non-judicial scrutiny process is the primary mechanism for ensuring the legality of government rules.[12] However, it also includes other administrative decisions such as appointments, urban plans, environmental permits, disciplinary sanctions, and even constitutional declarations of emergency.

7.3.2.3 Participants

The paradigmatic institutional actors that participate in the procedure are administrative agencies, which seek to enact the rules or the decisions under review. These administrative authorities include the President of the Republic and all the bodies in the central administration. However, a number of other authorities do not fall within the purview of this legality review procedure. Indeed, some regulatory agencies, the Central Bank, and the municipalities are excluded. Nonetheless, it is still the case that most of the components of the Chilean public administration fall under the comptroller-general's oversight via this non-judicial legal accountability mechanism.

An interesting aspect of the legality review procedure is whether affected parties can challenge or support administrative decisions in this forum. In other words, the issue here is whether non-governmental organisations have a voice. Neither the constitution nor the Comptroller's Organic Law explicitly regulates the issue of private party access. Nonetheless, a long-standing practice recognises the possibility of the affected parties' intervention. As early as the 1960s, a leading commentator explained, 'There is no procedure for this remedy, but in practice it is accepted, and on occasions the Comptroller-General has adopted

---

time, the constitution was silent regarding this legislative practice. As a result, it was unclear if the comptroller-general had jurisdiction over reviewing this type of regulation. For that reason, when the congress delegated regulatory powers, it often explicitly stipulated that the comptroller-general was endowed with the power to check whether the secondary legislation was consistent with the enabling statute (Daniel 1960, pp. 36ff.).

12 There are remarkable parallels with the scrutiny by the Joint Committee on Statutory Instruments. See Page 2001, ch. 8.

decisions rejecting administrative decisions on grounds raised precisely by interested parties' (Daniel 1960, pp. 43–44). The commentator pointed out that regarding regulations of general interest (i.e., administrative rules), it was very difficult when directly affected parties only learned through the media that a procedure of this kind was being conducted.

Currently, both officers and litigants report that affected parties' participation is just a matter of informal contacts among the regulators, the regulated, comptroller officers, and third parties. However, in legal terms, the right to make petitions in the legality review process is remarkably weak (Cordero 2010, p. 183). For instance, the comptroller-general has decided that the lodging of ex parte briefs does not interrupt the process and that neither the Office of the Comptroller-General nor the regulators have to address the concerns raised by affected third parties (Ruling 27,272, 2008). Thus, private parties can be heard, but there will not necessarily be an adversarial process. This discouraging attitude towards private party participation is explained by the fear of excessive judicialisation of this legality review process (Vergara 2012, pp. 106–107).

7.3.2.4 Standard of review

The decrees or the regulations examined by the comptroller-general through this procedure are judged under legal and constitutional standards. This implies that administrative decisions are assessed in the light of statutory and constitutional provisions (Constitution, Art. 99). Underpinning the nature of the comptroller-general as an independent legal check, not an advisory body, it is not allowed to review the merits of the decision under examination (Organic Law, Art. 21B; Bordalí and Ferrada 2008, pp. 34–35). However, there is a long-standing view that the check by the comptroller-general must go beyond mere legality. For instance, an influential scholar has argued that in this procedure, the administration is required to demonstrate not only the legality of the measures but that the outcome is the right solution to address the social problem at stake (Soto-Kloss 2012, p. 203). Thus, in this viewpoint, the scrutiny should encompass both legality and merit. More recently, some scholars have argued that the examination under the legality review procedure should embrace broader notions of good administration, not only formal legality (Vergara 2012, p. 106).

The comptroller-general lacks investigatory powers during the legality review procedure. However, he or she can request officers of any administrative department to provide information related to the service (Organic Law, Article 9). Additionally, it is a well-established practice that the office can require supporting factual evidence before deciding on the legality of an administrative decision (see, e.g., cases mentioned in Millar 2000).

7.3.2.5 The insistence mechanism—the presidential override

The influence of the Office of the Comptroller-General on public administration is significant. One reason for this is that it works closely with administrative

114   *Guillermo Jiménez*

agencies. However, its main source of power resides in the fact that it can paralyse administrative action, including presidential regulations. This may be surprising because this checking body does not have the last word on the legality of administrative acts. As mentioned, if the comptroller-general rejects an executive decision on legality grounds, the president can, under certain conditions, insist on overriding the former's determination. This mechanism is often called 'presidential insistence'. If the rejection is based on constitutional grounds, the president can request the Constitutional Tribunal to adjudicate the dispute.

Currently, presidential insistence is regulated at both the constitutional and the legal levels (Constitution, Article 99; Organic Law, Article 10). It has been argued that this procedure expresses a non-legalistic conception of political disagreements (Atria 2012).[13] While a legalist conception conceives a disagreement as a technical controversy to be solved in a technical forum, a political or reflexive conception claims that political controversies must be decided (in the last instance) by political bodies, such as presidents or parliaments (Atria 2012, p. 331). In this viewpoint, the importance of the presidential override is that despite being politically costly for the president to take his or her preferred course of action, it does not prevent him or her from having the last word (Atria 2012, p. 333) Therefore, if the president insists, he or she will escalate the conflict, transforming it from a technical legal controversy to a political disagreement in which public opinion and other political actors might be engaged. However, this new dimension of the conflict will be informed and enriched by the perspective of the comptroller-general and other technical instances that may have been heard in the meantime.

In concrete terms, in politically controversial times, the president has intensively exercised his or her powers to prevail over the comptroller-general's opposition by insisting on his or her previous determinations. One such period was during Salvador Allende's socialist government in the 1970s (Faúndez 2007a, ch. 9, 2007b). However, this complex institutional device has not been used over the last few decades. Indeed, the last time a decree of insistence was enacted by the executive was in 1990, just after the end of Pinochet's dictatorship, when the President of the Republic intended to remove the head of a public university. An explanation for the president's unwillingness to exercise his override power may lie in the relative consensual politics that have been commonplace in Chile since Pinochet's dictatorship. In contrast to the situation in previous decades, the political elites' disagreement concerning the boundaries of legality has not reached critical levels (see Figure 7.1). An alternative explanation may simply be that it is rare for the comptroller-general to reject administrative decisions (Garcés and Rajevic 2009).

---

13 This view seems to be inspired by discussions about legislative overrides in commonwealth constitutionalism. For this discussion, see Gardbaum (2001).

Non-judicial legal accountability 115

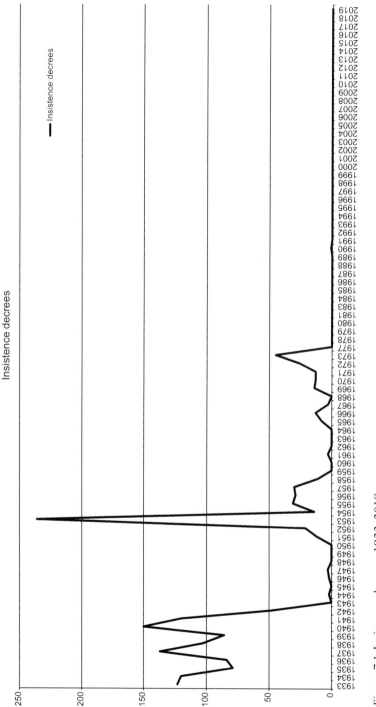

Figure 7.1 Insistence decrees, 1933–2019

116 *Guillermo Jiménez*

7.3.3 *The power of dispute resolution*

7.3.3.1 *Basic provisions*

The dispute-resolution function of the Office of the Comptroller-General is based on its power to provide legal opinions interpreting administrative legality. The office's interpretive power (*potestad dictaminante*) may be defined as the non-judicial power to issue binding legal opinions in case of any doubt or uncertainty about the proper interpretation of the statutes that regulate public services. In contrast to the ex-ante power of the legality review (*toma de razón*), no constitutional provisions regulate this interpretive power. Nevertheless, although with a different language, it has been regulated in the comptroller-general's Organic Law since the inception of the institution. However, the contemporary features of this power only crystallised in the 1950s.

This power is currently primarily contained in Article 6 of the comptroller-general's Organic Law in the following terms:

> It is only for the Comptroller-General to report about salaries, rewards, allocations, evictions, pensions, retirements . . . and in general about the matters related to the statute of public employees, and about the functioning of public services under its oversight, in order to ensure the proper application of the statutes and the regulations that govern them.
>
> Equally, it is for the Comptroller-General to inform about any other issue related to or that may relate to the expenditure or commitments of public funds, as long as doubts arise over the proper application of the respective statutes.
>
> The Comptroller-General shall neither intervene nor report on issues that either by their nature are of litigious character or that fall under the domain of the courts of justice, or that fall under the remit of the State Defence Council, notwithstanding the powers that, regarding judicial matters, this law grants to the Comptroller.
>
> According to the foregoing, only the decisions and reports of the Comptroller-General of the republic could be invoked as administrative jurisprudence in the matters referred to in Article 1.

This somewhat confusing provision has been interpreted in the following manner. On one hand, it ensures the comptroller-general's interpretive domain in matters relating to public administration. It conceives the institution as the primary non-judicial interpreter of administrative legality. Moreover, its determinations are binding on administrative officers and institutions: they constitute 'administrative jurisprudence'. On the other hand, the interpretive powers of the office must not invade the judicial domain. Although it offers no guidance for drawing boundaries, the provision assumes the separation between administrative issues and judicial disputes. Certainly, there are historical reasons for interpreting the provision in this way. As stated, for decades, the Office of the Comptroller-General has acted as a court substitute due to the restricted regime of judicial review in the country, and the ambiguity of this legal provision has allowed political actors to justify the office's adjudicatory functions.

7.3.3.2 Aims and functions

In principle, this power operates regardless of any concrete administrative decision. Originally, it was not designed as a power to challenge administrative action directly but as a power to provide authoritative interpretations of the statutes governing the use of administrative power. However, over the years, the function has become more complex. Currently, through its statements, the Office of the Comptroller-General can render interpretive opinions about the rules that regulate the civil service, solve conflicts of jurisdiction among public bodies, coordinate internal control procedures of administrative agencies, and, importantly, adjudicate disputes between public bodies and private parties (Letelier 2015; De la Cruz 2019). Beyond academic disagreement about boundaries, the Office of the Comptroller-General currently operates as a site for the protection of rights against administrative action on a daily basis (Valdivia 2017, p. 351).

According to the literature, this power is aimed to ensure that public law is properly and uniformly interpreted and applied across administrative agencies (Cordero 2010, p. 171). In exercising this power, the Office of the Comptroller-General operates as a centralised interpretive non-judicial forum. Consequently, this institution may reduce with a general effect the ambiguity of legislation, avoid further litigation, and make administrative action more predictable (Letelier 2015; Cordero 2010, pp. 180ff.). In addition to its interpretive role, the institution has also performed more ambitious, creative tasks. For instance, some commentators have explained that the Office of the Comptroller-General has acted as a 'positive legislator', filling the gaps left by a legislature that has been unable to provide enough basic general regulation for public administration (Cordero 2010, pp. 180ff.).

An illustration of this creative power is the role of the Office of the Comptroller-General in administrative procedures (Jara 2013; González 2012; Pierry 2002, p. 389). Indeed, through its interpretive function, the office filled numerous gaps of the Chilean regime of administrative procedures before the promulgation of a general piece of legislation in 2003. According to some commentators, the institution has played a 'generalising role' (Jara 2013, p. 64). By adjudicating complaints from individuals or responding to agencies' requests for clarification of questions of law, the Office of the Comptroller-General has constructed a complete regime of administrative procedures in the absence of statutory legislation. Drawing on the constitutional right of petition, it developed the right to obtain a response from administrative agencies. According to the office, the administrative bodies have the duty to provide proper responses to petitions filed by citizens (Jara 2013, p. 77). Furthermore, an administrative response should meet certain requirements, such as being written, timely, and conclusive. A written copy of the response should also be provided to the affected party. The other important areas

118   *Guillermo Jiménez*

developed by this body have been publicity, the means of internal reviews, and due process in disciplinary proceedings and in public procurement (Jara 2013, p. 70). More recently, when the legislature has intervened by providing statutory legislation, it has taken inspiration from the rules and the principles already elaborated by the office. Even after the enactment of the Chilean Administrative Procedure Act 2003, the comptroller-general has continued to play a leading role in the clarification of the alleged obscurities in the law. The comptroller-general has issued interpretive statements regarding several matters, such as the scope of the law, the content of the principles of procedure, the means of invalidation by the administration itself, internal complaints procedures, administrative inaction, and so forth (Jara 2013). Further areas of involvement are local government, government information and advertising, urban planning, probity and conflict of interests, state enterprises, and public procurement, among many others.

This feature echoes the function performed by the Conseil d'Etat in France. For instance, Bell explains that 'the role of the *Conseil d'Etat* has very much been to supplement the rules laid down by the legislator' since '[its function] is both to create and enforce standards' (Bell 2001, p. 156). Similarly, Hamson indicates that the French institution has created a body of precedents 'to secure a proper and decent standard of behaviour in the French administration' (Hamson 1954, pp. 126–127; Edley 1992, p. 242). As Edley states it, the Conseil d'Etat has developed 'extrastatutory doctrines of quasi-constitutional administrative law' (Edley 1992, p. 242).

In contrast to the Chilean judiciary, the Office of the Comptroller-General has a strong doctrine of precedents (Marín 2012; Astorquiza 2012). Based on a narrow reading of the Chilean Civil Code, the courts usually maintain that their rulings apply only to the case under consideration. Thus, judicial decisions have no general application, and courts do not abundantly cite them in their reasoning. This implies that it is not difficult to find contradictory decisions within the same court. In contrast, the Office of the Comptroller-General usually makes constant and profuse references to its previous decisions on the same issue. It also explicitly declares when a criterion has changed. This practice is based on a reading of the office's Organic Law, as Article 6 states that only its decisions could be invoked as binding administrative precedents. For the purpose of keeping its precedents up to date, it administers an enormous database containing its previous decisions on a range of topics.[14] As a result, practitioners usually consult the office's database to anticipate the actions of the comptroller-general and administrative agencies.

7.3.3.3 Access

As for access, Article 5[3] of the Organic Law provides a general clause that allows intervention by public and private parties. It stipulates that the Office of the

---

14 The origin of the use of precedents in the office is essentially bureaucratic rather than judicial. Former Comptroller-General Enrique Silva Cimma reports that as a result of internal bureaucratic needs, a crucial device for the institution's doctrine of precedents was created in the 1950s (Silva Cimma 2000, p. 119; Marín 2012, p. 149).

Comptroller-General will issue 'interpretive statements' (*dictámenes*) upon the request of affected parties, heads of public services, or any other authorities. A well-established interpretation of this regulation is that both public agencies and private parties can ask the Office of the Comptroller-General to issue statements that provide authoritative interpretations of administrative legality. Moreover, the office usually issues statements about the legality of administrative decisions if it detects an illegality. In these cases, it intervenes on its own initiative.

This interpretive power has become increasingly important over the last few decades because it further allows private avenues to challenge administrative decisions. Thus, while an ex ante legality review is conducted mainly through a procedure with limited private party participation, the exercise of this interpretive power enables private individuals to voice their grievances and complaints against the administration (Bermúdez 2011, pp. 403ff.). For instance, between 2007 and 2014, over 70% of the cases involving interpretive power were initiated by petitions from private parties or public employees (see Comptroller-General Annual Reports).

Private access to the comptroller-general's remedies through this procedure is not only a matter of fact but also a matter of law. Since 1974, the comptroller-general has accepted the jurisdiction to intervene if the request is based on a previous refusal or a delayed response by an administrative agency (see rulings 24,841, 1974 and 61,598, 2011). In other words, the affected party first has to seek relief from the primary decision maker and only subsequently from the comptroller-general. Of course, this criterion echoes the rule of the 'prior decision' in French administrative law (Brown and Bell 1998, pp. 165–166). However, today's access is even greater. In March 2015, the Office of the Comptroller-General issued a new statement that would determine the rules governing the request for an interpretive opinion (ruling 24,143, 2015). According to this scheme, government bodies can request the office's legal opinions only in matters that fall under their jurisdiction or that have a direct impact on their powers. Moreover, they must previously submit a legal report drafted by their internal advisors and clearly and precisely state their request. As for private parties and administrative officers, in their personal capacity, they can only request for legal opinions on affairs in which they have rights or specific interests, either individual or collective, at stake. Although this represents a narrow view of locus standi, it eliminates the need for a previous complaint against the administration in order to lodge a request with the comptroller-general. Moreover, the new regulation gives the institution the discretion to issue a legal opinion—when the nature and the circumstances of the case call for it—despite the complainant's failure to meet the previously mentioned conditions. Hence, this last provision opens the possibility for public interest standing before the office.

7.3.3.4 Legal authority and limits

Compliance with the comptroller-general's rulings is mandatory for administrative agencies. They are not mere guidance or advisory opinions. Indeed, Article 9

120 *Guillermo Jiménez*

of the Organic Law states that the comptroller-general's 'interpretive opinions are binding to the respective officers, in the case or cases they refer on'. Article 19 also states that lawyers and in-house counsel in every department of the public administration or in institutions under the oversight of the comptroller-general, who do not represent the government in courts, will be subjected to the technical supervision of the office, whose jurisprudence and resolutions must be observed. Disregard for the legal interpretation issued by the office may result in disciplinary or even criminal proceedings (Cordero 2010, p. 170; Aldunate 2005). In other words, the rulings cannot be enforced directly but through disciplinary proceedings (Marín 2012, p. 153).

In practical terms, the comptroller-general's statements consist of clarifications of legal provisions. According to the office's doctrine, these rulings merely declare what is already implicit in the law. As they are mere interpretations, they do not change the law (Cordero 2013, pp. 264–265). As a result, it has been argued that these interpretations have retroactive effect. In other words, they merely declare the proper interpretation of the statute's meaning and intent since its enactment (Pallavicini 2010, p. 127; Aróstica 1989, p. 541). Nevertheless, the office can quite flexibly reconsider its own interpretive opinions.[15] Thus, in contrast to the judiciary, the principle of res judicata does not apply to the interpretations issued by the office. As a commentator expressed it in 1963, the office has the duty to actively seek the right interpretation of the law and address reconsideration petitions filed by affected parties because 'it is not possible to persist in error if subsequently one becomes fully aware of it' (ruling 62,927, 1963, cited by Marín 2012, p. 153). To avoid harming legitimate expectations, the office has recently developed a doctrine according to which its reconsiderations only apply prospectively.

The Organic Law states an important limit to the otherwise extensive powers of the comptroller-general. Article 6.3 states that the office shall neither intervene nor report on issues that by their nature are either litigious or subjected to the jurisdiction of the courts of justice. The provision adds that these issues fall under the remit of the Council of Defence of the State, the agency in charge of the legal representation of the treasury before the courts. According to the traditional interpretation, this provision sets the boundaries within which the Office of the Comptroller-General can act. Beyond that, it would interfere in the judicial arena (Silva Cimma 1995, p. 172).

7.4 Conclusion

This chapter has provided an overview of the structure, functions, and powers of the Chilean Office of the Comptroller-General as a non-judicial mechanism for legal accountability. This brief outline helps broaden the understanding of the

---

15 However, Soto-Kloss has adopted the extreme position that the Office of the Comptroller-General cannot deviate from its prior opinions. See Soto-Kloss (1999, p. 399).

institutional forms of holding administrative power to account beyond the traditional court system, drawing on previous work about non-judicial legal accountability in Latin America and elsewhere.

This Chilean institution of non-judicial legal accountability exhibits the following three main features. First, the institution is governed by rigid legal arrangements, which are difficult to modify without a high degree of political and inter-institutional consensus. This has also entailed the survival of old-fashioned legal structures with little room for adjustment to new circumstances. Second, the institution enjoys a high degree of independence from the other branches of government. Although a component of the executive branch, it is conceived as autonomous from the President of the Republic. This independence is reflected in the appointment, tenure, and everyday operation of the institution. The Office of the Comptroller-General is equally independent of the judiciary and the congress. Its constitutional status has prompted some commentators to regard it as the fourth branch of government in the Chilean political system. Internally, the office displays a hierarchical structure, concentrating power in the office head. However, a large bureaucracy works within the institution that for historical and functional reasons has enjoyed a good reputation.

Third, the Office of the Comptroller-General can be described as a multitasking institution. It performs expert financial and legal accountability functions, and its role as a financial oversight body is a feature shared with comparable organisations elsewhere. What is distinctive about the Office of the Comptroller-General is its non-judicial legal accountability role. It intervenes in reviewing major government rules and administrative decisions before their promulgation, wielding a remarkable veto power. To avoid the risk of administrative deadlock, under certain conditions, the executive branch can override adverse determinations of the comptroller-general. The institution also performs adjudicatory functions, acting as an arbiter in disputes among public bodies or between them and private parties. This dimension of the office has been developed by interpreting its ambiguous organic legislation, with the view of broadening access to the limited forms of administrative justice existing in Chile.

In brief, the Office of the Comptroller-General has developed as a hybrid institution that has adapted to demands for legality in the context of dysfunctional administrative justice arrangements. Despite its non-judicial nature, the body has operated to promote distinctive legal accountability values such as consistency, rule interpretation, impartiality, publicity, and aggrieved parties' access to redress. Its unplanned growth has given the office some distinctive organisational and functional features that have made it a non-judicial institutional entity worthy of closer inspection.

References

Ackerman, J. (2011). Understanding independent accountability agencies. In: Rose-Ackerman, S. and Lindseth, P. T. eds. *Comparative Administrative Law*. Cheltenham: Edward Elgar Publishing.

122 *Guillermo Jiménez*

Adler, M. (2010). Understanding and analysing administrative justice. In: Adler, M. ed. *Administrative Justice in Context.* Oxford: Hart Publishing.

Aldunate, E. (2005). La evolución de la función de control de la Contraloría General de la República. *Revista de Derecho*, 26 (Pontificia U. Católica de Valparaíso), pp. 19–20.

Aróstica, I. (1989). Notas sobre los dictámenes de la Contraloría General de la República. *XX Jornadas de derecho público*, 531 (U de Valparaíso), pp. 531–553.

Asimow, M., Bocksang, G., Cirotteau, M., Dotan, Y. and Perroud, T. (2020). Between the agency and the court: Ex Ante review of regulations. *The American Journal of Comparative Law*, 68(332), pp. 332–375.

Astorquiza, G. (2012). A propósito de la Contraloría General de la República y de su quehacer interpretativo del ordenamiento jurídico. Criterios. In: Contraloría General de la República ed. *La Contraloría General de la República y el estado de derecho. 75 años de vida institucional (1927–2002).* Contraloría General de la República, pp. 193–215.

Atria, F. (2012). Legalismo y reflexividad: La contraloría como modelo. In: *La Contraloría General de la República y el Estado de Derecho. 75 años de Vida Institucional 1927–2002.* Contraloría General de la República, pp. 317–344.

Bell, J. (2001). *French Legal Cultures.* London: Butterworths.

Bermúdez, J. (2011). *Derecho Administrativo General.* 2nd ed. Santiago: Legal Publishing.

Bordalí, A. and Ferrada, J. C. (2008). *Estudios de Justicia Administrativa.* Santiago: Lexis Nexis.

Bovens, M. (2007). Analysing and assessing accountability: A conceptual framework. *European Law Journal*, 13, pp. 447–468.

Brown, L. N. and Bell, J. (1998). *French Administrative Law.* 5th ed. Oxford: Clarendon Press.

Cane, P. (2010). *Administrative Tribunals and Adjudication.* Oxford: Hart Publishing.

Carey, J. M. and Shugart, M. S. (1998). Calling out the tanks or filling out the forms? In: Carey, J. M. and Soberg Shugart, M. eds. *Executive Decree Authority.* New York: Cambridge University Press.

Carmona, C. (2005). *El principio de control. El control externo, jurídico y no jurisdiccional de la administración.* Santiago: Universidad de Chile.

Comptroller General (2015). *Annual Report.* Santiago: Comptroller-General Office Publications.

Cordero, L. (2007). La Contraloría General de la República y la Toma de Razón: Fundamento de Cuatro Falacias. *Revista de Derecho Público (U. de Chile)*, 69, pp. 153–166.

Cordero, L. (2010). La jurisprudencia administrativa en perspectiva: Entre legislador positivo y juez activista. *Anuario de Derecho Público UDP 165.*

Cordero, L. (2013). Nulidad y dictaminación de Contraloría. Nuevas formas de declaración de ilegalidad. Comentario a las sentencias del caso CMPC. *Anuario de Derecho Público UDP 256.*

Daintith, T. and Page, A. (1999). *The Executive in the Constitution: Structure, Autonomy, and Internal Control.* Oxford: Oxford University Press.

Daniel, M. (1960). *El Control Jurídico de la Administración. Nociones Fundamentales.* Santiago: Editorial Universitaria.

De la Cruz, A. (2019). *Contraloría General de la República: ¿Jurisdicción contenciosa administrativa?* Santiago: Ediciones Der.

Doyle, M. and O'Brien, N. (2020). *Reimagining Administrative Justice Human Rights in Small Places.* London: Palgrave Macmillan.

Edley, C. F. (1992). *Administrative Law: Rethinking Judicial Control of Bureaucracy.* New Haven: Yale University Press.

Elliott, C., Vernon, C. and Jeanpierre, E. (2006). *French Legal System.* 2nd ed. London: Pearson Longman.

Faúndez, J. (2007a). *Democratization, Development, and Legality: Chile, 1831–1973.* London: Palgrave Macmillan.

Faúndez, J. (2007b). The fragile foundations of administrative legality: Chile between 1932 and 1973. *Journal of Comparative Law*, 2, pp. 77–94.

Ferrada, J. C. (2018). Las recientes contiendas de competencia entre la Contraloría General de la República y los tribunales de justicia: una disputa en las sombras. *Anuario de Derecho Público UDP 329.*

Garcés, M. F. and Rajevic, E. (2009). Control de legalidad y procedimiento de toma de razón. In: Tomicic, V. and Garcia, C. eds. *Un Mejor Estado para Chile: Propuestas de Modernización y Reforma.* Consorcio para la Reforma del Estado.

Gardbaum, S. (2001). The new commonwealth model of constitutionalism. *The American Journal of Comparative Law*, 49(707), pp. 707–760.

Gellhorn, W. (1966a). *Ombudsmen and Others: Citizens Protectors in Nine Countries.* Cambridge: Harvard University Press.

Gellhorn, W. (1966b). *When Americans Complain: Governmental Grievance Procedures.* Cambridge: Harvard University Press.

González, M. (2012). El procedimiento administrativo en Chile. Aporte de la Contraloría General. In: *La Contraloría General de la República y el Estado de Derecho. 75 años de Vida Institucional 1927–2002.* Contraloría General de la República, pp. 377–392.

Hamilton, A., Madison, J. and Jay, J. (2009). *The Federalist.* Belknap Press of Harvard University Press.

Hamson, C. J. (1954). *Executive Discretion and Judicial Control: An Aspect of the French Conseil D'etat.* London: Stevens.

Hertogh, M. (2001). Coercion, cooperation, and control: Understanding the policy impact of administrative courts and the ombudsman in the Netherlands. *Law & Policy*, 23(47), pp. 47–67.

Jara, J. (2013). La Contraloría General de la República y su contribución al surgimiento y evolución del procedimiento administrativo en Chile. *Revista de Derecho Público (U. de Chile)*, 78, pp. 63–77.

King. J. (2012). *Judging Social Rights.* Cambridge: Cambridge University Press.

Landau, D. (2013). Checking institutions and the institutional control of politics. *Int'l J. Const. L. Blog* [Online]. Available from: www.iconnectblog.com/2013/12/checking-institutions-and-the-institutional-control-of-politics [Accessed 13 December 2013].

Letelier, R. (2015). La Contraloría General de la República. In: Viera, Ch., Bassa, J. and Ferrada, J. C. eds. *La Constitución Chilena. Una revisión crítica a su práctica política.* Santiago: Lom Ediciones.

Marín, U. (2012). La jurisprudencia administrativa de la Contraloría General y su relación con la de los tribunales y de otros organismos estatales. *Contraloría General de la República: 85 Años de Vida Institucional.* Contraloría General de la República, pp. 149–156.

Mashaw, J. (1983). *Bureaucratic Justice: Managing Social Security Disability Claims.* New Haven: Yale University Press.

124 *Guillermo Jiménez*

Metzger, G. E. and Stack, K. M. (2017). Internal administrative law. *Michigan Law Review*, 115(1239), pp. 1239–1307.

Millar, J. (2000). Alcance del control de legalidad. Su evolución a propósito de los actos administrativos requisitorios, durante 1970–1973. *Revista de Derecho (Universidad Austral de Valdivia)*, 11, pp. 83–94.

Navot, S. (2014). *The Constitution of Israel: A Contextual Analysis*. Oxford: Hart Publishing.

O'Donnell, G. A. (1999). Horizontal accountability in new democracies. In: Schedler, A., Diamond, L. and Plattner, M. eds. *The Self-Restraining State: Power and Accountability in New Democracies*. Boulder: Lynne Rienner Publishers.

O'Donnell, G. A. (2013). Horizontal accountability: The legal institutionalization of mistrust. In: Welna, Ch. and Mainwaring, S. eds. *Democratic Accountability in Latin America*. Oxford: Oxford University Press.

Page, E. C. (2001). *Governing by Numbers: Delegated Legislation and Everyday Policy-Making*. Oxford: Hart Publishing.

Pallavicini, J. (2010). Control de constitucionalidad de la Contraloría General de la República. *Revista de Derecho Público (U. de Chile)*, 72(108), pp. 108–132.

Parrillo, N. R. ed. (2017). *Administrative Law from the Inside Out: Essays on Themes in the Work of Jerry L Mashaw*. Cambridge: Cambridge University Press.

Pierry, P. (2002). Las transformaciones del derecho administrativo en el siglo XX. *XXIII Revista de Derecho (Universidad Católica de Valparaíso)*, 377, pp. 377–404.

Prosser, T. (2014). *The Economic Constitution*. Oxford: Oxford University Press.

Sadek, M. T. and Cavalcanti, R. B. (2003). The new Brazilian public prosecution: An agent of accountability. In: Welna, Ch. and Mainwaring, S. eds. *Democratic Accountability in Latin America*. Oxford: Oxford University Press.

Santiso, C. (2009). *The Political Economy of Government Auditing: Financial Governance and the Rule of Law in Latin America and Beyond*. Abingdon: Routledge-Cavendish.

Shapiro, S. A. and Wright, R. F. (2011). The future of the administrative presidency: Turning administrative law inside-out. *University of Miami Law Review*, 65(577), pp. 577–620.

Silva Bascuñán, A. (1997). *Tratado de derecho constitucional*, vol. 9. Santiago: Editorial Jurídica de Chile.

Silva Bascuñán, A. (2000). *Tratado de derecho constitucional. Congreso Nacional. La función legislativa*, vol. 7. Santiago: Editorial Jurídica de Chile.

Silva Cimma, E. (1995). *Derecho administrativo chileno y comparado. El control público*. Santiago: Editorial Jurídica de Chile.

Silva Cimma, E. (1996). *Derecho administrativo chileno y comparado. Introducción y fuentes*. Santiago: Editorial Jurídica de Chile.

Silva Cimma, E. (2000). *Memorias privadas de un hombre público*. Santiago: Editorial Andrés Bello.

Soto-Kloss, E. (1999). Acerca de la obligatoriedad de los precedentes en la actividad administrativa del estado. *Revista Chilena de Derecho*, 26(399), pp. 399–403.

Soto-Kloss, E. (2012). La toma de razón y el poder normativo de la Contraloría General de la República. *La Contraloría General de la República. 50 años de vida institucional 1927–1977*. Contraloría General de la República, pp. 181–206.

Stone Sweet, A. (1992). *The Birth of Judicial Politics in France: The Constitutional Council in Comparative Perspective*. Oxford: Oxford University Press.

Tushnet, M. (2020). Institutions protecting constitutional democracy: Some conceptual and methodological preliminaries. *University of Toronto Law Journal*, 70(95), pp. 95–106.

Valdivia, J. M. (2017). Reflexiones sobre las acciones en derecho administrativo. In: Schopf, A. and Marín, J. C. eds. *Lo público y lo privado en el derecho. Estudios en homenaje al profesor Enrique Barros Bourie*. Santiago: Thomson Reuters.

Vergara, A. (2012). El rol de la Contraloría General de la República: Desde el control de legalidad a los nuevos estándares de buena administración. *Contraloría General de la República: 85 Años de Vida Institucional (1927–2012)*. Contraloría General de la República, pp. 103–110.

Vermeule, A. (2017). Bureaucracy and distrust: Landis, Jaffe and Kagan on the administrative state. *Harvard Law Review*, 130, pp. 2463–2488.

Part III
Authority

8 Presidents' (mis)use of public accountability

Going-public tactics in European semi-presidential regimes

Thomas Sedelius

8.1 Introduction

There has been a steady rise in the number of countries with directly elected presidents in recent decades and, similarly, an increasing research focus on the concentration of power around single executive leaders (Passarelli 2015, 2018; Poguntke and Webb 2005). Semi-presidentialism, where a directly elected president shares executive power with a prime minister, is currently the constitutional model in about 20 European countries.[1] The dual executive structure of semi-presidentialism poses some specific challenges of accountability, as the voters elect a president who appoints a prime minister who in turn relies on the confidence of the parliament in order to survive. Thus defined, the prime minister in a semi-presidential system serves as an agent of two directly elected principals (the parliament and the president) creating a built-in potential for institutional conflict. Moreover, and in contrast to a presidential system where the president's responsibility for government policy is more direct and transparent, a dual executive structure allows the president to either claim credit for successful policies or escape policy responsibility by publicly criticising the cabinet, depending on how it may serve his or her future electoral prospects. Thus, in terms of accountability to the electorate—that is, to what extent the voters can discern whether the executives are acting in their interest and sanction them appropriately—the dual executive structure is more ambiguous than parliamentary and presidential systems.

Hence, comparative political research on semi-presidentialism has paid considerable attention to regime stability and how presidential power and a divided government affect democratic performance (e.g., Cavatorta and Elgie 2010; Cheibub et al. 2014; Elgie 2011; 2016; Sedelius and Linde 2018). A number of studies have focused on intra-executive conflicts between the president and the prime minister (Elgie 2018b; Protsyk 2006; Sedelius and Mashtaler 2013). Evidently, intra-executive conflicts have caused disruptive policy-making processes, repeated

---

1 These countries are Austria, Belarus, Bulgaria, Croatia, the Czech Republic, Finland, France, Iceland, Ireland, Lithuania, Macedonia, Moldova, Montenegro, Poland, Romania, Serbia, Slovakia, Slovenia, Russia, and Ukraine.

130 *Thomas Sedelius*

constitutional reforms, and even political instability in some cases (e.g., Poland in 1995 and 2007; Romania in 2012, 2017–2018; Ukraine in 2006–2010).

Semi-presidential constitutions in Europe predominantly favour the prime minister over the president, with presidential prerogatives largely restricted to representative functions and co-shared leadership in foreign, security, and defence policies (Raunio 2012). However, contrary to what constitutional power reveals, political outcomes of intra-executive tensions are often in the president's favour (Raunio and Sedelius 2019). The reasons why the president often prevails over the prime minister may vary, but they often directly or indirectly relate to the perceived moral authority and public support enjoyed by the president. The president is directly accountable to the people and typically more popular than the prime minister (and other party politicians), and aggressive use of public grandstanding may work in the president's favour. However, few studies, if any, have systematically examined to what extent going-public tactics really matter to intra-executive relations in semi-presidential systems. Previous research on presidential strategies has been primarily based on presidential systems in the US and Latin America (cf. Kernell 2013), where no dual executive structure exists. From these studies, it appears that presidents can effectively use the option of public addresses to strengthen their bargaining position and do so by illustrating the potential electoral costs to opponents (Cox and Kernell 1991). In semi-presidential systems, this option should intuitively be attractive to presidents, considering their more limited constitutional powers but the usually strong public support for them. Additionally, in the absence of a detailed constitutional division of labour and coordination between the president and the prime minister, the president is likely to exploit public opinion in order to possibly intervene in matters falling under the competence of the government. However, just as going-public tactics may contribute to resolving conflicts, they may also further exacerbate conflicts and tensions between the executive leaders.

Hence, in this chapter I examine the link between the presidents' use of going-public tactics and intra-executive conflicts in European semi-presidential regimes. The idea is to investigate when and how perceived popular legitimacy by the president impedes and sometimes even outperforms formal constitutional power in intra-executive relations. Using both primary and secondary data on president-cabinet relations and intra-executive conflicts, including expert interview materials from three countries (Finland, Lithuania, and Romania), I examine how presidents with relatively weak constitutional powers use informal strategies of going public to increase their influence on government and policy. The empirical analysis covers the period from the early 1990s to 2019 and highlights a number of intra-executive confrontations where the presidents' perceived popular legitimacy has played a role in the direction and outcome of conflicts.

In the next section, I present this study's comparative design and data, followed by definitions and theoretical standpoints, where I briefly elaborate on how to define semi-presidentialism but discuss in more detail the built-in institutional logic of semi-presidentialism, including how the president's popular mandate is relevant to intra-executive relations. In the subsequent empirical section, I

(Mis)use of public accountability 131

cover a contextual presentation of the three countries' semi-presidential systems, followed by the analysis, in which I examine a number of intra-executive conflicts where the presidents have used going-public tactics to influence political outcomes in their favour. Finally, I discuss how the popular mandate and the perceived popular support of the president function as an informal institution and an accountability mechanism where popular opinion has a determining effect on political behaviour between elections.

8.2 Research design and data

This research is based on a comparative case study design, including two Central European countries (Lithuania and Romania) on one hand, and Finland as a long-lasting case of European semi-presidentialism on the other. Finland aside, Lithuania and Romania have the shared legacy of systemic communism, their subsequent transition to democracy and a market economy in the 1990s, and their European Union (EU) and North Atlantic Treaty Organization (NATO) accession processes in the 2000s. However, each country represents a unique semi-presidential trajectory: high levels of institutionalisation and the weakening of a historically strong presidency in Finland since the early 2000s; general intra-executive stability under a personalised political system in Lithuania; and party system instability, strong presidential influence, and high institutional tensions in Romania. By examining the conditions and the implications of going-public tactics used by ten presidents in these three countries, I am especially interested in the extent to which the presidents' (perceived) popular legitimacy impedes and even outperforms formal constitutional power in the intra-executive relations between the presidents and the prime ministers. A guiding assumption in this study is that the impact of the presidents' going-public strategies is conditioned by formal constitutional powers, unified or divided governments (cohabitation), the presidents' influence on their parties, and the prevailing norms among the political elites regarding the presidents' role in the political systems.

The empirical materials consist of primary and secondary data on president-cabinet relations and intra-executive conflicts, including expert interviews covering the period from the early 1990s to 2019.[2] Written sources include official documents (e.g., constitutions, laws, rules of procedure), academic literature (e.g., comparative and case study-oriented articles, books, reports and updates)

---

2 The experts in each country were contacted in order to collect information on how the semi-presidential systems had worked in practice with regard to intra-executive relations and coordination mechanisms. The key objective of the interviews was to establish the actual role and importance of intra-executive institutions, and the data were primarily used for a project whose outcome is largely reported in Raunio and Sedelius (2020). The interviewees were willing to speak only under the condition of confidentiality. In total, 10 persons were interviewed in Finland, 9 in Lithuania and 12 in Romania. Many of them had experience in intra-executive coordination under two or more presidents. The interviewees' positions include current and former high-level civil servants, counsellors and advisors in the offices of the president and the prime minister, speakers and members of parliament (MPs), and ministers.

132 *Thomas Sedelius*

and additional secondary materials (e.g., online resources, such as the research-based blog *Presidential Power*).

8.3 Theory and definitions

Since Duverger's founding definition[3] of semi-presidentialism, there has been a contentious and drawn-out debate on how to categorise dual executive regimes with a popularly elected president and an indirectly elected/selected prime minister accountable to the parliament. Duverger's (1980, p. 4) non-institutional criterion, stating that in a semi-presidential regime 'the president possesses quite considerable powers', has caused confusion. Scholars have approached it differently, and classifications of semi-presidential countries have varied extensively. In response, Elgie (1999, p. 13) proposes a minimalist and strictly constitutional definition: 'semi-presidentialism is where a constitution includes a popularly elected fixed-term president and a prime minister and cabinet who are collectively responsible to the legislature'. In turn, Elgie's definition has triggered considerable critique for encompassing too many and disparate countries. For both theoretical and empirical reasons, there is a need to separate different forms of semi-presidentialism. Among the alternatives in the literature, Shugart and Carey's (1992) distinction between two sub-types of semi-presidentialism (premier-presidential and president-parliamentary regimes) has gained broad acceptance. In premier-presidentialism, (1) the president is elected by a popular vote for a fixed term of office and (2) the president selects the prime minister who shall head the cabinet, but (3) the authority to dismiss the cabinet rests exclusively with the parliament. In president-parliamentarism, (1) the president is elected by a popular vote for a fixed term of office, (2) the president appoints and dismisses the prime minister and other cabinet ministers, and (3) the prime minister and the cabinet ministers are subjected to parliamentary and presidential confidence (Shugart 2005, p. 333; Shugart and Carey 1992, pp. 23–24). Hence, the defining distinction is that under president-parliamentarism, the government is accountable to both the president and the parliament, whereas under premier-presidentialism, the government is accountable to the parliament only. In this study, I confine the analysis to premier-presidentialism and to three selected European cases.

Power sharing between the executives precludes a clear separation of powers, which may exacerbate constitutional ambiguity and conflict. Due to the parliament's exclusive power to dismiss the prime minister under premier-presidentialism, the government is likely to propose policy that the parliamentary majority can accept even when in conflict with the president's agenda. Therefore, intra-executive tensions between the president and the cabinet can be expected whenever the president and the parliament have different policy directions.

---

3 Duverger (1980, p. 4) defines semi-presidentialism based on three criteria: (1) The president is elected by universal suffrage. (2) The president possesses quite considerable powers. (3) The prime minister and other ministers also possess executive and governmental powers but can stay in office only with the consent of the parliament.

(Mis)use of public accountability   133

Empirical studies confirm this expectation, showing that intra-executive conflicts are conditioned by presidential powers, majority conditions in the parliament, and even the prime minister's presidential ambitions (Amorim Neto and Strøm 2006; Protsyk 2005, 2006; Schleiter and Morgan-Jones 2010). Sedelius and Ekman's (2010) study on the implications of intra-executive conflicts in Eastern Europe suggests that conflicts are associated with early resignation of governments. Cohabitation, 'where the president and prime minister are from opposing parties and where the president's party is not represented in cabinet' (Elgie 2011, p. 12), increases the likelihood of intra-executive conflicts (Sedelius and Mashtaler 2013). Cohabitation may cause tension and undermine general performance, especially in young democracies, or when no clear-cut constitutional provision sets out the distribution of power among the key actors (Elgie 2010; Gherghina and Miscoiu 2013; Shoesmith 2003).

Variations in formal presidential powers go a long way towards explaining key differences among semi-presidential regimes and to determining the power balance between the president and the prime minister. To what extent presidents actually use or need to use their formal powers certainly varies and does not only depend on the distribution of power, however. In this study, I am interested in how presidents try to influence politics through informal power and direct appeals to the public. Based on a study of Central and Eastern Europe, De Raadt (2009) argues that constitutional ambiguity about executive leadership provides the presidents with substantial room to manoeuvre, making it more difficult for citizens to determine whom to hold accountable. Such considerations are particularly relevant, as surveys have shown high levels of public trust in the presidents but outright distrust in other political leaders, including the prime minister and political parties (cf. Baltic Barometer 2014; Ekman et al. 2016).

Cooperation and overall smooth intra-executive relations have clear benefits, especially in terms of policy-making. However, regarding policy influence and vote-seeking, a smooth cooperation strategy is not self-evidently the most rewarding option (Lazardeux 2015). There are sometimes rational incentives for the president to avoid cooperation and instead go public with opinions that go against the prime minister, especially when he or she needs to claim credit or avoid blame for particular policies. The underlying motive might be to use the public as an intermediary to win support in order to illustrate that there is a potential electoral cost to the prime minister. In an analysis of American presidents, Kernell (2007, pp. 1–2) defines 'going public' as 'a strategy whereby a president promotes himself and his policies . . . by appealing directly to the . . . public for support'. Through public speeches and writings, the president 'seeks the aid of a third party—the public—to force other politicians to accept his preferences'. Aware of their popular support, presidents can effectively use the option of public addresses and make 'public commitments to particular positions in order to raise the costs of reneging and thereby strengthen their bargaining position' (Cox and Kernell 1991, p. 243). Although a gambling strategy, this can prove to be effective if the presidents are able to illustrate the potential electoral costs to their counterparts (Elgie 2001, p. 17). Furthermore, 'and possibly most

134 *Thomas Sedelius*

injurious to bargaining, going public undermines the legitimacy of other politicians' (Kernell 2013, p. 303). In a premier-presidential system, the president may find this option particularly attractive, considering that the constitutional powers of the presidency are limited, whereas support for the president is usually strong.

Diffuse conditions of accountability seem to favour the presidents in terms of both informal powers and citizen support (Raunio and Sedelius 2020). It might be that the presidents' higher popularity is attributed to their limited powers and to their status of being above party politics and thus somewhat elevated from day-to-day political quarrels. When seeking ways of converting their perceived authority into actual power, they have the option of going public to criticise the government without necessarily being held to account by the electorate in subsequent elections. In this way, formally weak presidents may compensate for their limited constitutional prerogatives by exploiting their perceived popular authority but retaining the option of shielding themselves behind the cabinet and avoiding blame for any failed policy.

8.4 Semi-presidentialism in Finland, Lithuania, and Romania

Table 8.1 presents indicators on the level of democracy and presidential powers in 17 premier-presidential regimes in Europe, including the three selected cases (in bold font). Finland, Lithuania and Romania all have democracy scores that are sufficient to be placed under the 'Free' category in Freedom in the World's 2020 measure but with varying degrees. As a long-established and prosperous democracy in Scandinavia, Finland continuously ranks at the very top of various democracy rankings (cf. EIU Democracy Index 2019; Lührmann et al. 2020). As a much younger democracy, post-Soviet Lithuania has performance scores that are overall stronger than Romania's, as also confirmed by Lithuania's earlier membership in the EU (2004)—three years ahead of Romania (2007).

Table 8.1 also lists presidential power scores, as recorded by Doyle and Elgie (2016). These scores measure the presidents' constitutional powers and are compiled and weighted based on 28 existing measures in the literature. The scores range from 0 (lowest) to 1 (highest) in separate time periods, following constitutional changes in a country's presidential powers. On this measure, Finland's post-2000 constitution provides the weakest presidential power scores (0.050) of all the listed countries, whereas the presidencies in Romania (0.250) and Lithuania (0.282) are among those with higher scores.

For the same set of countries, Table 8.2 reports a more detailed measure of presidential power, as developed by Shugart and Carey (1992). The index includes six 'legislative' and four 'non-legislative' powers, with scores ranging from a minimum of 0 to a maximum of 4 on each prerogative. These data confirm that premier-presidentialism in Europe provides (in general) relatively weak presidencies and that Finland's post-2000 constitution belongs to the group with little formal powers of the president. Lithuania and Romania score higher on both legislative and non-legislative powers. Presidential powers in Lithuania are

Table 8.1 Level of democracy and formal presidential powers in European semi-presidential (premier-presidential) regimes

Country	Year of adoption of semi-presidential constitution	Democracy 2020 Freedom in the World aggregate scores	Year of EU membership	Presidential power scores, Doyle and Elgie (2016), Prespow1 normalised score (standard error) year interval
Bulgaria	1991	80/100 (F)	2007	0.183 (0.044) 1992–present
Croatia	2001	85/100 (F)	2013	0.291 (0.074) 2001–present
Czech Republic	2012	91/100 (F)	2004	—
Finland	**1919**	**100/100 (F)**	**1995**	**0.050 (0.035) 2000–present**
France	1962	90/100 (F)	1958	0.131 (0.020) 1963–present
Ireland	1937	97/100 (F)	1973	0.062 (0.048) 1938–present
Lithuania	**1992**	**91/100 (F)**	**2004**	**0.282 (0.044) 1993–present**
Moldova	1994, 2016	60/100 (PF)	Non-member	0.240 (0.059) 1995–2000
Montenegro	2007	62/100 (PF)	Non-member	—
North Macedonia	1991	63/100 (PF)	Non-member	—
Poland	1997	84/100 (F)	2004	0.241 (0.044) 1997–present
Portugal	1976	96/100 (F)	1986	0.197 (0.016) 1983–present
Romania	**1991**	**83/100 (F)**	**2007**	**0.250 (0.033) 1992–present**
Serbia	2006	66/100 (F)	Non-member	—
Slovakia	1999	88/100 (F)	2004	0.189 (0.139) 2002–present
Slovenia	1991	94/100 (F)	2004	0.118 (0.019) 1992–present
Ukraine	2006, 2014	62/100 (PF)	Non-member	0.329 (0.206) 2005–2010

Note: Freedom House annually measures civil liberties and political rights and provides an aggregated 'Freedom Score', ranging from 0 (least free) to 100 (most free). F = free; PF = partly free. Doyle and Elgie's scores measure the presidents' constitutional powers and are compiled and weighted based on 28 existing measures in the literature. The scores range from 0 (lowest) to 1 (highest).

Sources: Doyle and Elgie (2016); Elgie (2015); Freedom House (2020).

136 Thomas Sedelius

Table 8.2 Shugart and Carey's presidential power scores for European semi-presidential (premier-presidential) regimes

Country	PKV	PTV	DC	EXL	BUD	REF	CF	CD	CEN	DIS	Total
Ireland	0	0	0	0	0	0	0	0	0	0	0
Finland	0	0	1	0	0	0	0	0	0	0	1
Macedonia	1	0	0	0	0	0	1	0	0	0	2
Bulgaria	1	0	1	0	0	0	0	0	0	0	2
Slovakia, 1999–present	1	0	0	0	0	0	1	0	0	1	3
Slovenia	0	0	1	0	0	0	1	0	1	1	4
France	0	1	0	0	0	0	1	0	0	3	5
Lithuania	1	0	1	0	0	0	1	0	2	1	6
Poland	1	0	0	0	0	2	1	0	1	1	6
Ukraine, 2006–2010, 2014–present	2	0	1	0	0	2	0	0	0	1	6
Moldova, 1991–2000, 2016–present	0	0	1	0	0	4	1	0	0	1	7
Croatia, 2001–present	0	0	1	0	0	2	1	0	2	1	7
Romania	0	0	1	0	0	4	1	0	0	1	7
Portugal	2	0	0	0	0	0	1	2	0	3	8

Note: Countries arranged in order of total scores. Shugart and Carey's measure of presidential power separates six legislative powers (PKV = package veto, PTV = pocket veto, DC = decree power, EXL = exclusive initiative of legislation, BUD = budgetary powers, REF = referendum initiative) and four non-legislative powers (CF = cabinet formation, CD = cabinet dismissal, CEN = cabinet censure; DIS = dissolution of parliament). Each power is scored from 0 to 4, with a total maximum power score of 40. For a full explanation of the scoring scheme, see Shugart and Carey (1992, pp. 148–152).

Source: Raunio and Sedelius (2020); Shugart and Carey (1992).

distributed across five categories: package veto, decree power, cabinet formation, cabinet censure, and dissolution of parliament. The total score in Romania is distributed across four of the included categories: decree power, referendum initiative, cabinet formation, and dissolution of parliament.

Despite their limited legislative and policy powers, the presidencies in Finland, Lithuania, and Romania are assigned a number of representative functions and have a political voice in national security and foreign affairs. Article 93 of the Constitution of Finland states that 'the foreign policy of Finland is directed by the President . . . in co-operation with the Government'. Similarly, the president of Lithuania shall 'settle basic foreign policy issues and, together with the Government, implement foreign policy' (Art. 84, para. 1). Likewise, Article 80, para. 1 of the Constitution of Romania declares that the president 'shall represent the Romanian State and is the safeguard of the national independence, unity and territorial integrity of the country'. The Romanian Constitution (Article 80, para. 2), furthermore, requires the president to 'guard the observance of the

(Mis)use of public accountability   137

Constitution and the proper functioning of the public authorities' but differs from the Constitutions of Finland and Lithuania by also assigning the president to 'act as a mediator between the Powers in the State as well as between the State and society'. Additionally, the presidents in all three countries possess power to appoint high-level officials to various offices in public administration. Usually, such appointment powers are shared with the prime minister or other government institutions and include the right to nominate judges to the Constitutional Court, the Chairman of the National Bank, the Commander of the Army, the Head of the Security Service, and the Prosecutor General.

Finland, Lithuania, and Romania share similar semi-presidential constitutions but have very different semi-presidential experiences. Until the late 1980s, Finland had been characterised by powerful presidents with a strong executive role in managing the country's sensitive relations with the Soviet Union—both formally and informally. However, since the end of the Cold War, there has been a gradual marginalisation of the president's position in the political system. Finland adopted a new constitution in 2000, which has considerably restricted the president's role by limiting presidential authority in government formation and dissolution matters, decision-making, decree power, and vetoing legislative bills. Hence, Finland represents a contemporary case of a constitutionally weak presidency embedded in a legacy of strong and powerful presidents.

In contrast to its Baltic neighbours, Estonia and Latvia, which established parliamentary systems in the early 1990s, Lithuania opted for a semi-presidential constitution, ratified in 1992, in the post-Soviet context of deep ideological cleavages, weak parties, and personality-based politics. To some extent, inter-war experiences of powerful presidencies carrying symbolic references of national independence influenced the establishment of direct presidential elections. Previous analyses of semi-presidentialism in Europe suggest that Lithuania is one of the countries with the lowest frequency of intra-executive conflicts (Elgie 2018a; Sedelius and Mashtaler 2013). However, the relations between the president and the government have shifted quite significantly during the post-Soviet period, and despite the relative stability of the Lithuanian political system, scholars have characterised it as personality-centred (Duvold and Jurkynas 2013). Personality-centred politics indeed creates favourable conditions for presidential activism.

Romania ratified its semi-presidential constitution in 1991 in the context of a violent transition. Although the president's role in policy-making is constitutionally limited, the presidents to date have exercised considerable influence on Romanian politics. The country has faced severe transitional challenges and is still struggling with ineffective policy-making, widespread corruption, and recurring political crises. Cohabitation in Romania has repeatedly generated high levels of institutional conflict and has twice (2007, 2012) resulted in impeachment procedures against the president.

Similar to the cases of other Central and Eastern European countries, the political systems in Lithuania and Romania have been characterised by personalisation and relatively low levels of institutionalisation (Crowther and Suciu 2013; Duvold and Jurkynas 2013). For most of the post-1991 period, a high

138   *Thomas Sedelius*

percentage of citizens appears to favour the presidency over other institutions, including the office of the prime minister and political parties (cf. Baltic Barometer 2014; Ekman et al. 2016; New Baltic Barometer 1993, 1995, 1996, 2000, 2001, 2004; New Europe Barometer 2001, 2004). Despite its formally weak powers, the presidency in both countries is considered the major prize for ambitious political leaders, which enhances the importance of personalities (Duvold and Jurkynas 2013). In this sense, a presidentialisation component is involved, where political parties have often been organised around individuals with political ambitions related to personal interests and to the presidency (cf. Samuels and Shugart 2010).

8.5 Analysis

In this section, the empirical findings are reported. The analysis starts from a general presentation of previously recorded intra-executive conflicts involving the three cases. I examine some of these conflicts more closely to identify when and how presidents have employed going-public tactics.

8.5.1 *Presidents, cabinets, and intra-executive conflicts*

The three cases show notable variations in intra-executive conflicts. Upon a closer examination of the president-cabinet relations in the three countries, their presidents, prime ministers, governing parties, cohabitation (yes/no) and intra-executive conflicts (low/high) are reported in Table 8.3. Using both expert survey estimations and secondary sources, Sedelius and Mashtaler (2013, p. 113) define a 'high level' of intra-executive conflict as observable instances of 'manifest and durable tensions between the president and the cabinet' (cf. Elgie 2018a).

8.5.2 *A strictly constrained but highly popular presidency in post-2000 Finland*

Finland has only one instance of a high-level conflict recorded in the data, which concerned the period of cohabitation between President Tarja Halonen and Prime Minister Matti Vanhanen, when the two openly disputed about who would represent Finland in the European Council in 2009. Before the Lisbon Treaty, the president had participated in the majority of the European Council meetings, usually together with the foreign minister, but the Lisbon Treaty required a single representative. Ultimately, the conflict was resolved when the parliament adopted a bill to amend the Constitution, stating that the prime minister would represent Finland in the European Council. Overall, executive relations in Finland are characterised by consensus seeking and by highly regulated relations between the president and the prime minster. Detailed regulations and the political elites' shared understanding about maintaining strict limits to presidential interference in policy-making have limited presidential activism since the 2000 constitutional reform.

Table 8.3 Intra-executive conflicts and periods of cohabitation: Finland, Lithuania, and Romania

President (party) term in office	Prime minister (term in office)	Prime minister's party	Cohabitation	Intra-executive conflict
Finland				
Mauno Koivisto (SDP) Jan. 1982–Mar. 1994	Kalevi Sorsa (Feb. 1982–Apr. 1987)	SDP	N	—
	Harri Holkeri (Apr. 1987–Apr. 1991)	KOK	N	—
	Esko Aho (Apr. 1991–)	KESK	**Y**	—
Martti Ahtisaari (SDP) Mar. 1994–Mar. 2000	Esko Aho (Apr. 1995)	KESK	**Y**	Low
	Paavo Lipponen (Apr. 1995–)	SDP	N	Low
Tarja Halonen (SDP) Mar. 2000–Mar. 2012	Paavo Lipponen (Apr. 2003)	SDP	N	Low
	Matti Vanhanen (June 2003–June 2010)	KESK	**Y**	**High**
	Mari Kiviniemi (June 2010–Jun. 2011)	KESK	**Y**	Low
	Jyrki Katainen (June 2011–)	KOK	N	Low
Sauli Niinistö (KOK) Mar. 2012–present	Jyrki Katainen (–June 2014)	KOK	N	Low
	Alexander Stubb (June 2014–May 2015)	KOK	N	Low
	Juha Sipilä (May 2015–Dec. 2019)	KESK	N	Low
	Sanne Mirella Marin (Dec. 2019–)	SDP	Y	—
Lithuania				
Algirdas M. Brazauskas (LDDP) Nov. 1992–Feb. 1998	Adolfas Šleževičius (Mar. 1993–Feb. 1996)	LDDP	N	Low
		LDDP	N	Low
	Laurynas Stankevičius (Feb. 1996–Dec. 1996)	TS-LK	**Y**	Low
	Gediminas Vagnorius (Dec. 1996–)			
Valdas Adamkus (formally non-party) Feb. 1998–Feb. 2003	Gediminas Vagnorius (May 1999)	TS-LK	N	**High**
	Rolandas Paksas (June 1999–Oct. 1999)	TS-LK	N	—
	Andrius Kubilius (Nov. 1999–Nov. 2000)	TS-LK	N	Low
		TS-LK	N	**High**
	Rolandas Paksas (Nov. 2000–Jun. 2001)	LSDP	N	Low
	Algirdas M. Brazauskas (July 2001–)			

(Continued)

Table 8.3 (Continued)

President (party) term in office	Prime minister (term in office)	Prime minister's party	Cohabitation	Intra-executive conflict
Rolandas Paksas (LLDP) Feb. 2003–Apr. 2004	Algirdas M. Brazauskas	LSDP	Y	High
Valdas Adamkus (formally non-party) July 2004–July 2009	Algirdas M. Brazauskas (June 2006)	LSDP	N	High
	Gediminas Kirkilas (July 2006–Dec. 2008)	LSDP	N	Low
	Andrius Kubilius (Dec. 2008–)	TS-LKD	N	Low
Dalia Grybauskaitė (formally non-party) July 2009—July 2019	Andrius Kubilius (Dec. 2012)	TS-LKD	N	Low
	Algirdas Butkevičius (Dec. 2012–Dec. 2016)	LSDP	N	High
	Saulius Skvernelis (Dec. 2016–)	LVZS	N	Low
Gitanas Nausėda Jul. 2019–present	Saulius Skvernelis (Dec. 2016–)	LVZS	N	—
Romania				
Ion Iliescu (FSN, 1992; FSDN, 1996, PDSR) Dec. 1989–Nov. 1996	Petre Roman (Dec. 1989–Oct. 1991)	FSN	N	High
	Theodor Stolojan (Oct. 1991–Nov. 1992)	PNL	N	Low
	Nicolae Vacaroiu (Nov. 1992–)	Non-party; 1993 PDSR	N	Low
Emil Constantinescu (PNT-CD) Nov. 1996–Dec. 2000	Nicolae Vacaroiu (Dec. 1996)	PDSR	N	Low
	Victor Ciorbea (Dec. 1996–Mar. 1998)	PNT-CD	N	Low
	Radu Vasile (Apr. 1998–Dec. 1999)	PNT-CD	N	High
	Constantin Isarescu (Dec. 1999–Dec. 2000)	Non-party	N	Low
Ion Iliescu (PDSR, 2001; PSD, PD, 2004) Dec. 2000–Dec. 2004	Adrian Nastase (Dec. 2000–Dec. 2004)	PDSR; 2001 PSD	N	Low
Traian Băsescu (PD) Dec. 2004–Dec. 2014	Calin Popescu-Tăriceanu (Dec. 2004–Dec. 2008)	PNL	Y	High
	Emil Boc (Dec. 2008–Feb. 2012)	PDL	N	Low
	Victor Ponta (May 2012–)	PSD	Y	High

Klaus Iohannis (PNL) Dec. 2014–present	Victor Ponta (Nov. 2015)	PSD	Y	**High**
	Dacian Cioloș (Nov. 2015–Jan. 2017)	Non-party	N	—
	Sorin Grindeanu (Jan. 2017–June 2017)	PSD	Y	—
	Mihai Tudose (June 2017–Jan. 2018)	PSD	Y	—
	Vasilica Dăncilă (Jan. 2018–Nov. 2019)	PSD	Y	**High**
	Ludovic Orban (Nov. 2019–)	PNL	N	—

Notes: Cohabitation is defined here as the situation 'where the president and prime minister are from different parties and where the president's party is not represented in cabinet' (Elgie 2011, p. 12).

Party abbreviations: *Finland: KESK* = Suomen Keskusta (Centre of Finland), *KOK* = Kansallinen Kokoomus (National Coalition, centre-right), *SDP* = Suomen Sosialidemokraattinen Piolue (Social Democratic Party of Finland). *Lithuania: LDDP* = Lietuvos Demokratinė Darbo Partija (Democratic Labour Party of Lithuania), *LLS* = Lietuvos Liberalų Sąjung (Liberal Union of Lithuania), *LSDP* = Lietuvos Socialdemokratų Partija (Social Democratic Party of Lithuania), *LVŽS* = Lietuvos Valstiečių ir Žaliųjų Sąjunga (Lithuanian Peasant and Greens Union, agrarian, centrist, Green conservative), *TS-LK* = Tėvynės Sąjunga-Lietuvos Konservatoriai (Homeland Union-Conservatives of Lithuania), *TS-LKD* = Tėvynės Sąjunga-Lietuvos Krikščionys Demokratai (Homeland Union-Christian Democrats of Lithuania). *Romania: FSN* = Frontul Salvării Naționale (National Salvation Front, split from *PCR* = Partidul Comunist Român [Romanian Communist Party], 1989–1993, then PD), *PD* = Partidul Democrat (Democratic Party, Social-Democratic, former FSN, 1993–2007, merged into PDL), *PDL* = Partidul Democrat Liberal (Democratic Liberal Party, centre-right, merger of PD and Partidul Liberal Democrat [Liberal Democratic Party]), *PDSR* = Partidul Democrației Sociale din România (Party of Social Democracy in Romania, ex-Communist, former FSDN, 1993–2001, merged into PSDR), *PNL* = Partidul Național Liberal (National Liberal Party, liberal, centre-right), *PNT-CD* = Partidul Național Țăranesc Creștin Democrat (Christian Democratic National Peasants' Party, Christian-Democratic, PNT successor), *PSD* = Partidul Social Democrat (Social Democrat Party, Social-Democratic, merger of PDSR and PSDR, established 2001), *PSDR* = Partidul Social Democrat Român (Romanian Social Democratic Party, Social-Democratic, merged with PMR, restored 1990–2001, merged into PSD), *UNPR* = Uniunea Națională pentru Progresul României (National Union for the Progress of Romania, Social-Democratic, split from PSD, established 2010).

Sources: Data adapted and updated from Elgie (2018a, 2018b); Raunio and Sedelius (2020); Sedelius and Mashtaler (2013); World Statesmen (2020).

142 *Thomas Sedelius*

Rarely do Finnish presidents criticise the government publicly. Certainly, there are differences of opinion, particularly under cohabitation, but the presidents have largely refrained from publicly attacking the prime minister and the cabinet. The exceptions are issues falling under the foreign policy co-leadership between the president and the government, where on rare occasions President Halonen and President Sauli Niinistö have publicly questioned the comments made by cabinet ministers. When the Social Democratic Halonen shared power with centre-right prime ministers from 2003 to 2012, she often emphasised different topics in her speeches, but even in cases of open clashes, such as over some civil service appointments or representation in the European Council, she did not try to delegitimise the government.

President Niinistö, who was a finance minister from 1996 to 2003 and the chair of the National Coalition from 1994 to 2001, has in turn often commented on the state of the economy, but such comments have mainly been general and not specifically directed at the government. In his official speeches, Niinistö has mainly referred to matters under the jurisdiction of the president. Generally, in their speeches and interviews, Finnish presidents primarily focus on foreign and security policy issues, thus leaving domestic politics—and mainly EU matters—to the prime minister and the cabinet (Hämäläinen 2013).

While the 'spirit of the constitution' is held in high esteem by the political elites, the popularity of the presidents must be kept in mind. Presidents are typically more popular than prime ministers and other 'party politicians' in Finland. According to survey data, public opinion consistently favours assigning the president a stronger role in politics—including domestic politics and EU affairs (Arvo-ja asennetutkimus/EVA Attitude and Value Survey 2018). Figure 8.1 shows that this trend strengthened over the period following the president's weakening executive role in both domestic and EU affairs, and the share of respondents

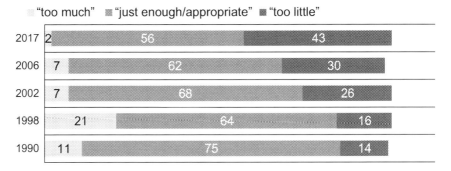

Figure 8.1 Public evaluation of the powers of the president in Finland, 1990–2017, in percentage

Source: Arvo-ja asennetutkimus/EVA Attitude and Value Survey (2018).

(Mis)use of public accountability   143

who considered that the president had 'too little' power rose from 14% in 1990 to 43% in 2017.

President Niinistö has been particularly trusted by the citizenry, enjoying broad support across the political spectrum. Furthermore, the constitution leaves the window open for presidential activism. For example, regarding government formation, the constitution simply states that the president appoints the prime minister (and the other ministers) after approval by the Eduskunta (parliament). The constitution therefore does not rule out presidential interference in government formation.

8.5.3 The presidency in Lithuania: popular leadership as a lever for power grabs

Power sharing with low levels of conflict has characterised the president–prime minister relationship for the most part in Lithuania. Nonetheless, since the country's independence, all presidents have at some point openly conflicted with the prime minister. Since 1992, Lithuania has been under five presidents: Algirdas Brazauskas, Valdas Adamkus, Dalia Grybauskaitė, Rolandas Paksas, and Gitanas Nausėda. I limit my analysis essentially to the first three, given the short-lived presidency of Paksas, and as of this writing, I do not have enough data on the recent presidency of Nausėda.

Previous research has described the first office holder, Brazauskas, as a constructive leader. He held the position as head of state carefully, without any open conflict with the prime minister or the Seimas (parliament). While Brazauskas was very much a party politician, he was also a key figure in the transition to democracy and remained popular throughout his political career, including from 2001 to 2006 as the prime minister (Raunio and Sedelius 2019). Brazauskas also favoured an open style of leadership, including active contacts with ordinary citizens. Brazauskas (2007, p. 70) himself noted that due to the limited constitutional powers of the president, he tried to influence the Seimas and the government with his 'political authority' and the people's support. This was easier during the first four years of his presidency, when his Social Democratic Party (LDDP) was in government and controlled the parliamentary majority. However, following the 1996 Seimas elections, matters became more difficult under the centre-right coalition of the Homeland Union and the Christian Democrats, and the president essentially limited his actions to foreign affairs. Brazauskas faced difficulties in establishing contacts with the ruling coalition, and while he regularly held meetings with Prime Minister Gediminas Vagnorius (Homeland Union), the latter emphasised the need to respect the jurisdictional limits set by the constitution.

Adamkus came from a very different background, having served in the US Environmental Protection Agency for nearly two decades. Elected on an independent ticket in both the 1998 and the 2004 presidential elections, Adamkus (2004, p. 38) wrote that he needed to 'create traditions' for the presidency. Having observed Brazauskas' weak position towards the end of his presidency, Adamkus

144 *Thomas Sedelius*

strived to act as a 'counterweight' to the government. In 1999, an intense conflict occurred between Adamkus and Prime Minister Vagnorius when the president openly criticised Vagnorius about economic reform. As the president had no supportive majority in the Seimas, he leaned heavily on his popular support. The opinion polls at that time showed approval rates of over 80% for the president and less than 20% for the prime minister (Sedelius 2006, p. 149). Adamkus publicly voiced his distrust in the prime minister, stating that he could not perform his duties as long as Vagnorius stayed in office. Following the Russian economic crisis, the sharp decline of the economy gave the president the upper hand, and he could effectively insist—although without formal dismissal powers—on the resignation of Vagnorius. This outcome was indeed an important moment in strengthening presidential leadership in Lithuania.

During his second term, Adamkus adopted a less assertive stance, with the balance of power more in favour of the prime minister, even during the minority government of Gediminas Kirkilas (2006–2008). Adamkus co-shared executive power with prime ministers and cabinets from opposing political camps for most of the period. Support ratings mattered, as Brazauskas was also an unusually popular politician in Lithuania during his tenure as the prime minister. Nonetheless, in 2006, Adamkus again resorted to a statement on national television, questioning whether the government still enjoyed the confidence of the Seimas, with Prime Minister Brazauskas resigning afterwards. In 2005, Adamkus had also intervened in the conflict between Viktor Uspaskich, the leader of the Labour Party and the minister of economic affairs, and Artūras Zuokas, the mayor of Vilnius and the chair of the Liberal and Centre Union. In yet another television appearance, Adamkus requested the resignations of the quarrelling politicians from their public offices, with Uspaskich indeed deciding to leave his ministerial post.

President Grybauskaitė, who was also elected as an independent candidate in both the 2009 and the 2014 elections (although in 2009, she was supported by the centre-right parties, Homeland Union-Lithuanian Christian Democrats and the Liberal Movement), became more powerful than her predecessors. Throughout her terms of office, her leadership style was more assertive and confrontational. With the exception of the period 2009–2012, Grybauskaitė shared power with prime ministers from opposing camps, which certainly influenced her strategies. She had a policy profile leaning towards the EU and economic affairs, as she had previously served as the Finance Minister and the Commissioner for Financial Programming and the Budget. From late 2012 to 2016, Grybauskaitė shared power with Algirdas Butkevičius' Social Democratic-led coalition and from 2016 onwards, with the cabinet led by Prime Minister Saulius Skvernelis that brought together the Peasant and Greens Union and the Social Democrats. By 2018, the relations between Grybauskaitė and Skvernelis deteriorated due to various disputes. Grybauskaitė was on particularly bad terms with the chair of the Peasant and Greens Union, Ramūnas Karbauskis. In her state of the nation address in the Seimas in June 2018, the president focused on the then ongoing corruption scandals and unleashed a strong attack on the government and the Seimas for

(Mis)use of public accountability 145

failing to address major societal problems. Simultaneously she called on the main political actors to stop all the quarrelling for the sake of the national interest.

Hence, both Adamkus and Grybauskaitė did not hesitate to go public, often questioning the legitimacy of prime ministers and their governments. Article 84, para. 18 of the Lithuanian Constitution stipulates that the president 'shall make annual reports at the Seimas on the situation in Lithuania and the domestic and foreign policies of the Republic of Lithuania'. Adamkus—and even more frequently, Grybauskaitė—used such state of the nation addresses to criticise the government. The presidents attempted to mark their authority throughout their tenures and often emerged victorious from intra-executive conflicts. Similar to other semi-presidential regimes, periods of cohabitation reduce the influence of the president and result in more intra-executive disputes. Presidents have benefitted from their popularity, with Adamkus and Grybauskaitė further reinforcing this through their anti-party or anti-establishment rhetoric (Krupavičius 2013).

8.5.4 Challenged mediation, popular support, and intra-executive conflict in Romania

Romania has experienced more instances of severe intra-executive conflicts than both Finland and Lithuania (cf. Table 8.3). Although the president's role in policymaking is constitutionally weak, the Romanian presidents have exercised considerable political influence, although to different extents and for various reasons.

Ion Iliescu (1990–1996, 2000–2004) and Traian Băsescu (2004–2014) were presidents with high levels of activism and did not avoid institutional confrontations, whereas Presidents Emil Constantinescu (1996–2000) and Klaus Iohannis (2014—present) have adopted more cautious modes of operation. Overall, cohabitation has clearly mattered more in Romania than in Finland and Lithuania, with the presidents also utilising party contacts to a larger extent than in the other two cases.

Iliescu was a powerful and popular figure during the transition to democracy, which facilitated his subsequent activism in office. Iliescu used his strong party links for directing the government, as the National Salvation Front (FSN)/Social Democrats were dominant actors in Romanian politics and economy until the mid-1990s. With Prime Minister Petre Roman's cabinet faring poorly in the polls on account of failed economic reforms in 1991, Iliescu most likely orchestrated a miners' strike to force the resignation of Roman, who had been challenging Iliescu for influence within the FSN. Iliescu and Roman disagreed on several issues, and after ousting Roman, Iliescu secured the appointment of two loyal prime ministers, Theodor Stolojan and Nicolae Văcăroiu. Iliescu was clearly using his links to a variety of stakeholders, ranging from trade unions and large businesses to the intelligence services, and he even publicly criticised many court decisions. In 1994, the parliament initiated an impeachment procedure against Iliescu on account of his failure to respect the separation of powers among state institutions, especially regarding courts. However, the Constitutional Court ruled that Iliescu's public statements did not constitute 'grave acts infringing upon Constitutional

146 *Thomas Sedelius*

provisions' (Art. 95), and his friendly parliamentary majority voted against the impeachment (Gherghina 2013; Sedelius 2006; Verheijen 1999).

Similar to Iliescu, President Băsescu had considerable experience gained from party politics before assuming office. He had served as the minister of transport in several cabinets during the 1990s, as well as the mayor of Bucharest. Băsescu certainly did not shy away from confrontations with the government and used various channels to influence Romanian politics. In the 2004 parliamentary elections, the Social Democrats emerged as the largest party, but President Băsescu appointed as prime minister Călin Popescu-Tăriceanu from the National Liberal Party, which had formed an alliance with Băsescu's Democratic Party. Furthermore, Băsescu was able to persuade the Humanist Party to break their pre-electoral coalition with the Social Democrats and instead join the new government. Thus, Băsescu managed to avoid cohabitation while obtaining a friendly majority in the legislature. Băsescu basically even 'handpicked some of the ministers' (Anghel 2018, p. 111). However, by the end of 2006, the Humanists left the coalition, and the relations between the two leaders had soured. Băsescu wanted to topple Popescu-Tăriceanu, who fired the Democratic Party ministers from his cabinet, but the latter refused to resign. Băsescu publicly attacked the government while unleashing similar criticism against the Social Democrats, which by then were supporting the government. In a public speech, Băsescu accused Popescu-Tăriceanu of asking him to intervene in favour of Dinu Patriciu, a Liberal Party member who had been caught in a corruption case. Băsescu even presented excerpts from his private conversation with Popescu-Tăriceanu in a press conference that was widely covered by the media (Gherghina et al. 2016, p. 12). According to Elgie (2018b, pp. 127–149), this cohabitation produced one of the highest levels of intra-executive conflict across his examination of 21 European countries.

Following the 2008 parliamentary elections, Băsescu called for the formation of a grand coalition between the Democratic Liberal Party (PDL) and the Social Democrat Party (PSD). This coalition lasted until October 2009, when the Social Democrats left the coalition. Two months later, Băsescu was re-elected as president and was able to forge a legislative majority for his party (PDL), with the help of the Democratic Alliance of Hungarians (UDMR) and using 35 defecting members of parliament (MPs) from the PSD and the Liberals. As he did in 2004, Băsescu strongly influenced the formation of the new government under Prime Minister Emil Boc. From 2008 to 2011, Băsescu's position was indeed very strong and probably reached the peak in the presidentialisation of Romanian politics thus far. However, by early 2012, the government's popularity was quickly declining on account of austerity measures. Băsescu reacted by replacing Boc with Mihai Răzvan Ungureanu as the prime minister. The PDL did not appreciate this move, as many party insiders believed that the replacement of the prime minister had been decided unilaterally by the president. Following the successful motion of no confidence against the Ungureanu cabinet in April 2012, Băsescu was forced to appoint the Social Democrat Victor Ponta as the new prime minister.

(Mis)use of public accountability   147

Another example of Băsescu's activism involved the 2009 presidential elections. Băsescu, whose popularity had declined, campaigned on a strong discourse about state modernisation, arguing that existing political institutions were inefficient. According to Article 90 of the Constitution, the president 'may, after consultation with Parliament, ask the people of Romania to express, by referendum, their will on matters of national interest'. Băsescu thus used his constitutional right and called for two consultative referenda on introducing a single-chamber parliament and decreasing the number of MPs to 300. Both referenda were passed with strong majorities in favour of the president's positions; subsequently, the issues were linked to a larger constitutional reform that also gained the support of the government led by Prime Minister Boc. However, by 2011, when the constitutional reform bill was presented to the parliament, the ruling president-friendly coalition did not manage to obtain the required two-thirds majorities in both chambers. At the end, the bill was voted down in 2013 under the leadership of the second cabinet of Victor Ponta (Gherghina and Hein 2016, pp. 185–186).

However, it was this kind of presidential activism that led to the two impeachment cases against Băsescu. The reason behind both impeachments was his alleged misuse of presidential powers, especially the way that he allegedly overstepped the 'mediating' function prescribed by the constitution. It was argued that Băsescu unnecessarily interfered in the work of the government and the parliament and used his party connections in an unconstitutional manner, and in 2012, he was accused of violating the independence of the courts. There was also a serious dispute about who would represent Romania in the European Council. Băsescu also unleashed strong attacks against the media. The Constitutional Court criticised Băsescu for his failure to be neutral and to act as a 'mediator' in society. In the previous 2007 referendum, 74.5% of the voters were against impeachment. In 2012, however, 89% voted for impeachment, but the turnout at 46% was below the required threshold (Gherghina and Miscoiu 2013; Iusmen 2015; Perju 2015).

Presidents Constantinescu and Iohannis have behaved in a much less confrontational manner, but they have had their share of intra-executive tensions as well. Constantinescu's presidency was characterised by considerable social unrest and economic decline while he tried to consolidate democracy and a stronger administration in order to edge closer towards both EU and NATO memberships. Constantinescu shared power with three prime ministers: Victor Ciorbea (1996–1998, Christian Democratic-National Peasants Party), Radu Vasile (1998–1999, Christian Democratic-National Peasants Party), and Mugur Isărescu (1999–2000, independent). In 1999, Constantinescu attempted to oust Prime Minister Vasile from office. The Vasile cabinet was suffering from internal disputes and poor economic performance. Constantinescu asked Vasile to resign, but as the latter refused to comply, the president asked all other ministers to step down. The ministers obeyed Constantinescu, who then issued a presidential decree in which he sacked Vasile. Aware that the president had no such constitutional instrument, Vasile first refused to resign but finally gave in to pressure. Constantinescu's manoeuvres also seemed to have the support of the main political parties.

148 Thomas Sedelius

As a result of this incident, the constitution (Art. 107) was reformed in 2003 to explicitly prevent the president from dismissing the prime minister. However, as concluded by Perju (2015, p. 253), overall, Constantinescu preferred not to intervene in domestic matters.

President Iohannis, finally, had served as a mayor of a small town in Transylvania and was noted for his civil society activism. Iohannis had led the National Liberal Party for half a year before being elected as president, but similar to Constantinescu, he lacked the kind of party politics background that Iliescu and Băsescu possessed. Overall, Iohannis has maintained a rather loose connection to his party. His term has been plagued by the continuing instability of Romanian politics, including corruption charges against leading politicians, several court cases, various political scandals and profound distrust in the political elite. Iohannis has co-ruled with several prime ministers from opposing political camps: Victor Ponta (Social Democrat, 2012–2015); Dacian Cioloş (independent, leading a technocrat government, November 2015–January 2017); Sorin Grindeanu (Social Democrat, January–June 2017); Mihai Tudose (Social Democrat, June 2017–January 2018); and Viorica Dăncilă (Social Democrat, January 2018–present).

Elected on the basis of an anti-corruption campaign, Iohannis has mainly clashed with the government over corruption. Iohannis has constantly criticised the various cabinets for not tackling the problems and has refused to appoint to public positions those politicians with links to corruption. In January 2017, Iohannis unexpectedly attended a Grindeanu cabinet meeting that discussed an emergency decree to pardon certain detainees and amend the penal code. Four days later, the president joined widespread street protests against the planned government ordinance. Iohannis then announced that he would call a referendum if the government did not withdraw the bill. Iohannis has also intervened in government formation and termination. In 2015, tensions between Iohannis and Prime Minister Ponta surfaced repeatedly, with the president questioning governmental key policies, including a new fiscal plan, and publicly calling for Ponta's resignation after a criminal investigation opened against him. Following Ponta's resignation in the middle of nationwide anti-corruption protests in November 2015, Iohannis nominated the former EU Commissioner for Agriculture Cioloş as the new prime minister. In December 2016, Iohannis refused to nominate Sevil Shhaideh as the prime minister without publicly explaining the reasons behind his decision. The Social Democratic-Alliance of Liberals and Democrats coalition responded by threatening Iohannis with presidential impeachment. Iohannis subsequently appointed the second nominee of the Social Democrats, Grindeanu, as the prime minister. In early January 2017, Iohannis sharply attacked the government in a speech delivered on the occasion of the Grindeanu cabinet's taking office. Iohannis criticised the government for not addressing how it would deal with the budget deficit while promising to increase salaries and pensions and cut down value-added tax (Bucur 2017). In March 2017, the parliament retaliated by adopting a declaration accusing Iohannis of interfering in executive-legislative relations.

(Mis)use of public accountability   149

In the spring of 2018, Iohannis encountered serious cooperation problems with Prime Minister Dăncilă, which peaked over the decision to move the country's embassy in Israel from Tel Aviv to Jerusalem. After Dăncilă had repeatedly avoided meetings and phone conversations with Iohannis on both domestic and international issues, Iohannis asked Dăncilă to resign, arguing that 'she can't cope with the role of prime minister of Romania and is transforming the government into a vulnerability'. Iohannis also accused Dăncilă of taking orders from her political party, announcing that the prime minister had lost his confidence and that the Dăncilă cabinet should resign (Paun 2018). According to Iohannis, it was a 'political necessity' to replace the government, which he called a crash of Romanian democracy (Rettman 2018). Despite such intra-executive conflicts and public appearances calling for the government to resign, Iohannis has been more reserved in his use of informal channels of influence than Băsescu.

Romanian presidents use the going-public strategy in a fairly routine manner, blaming the government for various policy failures and commenting on issues under the jurisdiction of the cabinet. The majority of presidential speeches are widely covered by the media, and the public is quite attentive. An interesting feature in this regard constitutes the presidential speeches in the parliament. According to Article 88 of the Constitution, 'the President of Romania shall address Parliament by messages on the main political issues of the nation'. Such messages have become more numerous over time[4] and can be considered an agenda-setting device, with the president presenting his vision on the most important societal questions.

8.6 Conclusions

Presidents in semi-presidential systems have formal prerogatives, such as (limited) appointment and dismissal powers, veto and monitoring functions, as well as informal options, such as meeting with individual politicians, including party leaders and various interest groups. In this chapter, I have raised the question of when and how presidents in semi-presidential systems use their perceived popular support to go public. The option of going-public tactics by using public speeches and media addresses seems particularly appealing, considering that the constitutional powers of the presidency in semi-presidential systems are rather limited, whereas public support is usually strong. My analysis of the presidents' actions during intra-executive conflicts confirms this assumption and illustrates how the deliberate use of public grandstanding often works in the presidents' favour.

The presidencies of Finland, Lithuania and Romania have broadly comparable constitutional prerogatives, although the post-2000 Finnish presidency is somewhat weaker. The analysis reveals both similarities and variations in how

4 Between December 2014 and March 2016, Iohannis addressed MPs six times, in comparison to only once by Constantinescu (1996–2000), five times by Iliescu during his second term (2000–2004), and 17 times by Băsescu between 2004 and 2011 (Bucur 2016; Levai and Tomescu 2012).

the presidents have utilised the option of going public. Arguably, contextual differences are more salient than constitutional powers for understanding these variations.

Finland is an old democracy known for its political stability, highly formalised procedures, and low level of corruption. Lithuania and Romania are younger democracies that needed to adopt new constitutions in the heated circumstances of the early 1990s. Their party systems tend to be less stable and their politics more personalised. Both countries, particularly Romania, have also experienced serious problems with corruption. Hence, Finnish citizens tend to trust their political institutions to a greater extent than do Lithuanian and Romanian citizens. However, in Finland, the president is more popular than the prime minister most of the time. Nonetheless, historical experiences of very dominant presidential figures have formed the political elites' shared view about the highly restricted role of the Finnish president. In contrast, in Lithuania and Romania, it is considered both legitimate and appropriate for the president to take a stronger position and to interfere in matters that constitutionally belong to the competence of the government.

In Finland, the president rarely criticises the prime minister and the cabinet in public. Disagreements do occur but are largely handled behind the scenes, without public conflicts. In contrast, the Lithuanian and the Romanian presidents have adopted quite confrontational stances, repeatedly unleashing harsh attacks on the government. In many instances, such public grandstanding has taken place in official, ceremonial duties (e.g., when addressing the parliament). The presidents have questioned the government's competence and legitimacy and have requested the prime ministers' resignation. In both countries, it is largely considered appropriate for the president to be actively involved in issues falling under the jurisdiction of the cabinet. Indeed, such presidential activism is facilitated by the low trust in political parties and party politicians and a personality-centred political culture overall. Whether such presidential activism is beneficial for the country can be debated; nevertheless, it is a built-in logic of semi-presidentialism.

Power sharing between the president and the prime minister can provide much-needed checks and balances in the political system. In the context of serious societal turmoil, presidents can bring order and stability with their speeches, legislative vetoes, or other measures. However, presidential powers and activism are slippery slopes, and therein lies the danger of accumulation of power in the hands of the president. The combination of direct elections and strong popular support works in favour of the president, especially in the personality-centred political cultures found in Central and Eastern European regimes. In Romania, there have been attempts to decrease the constitutional prerogatives of the president, precisely because of the accumulation of power in the presidency and the strongly personalised political culture that it embodies.

This apparent gap between a constitutionally restricted presidency on the one hand and citizen support of a significantly stronger president on the other is effectively exploited by the presidents from time to time. In terms of accountability to the citizens, this is both a strength and a weakness of semi-presidentialism.

(Mis)use of public accountability 151

To the extent that citizens can hold their presidents accountable in subsequent elections, semi-presidentialism offers a separate democratic chain of delegation that is non-existent in a parliamentary system. However, the dual executive structure also diffuses power and responsibility, making it more difficult for citizens to determine who is responsible for various political outcomes.

References

Adamkus, V. (2004). Lithuania as a center of regional cooperation. *Lithuania Foreign Policy Review*, 13–14, pp. 17–20.

Amorim Neto, O. and Strøm, K. (2006). Breaking the parliamentary chain of delegation: Presidents and non-partisan cabinet members in European democracies. *British Journal of Political Science* [Online], 36(4), pp. 619–643. https://doi.org/10.1017/S0007123406000330 [Accessed 23 November 2020].

Anghel, V. (2018). 'Why can't we be friends?' The coalition potential of presidents in semi-presidential republics-insights from Romania. *East European Politics and Societies and Cultures* [Online], 32(1), pp. 101–118. https://doi.org/10.1177% 2F0888325417722829 [Accessed 23 November 2020].

Arvo-ja asennetutkimus/EVA Attitude and Value Survey. (2018). [Online]. Available from: www.eva.fi/eng [Accessed 13 December 2018].

Baltic Barometer. (2014). [Dataset]. Stockholm: Ekman Joakim, Södertörn University.

Brazauskas, A. (2007). *Ir Tuomet Dirbome Lietuvai: Faktai, Atsiminimai, Komentarai.* Vilnius: Knygiai.

Bucur, C. (2016, 16 March). Romania: President Iohannis' contested performance and a brief assessment of his exercise of constitutional powers. *Presidential Power Blog* [Online]. Available from: http://presidential-power.com/?p=4614 [Accessed 23 November 2020].

Bucur, C. (2017, 15 March). Romania: President postpones anti-corruption referendum. *Presidential Power Blog* [Online]. Available from: https://presidential-power.com/?p=6165 [Accessed 23 November 2020].

Cavatorta, F. and Elgie, R. (2010). The impact of semi-presidentialism on governance in the Palestinian Authority. *Parliamentary Affairs* [Online], 16(1), pp. 22–40. https://doi.org/10.1093/pa/gsp028 [Accessed 23 November 2020].

Cheibub, J. A., Elkins, Z. and Ginsburg, T. (2014). Beyond presidentialism and parliamentarism. *British Journal of Political Science* [Online], 44(3), pp. 515–544. https://doi.org/10.1017/S000712341300032X [Accessed 23 November 2020].

Cox, G. and Kernell, S. eds. (1991). *The Politics of Divided Government.* New York: Westview Press.

Crowther, W. and Suciu, O. V. (2013). Romania. In: Berglund, S., et al. eds. *The Handbook of Political Change in Eastern Europe.* 3rd ed. Cheltenham: Edward Elgar, pp. 369–406.

De Raadt, J. (2009). Contestable constitutions: Ambiguity, conflict, and change in East Central European dual executive systems. *Communist and Post-Communist Studies* [Online], 42(1), pp. 83–101. https://doi.org/10.1016/j.postcomstud.2009.02.003 [Accessed 23 November 2020].

Doyle, D. and Elgie, R. (2016). Maximizing the reliability of cross-national measures of presidential power. *British Journal of Political Science* [Online], 46(4), pp. 731–741. https://doi.org/10.1017/S0007123414000465 [Accessed 23 November 2020].

152 Thomas Sedelius

Duverger, M. (1980). A new political system model: Semi-presidential government. *European Journal of Political Research* [Online], 8(2), pp. 165–187. https://doi.org/10.1111/j.1475-6765.1980.tb00569.x [Accessed 23 November 2020].

Duvold, K. and Jurkynas, M. (2013). Lithuania. In: Berglund, S., et al. eds. *The Handbook of Political Change in Eastern Europe*. 3rd ed. Cheltenham: Edward Elgar, pp. 125–166.

EIU Democracy Index. (2019). *Democracy Index 2019*. The Economist Group 2020. Available from: www.eiu.com/topic/democracy-index [Accessed 23 November 2020].

Ekman, J., Duvold, K. and Berglund, S. (2016). *Social-Political Survey in Central Europe*. [Datafile]. Huddinge: Södertörn University.

Elgie, R. ed. (1999). *Semi-Presidentialism in Europe*. Oxford: Oxford University Press. https://doi.org/10.1093/0198293860.001.0001 [Accessed 23 November 2020].

Elgie, R. (2001). Cohabitation: Divided government French-style. In: Elgie, R. ed. *Divided Government in Comparative Perspective*. Oxford: Oxford University Press, pp. 106–126. https://doi.org/10.1093/0198295650.001.0001 [Accessed 23 November 2020].

Elgie, R. (2010). Duverger, semi-presidentialism and the supposed French archetype. In: Grossman, E. and Sauger, N. eds. *France's Political Institutions at 50*. London: Routledge, pp. 6–25.

Elgie, R. (2011). *Semi-Presidentialism: Sub-Types and Democratic Performance*. Oxford: Oxford University Press. https://doi.org/10.1093/acprof:oso/9780199585984.001.0001 [Accessed 23 November 2020].

Elgie, R. (2015). *Presidential Power Scores*. [Dataset]. Available from: https://presidential-power.com [Accessed 3 October 2018].

Elgie, R. (2016). Three waves of semi-presidential studies. *Democratization* [Online], 23(1), pp. 49–70. https://doi.org/10.1080/13510347.2014.960853 [Accessed 23 November 2020].

Elgie, R. (2018a). *Political Leadership: A Pragmatic Institutionalist Approach*. London: Palgrave Macmillan. https://doi.org/10.1057/978-1-137-34622-3 [Accessed 23 November 2020].

Elgie, R. (2018b). List of cohabitations: The semi-presidential one. *Semi-Presidentialism* [Online]. Available from: www.semipresidentialism.com [Accessed 7 October 2018].

Freedom House. (2020). *Freedom in the World 2020*. Available from: www.freedomhouse.org [Accessed 2 July 2020].

Gherghina, S. (2013). Formal and informal powers in a semi-presidential regime: The case of Romania. In: Hloušek, V., et al. eds. *Presidents above Parties? Presidents in Central and Eastern Europe: Their Formal Competencies and Informal Power*. Brno: Masaryk University, pp. 257–270.

Gherghina, S. and Hein, M. (2016). Romania. In: Fruhstorfer, A. and Hein, M. eds. *Constitutional Politics in Central and Eastern Europe: From Post-Socialist Transition to the Reform of Political Systems*. Wiesbaden: Springer, pp. 173–197. https://doi.org/10.1007/978-3-658-13762-5 [Accessed 23 November 2020].

Gherghina, S., Iancu, A. and Soare, S. (2016). Presidents and their parties: Insights from Romania. *Paper presented at the ECPR General Conference*, Prague, 2016.

Gherghina, S. and Miscoiu, S. (2013). The failure of cohabitation: Explaining the 2007 and 2012 institutional crises in Romania. *East European Politics and Societies and Cultures* [Online], 27(4), pp. 668–684. https://doi.org/10.1177%2F0888325413485621 [Accessed 23 November 2020].

(Mis)use of public accountability 153

Hämäläinen, U. (2013). Niinistö mukautui yhteisjohtajaksi. In: Tiihonen, S., et al. eds. *Presidentti johtaa: Suomalaisen valtiojohtamisen pitkä linja.* Helsinki: Siltala, pp. 279–300.

Iusmen, I. (2015). EU leverage and democratic backsliding in Central and Eastern Europe: The case of Romania. *Journal of Common Market Studies* [Online], 53(3), pp. 593–608. https://doi.org/10.1111/jcms.12193 [Accessed 23 November 2020].

Kernell, S. (2007). *Going Public: New Strategies of Presidential Leadership.* 4th ed. Washington, DC: CQ Press.

Kernell, S. (2013). Going public. In: Kernell, S. and Smith, S. S. eds. *From Principles and Practice of American Politics: Classic and Contemporary Readings.* 5th ed. Los Angeles: Sage, pp. 300–317.

Krupavičius, A. (2013). Lithuania's president: A formal and informal power. In: Hloušek, V., et al. eds. *Presidents above Parties? Presidents in Central and Eastern Europe: Their Formal Competencies and Informal Power.* Brno: Masaryk University, pp. 205–232.

Lazardeux, S. G. (2015). *Cohabitation and Conflicting Politics in French Policymaking.* Basingstoke: Palgrave Macmillan. https://doi.org/10.1057/9781137476906 [Accessed 23 November 2020].

Levai, M. C. and Tomescu, C. (2012). Atribuţiile Preşedintelui României în raport cu Parlamentul—aspecte teoretice şi practice. *Revista Transilvană de Ştiinţe Administrative,* 30(1), pp. 84–105.

Lührmann, A., Maerz, S. F., Grahn, S., Alizada, N., Gastaldi, L., Hellmeier, S., Hindle, G. and Lindberg, S. I. (2020). *Autocratization Surges: Resistance Grows: Democracy Report 2020.* University of Gothenburg: V-Dem Institute. Available from: www.v-dem.net/en/ [Accessed 23 November 2020].

New Baltic Barometer 1. (1993). CSPP School of Government & Public Policy at the University of Strathclyde. Available from: www.cspp.strath.ac.uk [Accessed 2 November 2018].

New Baltic Barometer 2. (1995). CSPP School of Government & Public Policy at the University of Strathclyde. Available from: www.cspp.strath.ac.uk [Accessed 2 November 2018].

New Baltic Barometer 3. (1996). CSPP School of Government & Public Policy at the University of Strathclyde. Available from: www.cspp.strath.ac.uk [Accessed 2 November 2018].

New Baltic Barometer 4. (2000). CSPP School of Government & Public Policy at the University of Strathclyde. Available from: www.cspp.strath.ac.uk [Accessed 2 November 2018].

New Baltic Barometer 5. (2001). CSPP School of Government & Public Policy at the University of Strathclyde. Available from: www.cspp.strath.ac.uk [Accessed 2 November 2018].

New Baltic Barometer 6. (2004). CSPP School of Government & Public Policy at the University of Strathclyde. Available from: www.cspp.strath.ac.uk [Accessed 2 November 2018].

New Europe Barometer. (2001). NDB VI Autumn. Dataset SPP 364. CSPP School of Government & Public Policy at the University of Strathclyde. Available from: www. cspp.strath.ac.uk/nebo.html [Accessed 15 September 2016].

New Europe Barometer. (2004). NDB VII Winter. Dataset SPP 404. CSPP School of Government & Public Policy at the University of Strathclyde. Available from: www. cspp.strath.ac.uk/nebo.html [Accessed 15 September 2016].

154 *Thomas Sedelius*

Passarelli, G. ed. (2015). *The Presidentialization of Political Parties: Organizations, Institutions and Leaders.* Basingstoke: Palgrave Macmillan. https://doi.org/10.1057/9781137482464 [Accessed 23 November 2020].

Passarelli, G. ed. (2018). *The Presidentialization of Political Parties in the Western Balkans.* London: Palgrave Macmillan. https://doi.org/10.1007/978-3-319-97352-4 [Accessed 23 November 2020].

Paun, C. (2018, 27 April). Romanian President Calls on Prime Minister to Resign. *Politico.* Available from: www.politico.eu/article/klaus-iohannis-viorica-dancila-romania-president-calls-on-prime-minister-to-resign [Accessed 2 June 2018].

Perju, V. (2015). The Romanian double executive and the 2012 constitutional crisis. *International Journal of Constitutional Law* [Online], 13(1), pp. 246–278. https://doi.org/10.1093/icon/mov011 [Accessed 23 November 2020].

Poguntke, T. and Webb, P. (2005). *Presidentialization of Politics: A Contemporary Study of Modern Democracies.* Oxford: Oxford University Press. https://doi.org/10.1093/0199252017.001.0001 [Accessed 23 November 2020].

Protsyk, O. (2005). Politics of intra-executive conflict in semi-presidential regimes in Eastern Europe. *East European Politics & Societies* [Online], 19(2), pp. 135–160. https://doi.org/10.1177%2F0888325404270672 [Accessed 23 November 2020].

Protsyk, O. (2006). Intra-executive competition between president and prime minister: Patterns of institutional conflict and cooperation under semi-presidentialism. *Political Studies* [Online], 54(2), pp. 219–244. https://doi.org/10.1111%2Fj.1467-9248.2006.00604.x [Accessed 23 November 2020].

Raunio, T. (2012). Semi-presidentialism and European integration: Lessons from Finland for constitutional design. *Journal of European Public Policy* [Online], 19(4), pp. 567–584. https://doi.org/10.1080/13501763.2011.614139 [Accessed 23 November 2020].

Raunio, T. and Sedelius, T. (2019). Shifting power-centres of semi-presidentialism: Exploring executive coordination in Lithuania. *Government and Opposition* [Online], 54(4), pp. 637–660. https://doi.org/10.1017/gov.2017.31 [Accessed 23 November 2020].

Raunio, T. and Sedelius, T. (2020). *Semi-Presidential Policy-Making in Europe: Executive Coordination and Political Leadership.* Basingstoke: Palgrave Macmillan, Springer Nature. https://doi.org/10.1007/978-3-030-16431-7 [Accessed 23 November 2020].

Rettman, A. (2018, 12 November). Romanian leaders trade jibes over upcoming EU presidency. *EUobserver.* Available from: https://euobserver.com/institutional/143357 [Accessed 4 April 2018].

Samuels, D. J. and Shugart, M. S. (2010). *Presidents, Parties, and Prime Ministers: How the Separation of Powers Affects Party Organization and Behavior.* Cambridge: Cambridge University Press. https://doi.org/10.1017/CBO9780511780882 [Accessed 23 November 2020].

Schleiter, P. and Morgan-Jones, E. (2010). Who's in charge? Presidents, assemblies, and the political control of semipresidential cabinets. *Comparative Political Studies* [Online], 43(11), pp. 1415–1441. https://doi.org/10.1177%2F0010414010371904 [Accessed 23 November 2020].

Sedelius, T. (2006). *The Tug-of-War between Presidents and Prime Ministers: Semi-Presidentialism in Central and Eastern Europe.* Örebro: Örebro Studies in Political Science, p. 15.

Sedelius, T. and Ekman, J. (2010). Intra-executive conflict and cabinet instability: Effects of semi-presidentialism in Central and Eastern Europe. *Government and Opposition* [Online], 45(4), pp. 505–530. https://doi.org/10.1111/j.1477-7053.2010.01325.x [Accessed 23 November 2020].

Sedelius, T. and Linde, J. (2018). Unravelling semi-presidentialism: Democracy and government performance in four distinct regime types. 25(1), pp. 136-157. https://doi.org/10.1080/13510347.2017.1334643 [Accessed 20 February 2021].

Sedelius, T. and Mashtaler, O. (2013). Two decades of semi-presidentialism: Issues of intra-executive conflict in Central and Eastern Europe 1991–2011. *East European Politics* [Online], 29(2), pp. 109–134. https://doi.org/10.1080/21599165.201 2.748662 [Accessed 23 November 2020].

Shoesmith, D. (2003). Timor-Leste: Divided leadership in a semi-presidential system. *Asian Survey* [Online], 43(2), pp. 231–252. https://doi.org/10.1525/as.2003.43.2.231 [Accessed 23 November 2020].

Shugart, M. S. (2005). Semi-presidential systems: Dual executive and mixed authority patterns. *French Politics* [Online], 3(3), pp. 323–351. https://doi.org/10.1057/palgrave.fp.8200087 [Accessed 23 November 2020].

Shugart, M. S. and Carey, J. M. (1992). *Presidents and Assemblies: Constitutional Design and Electoral Dynamics.* New York: Cambridge University Press.

Verheijen, T. (1999). Romania. In: Elgie, R. ed. *Semi-Presidentialism in Europe.* Oxford: Oxford University Press, pp. 193–215.

World Statesmen. (2020). Available from: www.worldstatesmen.org [Accessed 2 July 2020].

9 Ministerial criminal liability in the Greek legal order

A concise critical review

Eugenia Kopsidi and Ioannis A. Vlachos

9.1 Introduction

In modern democratic societies, the political responsibility and criminal liability of Members of the Cabinet are assessed individually, under different approaches and through distinct processes and procedures. While political responsibility refers to the investigation, through parliamentary scrutiny, of cabinet members' acts and omissions with regard to the public interest, criminal liability encompasses the investigation by judicial authorities of criminal offences punishable by provisions of the Criminal Code and special criminal legislation. In this sense, political responsibility is much broader than criminal liability, as it involves any misconduct attributable to a minister, even without his/her direct entrenchment therein. Although several legal orders distinguish between ministerial 'accountability' and 'responsibility'—with the latter suggesting an aspect of personal blame, the two terms are used indistinctively in the Greek political and legal discourse and are therefore interchangeably mentioned herein. In contrast, criminal liability is a subclass of legal liability substantiated when a minister's act or omission is classifiable as a criminal offence.

However, the bond between these two forms of accountability has always been particularly tight, as the legislature's prosecution of ministers originally served as a substitute to the conceptual lack of political responsibility. In particular, in the pre-democratic British parliamentary practice, when the institution of ministerial accountability first emerged, the monarch's absolute and unquestionable unaccountability regimen was offset by a parliamentary control mechanism against ministerial accountability by means of the institution of impeachment (Loverdos 1995, p. 50; Besila-Vika 1985, p. 11). At this early stage, such responsibility was joint, distinctive and separated from the common notion of criminal liability applicable to everyone else, which largely substantiated the strong political aspects of this extraordinary procedure.

Along these lines, the political responsibility of the members of the executive in its contemporary sense is the evolution of the initially uniform ministerial responsibility, which simultaneously incorporated elements of civil and criminal liability. The consolidation of parliamentarianism in the UK and its gradual prevalence in the larger part of continental Europe have led to the legislature's disengagement

Ministerial criminal liability in the Greek legal order 157

from dealing with ministerial criminal liability by drawing a clear distinguishing line between the notional aspects of political and criminal answerability and by envisaging the corresponding investigative competences.

Albeit ministerial criminal liability and political responsibility are currently acknowledged as two distinct and separate concepts in modern democracies, exploring the former (as this chapter aspires to do) inevitably entails a political facet that often justifies or at least explains its governing peculiarities.

The extraordinary regime governing ministerial criminal liability is a prickly and controversial issue that has persisted for decades in Greece, from both political and legal perspectives. Although its primary intent is not the enhanced fortification of ministers as natural persons but the good functioning of the polity, the institution of ministerial criminal responsibility has endured fierce criticism by political agents and legal theorists alike, as it seems to have failed in its core objective and has frequently been exploited in pursuit of political expediencies.

The specifics applicable to ministerial criminal liability are enshrined in Article 86 of the Greek Constitution, which stipulates:

> Only the Parliament has the power to prosecute serving or former members of the Cabinet or Undersecretaries for criminal offences that they committed during the discharge of their duties, as specified by law. The institution of specific ministerial offences is prohibited.

A special substantive and procedural regime is then established to handle the criminal liability of secretaries and undersecretaries for offences committed 'during the discharge of their duties', its key feature being the prosecution not by the judiciary but by the legislature, in apparent derogation from the principle of separation of powers. The whole process of investigating alleged criminal offences committed by ministers functions as an institutional guarantee in the sense that the primary objective is to safeguard the executive power and its members from unjust or malicious prosecution which would essentially obstruct the exercise of their powers.

The privileged exclusive framework governing ministerial criminal liability—including (until recently) the short limitation period and the so-called extinguishing deadline—is essentially rationalised by this intention to establish an institutional guarantee. Although the concept of ministerial criminal liability has often been abused and has repeatedly led to the 'penalisation of the political life' (as the political revolving doors between government and opposition have often led to the prosecution of the Cabinet's former members when their rivals win parliamentary majority in the future), it cannot be overlooked that the respective set of provisions remains preferential. Additionally, despite frequent prosecutions against former ministers, the perceptible inadequate assignment of accountability has exposed both an inherent systemic flaw and a political reluctance that, in turn, have recurrently resulted in immunity. Hence, the Greek model of handling ministerial criminal liability evidently reveals that both the high-profile political corruption and its declared antidote undermine several axiomatic principles shared by modern democracies, such as horizontal equality before the law, separation of powers, and accountability in decision-making, therefore contributing to the delegitimisation of the political system.

Despite the recent pompous public statements and the proclaimed broad consensus for the revision of Article 86 of the Constitution, eventually only the extinguishing deadline in para. 3 has been abolished. The exceptional regime has remained otherwise unchanged, substantially prolonging a system that has long been abused to the point of practical inefficiency and has historically mostly served the conservation of political privileges. Thus, a model principally dating back to the founding of the Greek State has remained unchanged once more, in times when the public's trust in the political system is quite tenuous and brittle, with the country still striving to overcome the dire corollaries of a decade-long economic crisis.

This contribution assesses the vulnerabilities of the current system, stemming not so much from the constitutional text and the pertinent legislation, but predominantly from their practical application since the adoption of the 1975 Constitution. By delving into the reasons which have led to the virtual non-implementation of the institution, this review of ministerial criminal liability aspires to critically investigate the demand for further revision of the applicable system. To this end, it is crucial to first examine the scope of Article 86 and its interpretative issues regarding the selective inclusion of specific ministerial offences within its exceptional regime. This is followed by a deliberation on the concerns arising from the short limitation period and the so-called extinguishing deadline, that is, the most idiosyncratic feature of the Greek system, considered by many as the singular root of a chronic evil. Next comes the matter of complicity in the sense of accessory impeachment under the exclusive procedure applicable to ministers, which raises additional issues of (un)equal treatment. Lastly, a new and different system is described and proposed, advising a radical amendment of Article 86 to draw an unambiguous line between political responsibility and criminal liability, assigning the latter to the sole competence of the judiciary.

9.2 The scope of ministerial offences under Article 86

Article 86, paras. 1 and 4 of the Constitution envisage a special competence of the Parliament and the Special Court to correspondingly prosecute and try criminal offences committed by incumbent or former members of the cabinet or undersecretaries during the discharge of their duties. In line with Article 86, para. 1, which also grants respective legislative delegation to the Parliament, Law 3126/2003 was passed to further regulate the field in detail. In its Article 1, para. 1, the constitutional reference to such 'criminal offences' is specified to include only 'misdemeanors and felonies' committed by said persons 'during the discharge of their duties'. It is thus initially derived and also expressly stated in Article 1 para. 3 that any other crime perpetrated by members of the cabinet or undersecretaries lies under the exclusive competence of ordinary criminal courts

Ministerial criminal liability in the Greek legal order   159

and calls for the application of the common criminal procedure, as the ordinary substantive criminal stipulations remain firmly enforceable (Charalambakis 2009, p. 769). Of course, this likewise agrees with the constitutional prohibition to establish special ministerial offences (i.e., *delicta sui generis*) in Article 86, para. 1.

Given the remarkably large number of such cases brought before the Greek Parliament since the late 1980s and the massive publicity they usually entail, the accurate interpretation of the phrase 'during the discharge of their duties' has become one of the principal issues of debate in the Greek political and legal domain. In the words of the former long-time minister and professor of constitutional law, E. Venizelos, these incidents 'triggered a widespread interpretative discord and friction, and brought a number of issues to light' (1993a, p. 463). Prior to discussing the more prevailing perceptions on the issue, it is elemental to provide a succinct outline of the optimal interpretative model for such an approach.

The distinctive handling of ministerial criminal violations establishes an extraordinary indictment regime which is commonly favourable to its subjects. As a special procedure, it falls within the general hermeneutic canon by which the interpretation of exceptional statutes must remain as narrow as possible.[1] In this sense, it should be exclusively restricted to incidents which fully correspond to the fundamental purpose of such atypical practices (Spyridakis 2014, p. 845). Furthermore, this exceptional treatment is not intended to safeguard cabinet members at the personal level but to guarantee the proper functioning of the executive branch's top tier. Therefore, the natural judge's competence is constitutionally circumvented only to serve the interests of the State and to neither endorse crypto-immunity for ministers nor encourage the micropolitical game. This aspect likewise calls for a narrow interpretation of the said provisions, as the natural judge principle (i.e., 'nobody can be removed from the natural judge established by law'; Neppi Modona 2012) is dominant in the Greek constitutional and penal doctrine and tradition.

Additionally, as both the separation of powers and the pertinent necessity for checks and balances are pillars of liberal democracies grounded in the rule of law, the constitutional deviation of Article 86 should also be approached with a restrictive mind, allowing the legislature to substitute the judiciary only when absolutely indispensable and befitting. As noted by Spyridakis:

> a narrow interpretation promotes the enforcement of the regular criminal provisions (i.e. those generally applicable to the public), with a corresponding expansion of the judiciary's powers. This 'burden' on the judiciary's back must not expose its members to the risk of involvement with political/partisan skirmishes. To steer clear of such peril, we should ensure that: legal proceedings against members of the Cabinet are not exploited or otherwise

---

1 In its 1/2011 ruling, the Judicial Council in Art. 86, para. 4 of the Constitution held that 'by general principle of law, exceptional provisions are interpreted narrowly. The Law on Ministerial Responsibility is, indeed, exceptional' (Anagnostopoulos 2011, p. 578).

160 *Eugenia Kopsidi and Ioannis A. Vlachos*

manipulated, consistent with the presumption of innocence; indictments against Ministers are not indiscriminately depicted as penalizations of the political life; the ministerial criminal liability maintains its individual/personal nature, and is not perceived as a symptom of a broader shared collective accountability of their political party or faction.

(2014, p. 846)

Reverting to the phrase 'during the discharge of their duties', it leaves room for three potential interpretations. Specifically, the offence (a) is committed during the ministerial tenure according to a strictly temporal criterion, or (b) is linked to the exercise of ministerial duties or (c) is in itself the act or the omission by which ministerial duties are discharged (Symeonidou-Kastanidou 2011, p. 496).

With respect to the first alternative, it is easily discredited by the rules of grammatical interpretation. In purely linguistic terms, 'discharge of duties' signifies the conduct through which the ministerial powers are exercised, whereas 'during' does not allude to time but to the process of implementing the said authority. Besides, such reading of the text would contradict both the obligation to impose restrictive construal tools and the rationale of the constitutional legislator. The latter acknowledges that such exceptions are tolerable only inasmuch as they defend the efficient and effective operation of the Government and the State, not when they offer an all-inclusive safe haven for ministerial criminality.[2] In principle, therefore, the special regime is reserved for offences that must somehow be associated with the discharge of ministerial duties.

According to Feloutzis (2005, p. 455), an offence is committed during the discharge of ministerial duties only when it is substantially linked to such exercise, not when it is merely perpetrated in the course of the minister's tenure. However, this nexus is not always as palpable as it initially appears. For example, it would prima facie seem that a minister's act of corrupting/seducing a minor in exchange for a material trade-off would not fall under Article 86, as such violation seems irrelevant to the discharge of ministerial duties. Nevertheless, in this case, if the victim is an irregular immigrant and the trade-off is a residence card which the minister can issue, then the crime does not seem detached from the exercise of ministerial powers. Hence, the law reasonably avoids a restrictive list of specific offences, leaving the examination of the aforementioned crucial element to the prosecuting body.

Useful inferences can be drawn from a comparative reading of the provision as it evolved in applicable legislation over time. Article 6 of Legislative Decree 802/1971 reads:

---

2 This inference is emphatically and unanimously held in the Greek Constitutional and Criminal Law doctrines and jurisprudence, in relevant case law and in the opinions traditionally expressed by Greek MPs in parliamentary committees and in the plenary, as chronicled in the minutes available at www.hellenicparliament.gr/Praktika/Anatheoriseis-Syntagmatos.

Ministerial criminal liability in the Greek legal order   161

Offences committed by members of the Cabinet and Deputies which are unrelated to their public duties are not subject to the provisions of this Decree. They shall be heard in the courts cited in the provisions of Articles 111 para 6 and 112 para 2 of the Code of Criminal Procedure.

An almost consistent phraseology also appears in Article 3 of the succeeding Law 2509/1997: 'Offences which are unrelated to the ministerial duties are tried in accordance with the provisions of the Code of Criminal Procedure by the competent courts'. Given that the current law diverges from the previous wording and instead, prefers the expression 'offences not committed during the discharge of their duties', it appears that crimes may exist which are not committed during the discharge of ministerial duties but are also not irrelevant to such functions, for which prosecution is handled under the ordinary regime. In affirmative terms, the text of the law denotes that some offences are *linked* to the fulfilment of the said duties but are not perpetrated *during* their implementation. Unsurprisingly, this premise bolsters the third and narrowest interpretation.

However, it is not only the special statutes that pave the way towards this evaluation. As evident in several of its provisions, the Penal Code also adopts the aforesaid distinction between acts committed during the discharge of ministerial duties and acts simply related to such practices. Article 235, paras. 1–3 on the passive bribery of public officials selectively read as follows:

> 1. A public official who, directly or through a third party, requests or receives or accepts the promise of any sort of illicit benefit for himself or for another in return for a future or completed act or omission *related to the discharge of his duties*, shall be sentenced to imprisonment and a pecuniary penalty.
> 2. If such act or omission of the perpetrator *breaches his duties*, he shall be sentenced to incarceration of up to ten years and a pecuniary penalty . . . .
> 3. A public official who requests or receives, for himself or for another, an illicit asset-related benefit by *exploiting his capacity*, shall be sentenced to imprisonment if the offense is not punishable under another penal provision.

As evident, neither the expression 'during the discharge of official duties' nor any equivalent thereof is included in the provision. Nonetheless, the legislator refers to acts or omissions that are either 'related to the discharge of' such duties or contravene them ('breaches'). Therefore, regardless of the permutations of passive bribery and their corresponding individual constituent elements, passive bribery of public officials is never committed 'during the discharge' of their duties.

Article 137A of Penal Code on torture also provides revealing feedback; it is therein envisaged:

> A public or military official whose duties include the prosecution of, interrogation for or investigation of offenses or disciplinary violations, or the execution of sentences or retention or custody of detainees, shall be sentenced to

incarceration up to ten years if, *during the discharge of said duties*, he tortures a person under his authority.

As Symeonidou-Kastanidou comments:

> It is apparent from the wording of the law that the act of torture must be carried out at the time when the official prosecutes, interrogates, investigates or detains a person, i.e. precisely at the time when he exercises the powers bestowed upon him by the law or by the competent authority. A different interpretative approach, which would assimilate criminal acts merely 'related' to these duties with those committed 'during' such discharge would constitute a contra legem reading to the detriment of the defendant, which is consequently intolerable.
>
> (2011, p. 498)

Others have also proposed a more restrictive approach to the issue (Margaritis 2011, pp. 490ff.), agreeing that the rationale behind Articles 137A and 235 of the Penal Code should be utilised as an interpretative benchmark, whereas the obsolete Article 6 of Legislative Decree 802/1971 and Article 3 of Law 2509/1997 could also provide serviceable guidance. Margaritis adds that another effective tool is the much pondered (in both theory and case law) 'civil liability in case of mistrial' found in Article 73 of the Introductory Law to the Code of Civil Procedure and in Article 6, para. 1 of Law 693/1977, where the expression 'during the discharge of duties ascribed to the judicial functions' is utilised. He concludes that the wording 'during the discharge of duties' encompasses only the acts that refer to the exercise of legally stipulated competences and the omissions to act according to legally stipulated functions. Margaritis argues:

> This assumption which detaches the crimes of bribery and money laundering from the exceptional regime, is not at odds with the letter of the law and certainly responds to the exceptional nature of the relevant regulatory framework.
>
> (2011, p. 492)

Anagnostopoulos (2011) disagrees with the above-mentioned arguments, maintaining that such approaches which lean towards a sweeping reduction of the offences to which Article 86 of the Constitution applies are 'suffocatingly narrow'. They mainly aim at mitigating the growing discomfort in the inability to prosecute former ministers due to the expiry of the constitution's special statute of limitations, appearing in the form of an extinguishing deadline (Anagnostopoulos 2011, p. 575).

Another line of reasoning which reinforces the application of the narrowest interpretation can be derived from the composition of the Special Court—a special

Ministerial criminal liability in the Greek legal order 163

judicial body competent to asses ministerial offences following parliamentary referrals. In accordance with the express constitutional provision of Article 86, para. 6:

> The Court competent for trying the relevant cases, at first and last instance is, as supreme court, a Special Court, which is composed for each case by six members of the Supreme Administrative Court and seven members of the Supreme Civil and Criminal Court.

One of several amendments to the system governing ministerial criminal liability after the 2001 constitutional revision relates to the composition of the Special Court. This court is composed not only of senior judges to the Supreme Court (*Areios Pagos*) who serve civil and criminal justice, but also of six members of the supreme administrative court (Council of State), who bring their constructive experience from participating in the disciplinary proceedings against civil servants, as well as their broad comprehension of public law, given that the prosecution usually contends with administrative acts. Moreover, the Special Court is assisted by a Judicial Council, comprised by two members of the Council of State and three members of the Supreme Court, who are barred from concurrent membership in the Special Court.

It is worth noting that according to the pan-European comparative report of the Committee on Democracy through Law (Venice Commission) of the Council of Europe in 47 Member States, it appears that Greece is moving into the 'main European trend', which includes national legal orders which have established a competent court composed exclusively of supreme justices, and not politicians (members of the House of Representatives or senators), as the case goes elsewhere. At any rate, this particular composition of the Special Court and the Judicial Council, involving exclusively high-profile judges, seems to correspond to the particularities accompanying the accountability of senior government officials.

It has been suitably argued that:

> The nature of the ministerial responsibility resides within both Criminal and Administrative Law, not only because the institution is incorporated in the Constitution, but because ministerial duties are essentially bound by rules set in public law, whose violation interpretatively matches the mens rea, the actus reus and the other conditions of criminal provisions.
>
> (Venizelos 1993b, p. 57)

Therefore, criminal acts referable to the Special Court may only be linked to the exercise of public authority and powers; otherwise, there would be no defensible claim for the participation of administrative judges, who obviously are unauthorised to hear non-administrative violations merely 'related to the discharge of ministerial duties'.

9.3 Statute of limitations and the extinguishing deadline: a hasty elimination of punishability

Until recently, a very challenging aspect of ministerial criminal liability in Greece related to a set of tight temporal boundaries, not only regarding the statute of limitations but also the expiration of the so-called extinguishing deadline. The former is a well-known concept shared by most legal orders; the latter, while seemingly procedural, had an annulling impact on prosecution as a whole, which would eventually lead to immunity via the abolition of punishability. Prior to the constitutional revision of 2019, Article 86, para. 3 stated that 'the Parliament may exercise its competence pursuant to paragraph 1 until the end of the second regular session of the parliamentary term commencing after the offence was committed'. This short time limit was put in place to prevent the lingering of pending criminal cases beyond the second national elections following the perpetration of the alleged offence. The provision practically meant that potential early dissolutions of the Parliament (i.e., adding up to less than the maximum of 8 years for two 4-year parliamentary sessions) would automatically and permanently cease prosecution for all applicable cases, irrespective of the severity of the alleged offences. In other words, the culmination of the second parliamentary session following the commitment of the act stripped the parliament of its competence to exercise prosecutorial powers, and the State could no longer advance in criminal proceedings against any offence committed by a minister or a deputy minister during the discharge of their duties (Chrysogonos 2003, p. 562).

The extinguishing deadline, in conjunction with the statute of limitations, has raised a number of interpretative issues which have often split theory and case law.[3] It is noteworthy that up until the previous constitutional revision of 2001, no reference had been made to the statute of limitations. This absence has since been cited as an excuse to prevent the procedural termination of prosecution, overlooking and possibly confusing it with the extinguishing deadline.[4] Nonetheless, the legal nature of the extinguishing deadline initiated a dogmatic dispute that has been the focus of intense scientific and political debates. In particular, it has been argued that it quite resembles the deadline for the timely filing of a criminal complaint for a non–ex officio indictable violation under Article 117 of the Criminal Code, after which criminal prosecution cannot be initiated

---

3 See Ruling no. 1943/2010 (Judicial Council of the Athens Court of Appeals; Pinikí Dikaiosíni 2011, p. 961). It refers to the accusations against the former minister of transport under K. Simitis' administration (September 1997–April 2000). Therein, it is especially noteworthy that the prosecutor's proposal to the Parliament views the statute of limitations and the extinguishing deadline as one and the same legal concept.

4 According to Art. 86, para. 5 of the Constitution:

> 5. Should the procedure on the prosecution of a serving or former member of the Cabinet or Undersecretary not be completed for any other reason whatsoever, including the reason of status of limitations, the Parliament may, at the request of the person itself or of its heirs, establish a special committee for investigating the charges in which highest magistrates may also participate.

Ministerial criminal liability in the Greek legal order 165

(Magkakis 1984, p. 283). It has also been asserted that the extinguishing deadline constitutes an 'atypical form of amnesty' as it practically encompasses the legislator's partiality for a particular category of acts 'in order to restore social peace or to appease political passions' (Jescheck and Weigend 1996, p. 923).[5] The most convincing view is that the extinguishing deadline is a sui generis case of a statute of limitations, on the grounds that they both eliminate punishability, thus rendering criminal prosecution inadmissible (Mantzoufas et al. 2014, p. 67).

Indeed, both time limits set a clear point beyond which criminal prosecution is impossible. The shorter (by default) cycle of the extinguishing deadline practically lasted from two to six years (in case of a ministerial offence committed in the beginning of a parliamentary term, the interval would eventually last for the entire four years plus an approximately two extra years for the two sessions of the next term, according to Article 53 of the Constitution), while the post-2011 statute of limitations now depends on the nature of the offence (5 + 3 years for misdemeanours, 15 or 20 + 5 years for felonies). However, until the adoption of Law 3961/2011, the exceptional statute of limitations was restricted to five years, irrespective of the nature or gravity of the offence. Therefore, a crucial characteristic of the different criminal jurisdiction for ministerial offences was the substantially privileged treatment of Cabinet members, as any parliamentary delay or procrastination in initiating the required proceedings triggered the elimination of punishability, due to either the expiry of the statute of limitations or the passing of the extinguishing deadline. To this day, the application of Article 86 has largely and essentially resulted in the inappropriate indirect impunity via expiration, which prevents scrutiny of ministerial criminal liability, and has thus confirmed that this constitutional provision notably undermines not only the separation of powers but also the constitutional principle of equality before the law (Koukiotis 2010, p. 1048).

9.4 Issues on complicity

Article 1, para. 2 of Law 3126/2003 states that 'accomplices are co-referred and tried according to the provisions herein'. Article 7, para. 1 mentions that the prosecution against the minister is extended to the accomplices, who are henceforth indicted and tried with the minister. Of course, the law follows the 2001 amendment of Article 86, para. 4, whereby 'in the case of impeachment before the Special Court of a serving or former member of the Cabinet or Undersecretary, any participants are also jointly indicted, as specified by law'.

However, according to para. 3:

If the House rejects the proposal to prosecute as manifestly unfounded . . . or decides to not prosecute . . . the ordinary criminal courts are still competent over the accomplices and the provisions herein do no longer apply.

---

5 See also Judgement no. 378/2005 (Athens Three-Judge Court-Marshal; *Piniká Khroniká* (55), p. 1089).

166 *Eugenia Kopsidi and Ioannis A. Vlachos*

Ergo, if a minister is the alleged principal offender and eventually avoids prosecution, this would mean that the procedure otherwise endures for his/her accomplices, even though their involvement may be comparatively lesser or even secondary. Apart from disturbing implications on equal treatment and proportionality, this absurdity also entails another possible setback: if the judges and the prosecutors consider such a case extremely serious (especially when significant damages have been incurred, to the public detriment), the exigency to punish the culprits and the frustration caused by the inability to prosecute the involved member of the Cabinet could lead to the draconian treatment of the accomplices (Kalogirou and Galetsellis 2009, pp. 46ff.)

A more equitable approach would call for an extension of equal treatment among all participants throughout every possible procedural outcome. In the words of Aravantinos, one of the founding fathers of modern constitutional theory in Greece:

> Convictions against the Minister's accomplices are an indirect conviction *sine iudicio* against the Minister and a stain on the Parliament, which tolerates the Minister and does not prosecute him, although his involvement was proven during the trial of the accomplices.
>
> (1880, p. 185)

Androulakis agrees and characteristically stresses that 'the Parliament . . . needs to rise up to the expectations and allow prosecution for all accomplices under the special regime, and thus contribute to the catharsis', adding:

> Accomplices to the same crime must generally be tried together, for a multitude of reasons (safer discovery of the truth when all parties are tried simultaneously, finer assessment of each defendant's liability, prevention of contradictory decisions).
>
> (1989, p. 69)

It is therefore imperative that the matter of complicity be also adjusted in line with the preceding remarks, as the procedural fragmentation essentially undermines the effectual handling of substantive aspects and culminates in breaches of the principle of isonomy.

9.5 In defence of amending Article 86

As scrutinised previously herein, the constitutional rationale behind the exceptional procedure against ministerial offences is embedded in an otherwise seemingly believable claim to avoid the likelihood of abuse by either governing majorities against formerly governing political antagonists or by oppositions on a mission to tarnish the credibility of a government by dragging its cabinet members behind criminal hearings which dominate the public discourse. However, the experience amassed from recent Greek political history and a simple reasoning pattern disprove this argument at its practical projection. On the latter, as fairly and laconically stated, 'if the political impartiality of the judiciary is uncertain or questionable, the political impartiality of MPs is, by definition, nonexistent' (Chrysogonos 1997, p. 459). Per the former, the sheer number of ministerial prosecutions brought before the Parliament over the last 45 years does not reveal signs of efficient abuse control. Of course, the very few cases which ended up in trials in comparison to the large number of prosecutions by parliamentary accord only add insult to injury.

In the words of Charalambakis:

> the parliamentary vote(: as regards ministerial prosecutions) is influenced by irrelevant aspects and policies or, more accurately, micro-political considerations entirely unrelated to the penal assessment, such as the degree of the suspect's popularity with the party leadership, or whether the cohesion of the governing majority hinges on the ballot outcome, etc. A typical example is the vote of May 5, 2009, on the prosecution of an MP of the then ruling party for acts allegedly committed during his stint as Minister, when—as admitted by almost all parliamentarians—their evaluation and, eventually, their choice was directly swayed by whether (depending on their affiliation to the government or the opposition) the outcome of the vote would result (due to the marginal parliamentary majority of the ruling party) to the loss of the governing majority and the eventual fall of the government. As all political analysts highlighted, the result of the vote would be completely different if the ruling party had the luxury of ampler parliamentary preponderance. However, this blunt confession leads to an apparent loss of credibility in the functioning of the Parliament, a brutal devaluation of parliamentarism as a cornerstone of polity and a digression of democracy towards treacherous paths.
>
> (2009, p. 777)

Furthermore, the supplementary claim that retaliation and vindictive micropolitical pettiness are essentially rooted in societies, where everyday politics stereotypically involve exaggeration and tartness, is also flawed. First, it arbitrarily conjures a hypothetical built-in societal flaw and thus oversees the fact that social constructs—much more, political ones—are not by any means subject to such deterministic and quasi-Darwinistic approaches. Behaviours, norms, and customs change over time and are basically outcomes of societal rather than natural variables. Second, it creates a zone of expedient idleness in favour of those who howsoever benefit from such advantages by trying to convince the public that these inherent imperfections are impossible to overcome. Of course, this promotes a highly detrimental institutional stagnation whose impact can range from parliamentary crises to constitutional derailments. Moreover, this assumption serves better as a counterargument, as it becomes self-contradictory by implying that the crucial competence to impeach ministerial offences should not only be awarded to a non-judicial body, in breach of the separation of powers, but essentially to members of Parliament (MPs) who are considered overreacting and

168 *Eugenia Kopsidi and Ioannis A. Vlachos*

vicious; that is, lacking the composed, unbiased, and impartial attributes typically required in such circumstances.

The extraordinary regimen also allegedly seeks to shield secretaries and undersecretaries from the mendacious litigiousness of those whose interests are practically debilitated by the exercise of governing powers, given that policy implementation is fundamentally a decision-making process which most frequently leaves certain individuals or groups displeased. In principle, this seems to be a rather convincing argument. Nevertheless, it loses significant momentum due to its quite restrictive outlook: decisions which may significantly obstruct important personal or collective pursuits are unquestionably not a ministerial monopoly. On a daily basis, hundreds of other political officials (directors, public enterprise CEOs, presidents of agencies, mayors and regional governors, etc.) take executive or quasi-executive action which may trigger the irritation or dissatisfaction of various stakeholders. Surprisingly, the legislature has never thought of lending an exceptional procedural hand to any such official, although it definitely should in terms of both equality and proportionality, as equivalent circumstances call for equivalent treatment, mutatis mutandis.

Reflecting on the presented facts and observations, a cohesive and credible proposal to transcend the pressing standoff (between fundamental principles, constitutional commitments, the rule of law, operative polity, and political functionalism) ostensibly lies in prioritising these contesting elements in terms of primacy—but not dominance—and in striking a fair balance between them by assessing the degree of compliance or defiance thereof. It is an almost joint conclusion that the constitutional and legal arsenal, albeit far from ideal in some aspects, is suitably equipped to sufficiently serve its alleged objectives. Still, it is almost unanimously admitted that the relevant provisions are consistently misread by the MPs through the lenses of arbitrary intentions and that the recurring abuses grimly impair legality, justice, the Greek political system, and society's perception of and confidence in its institutions. The abolition of the extinguishing deadline via the recent constitutional amendment is an upgrade in principle but not a warranty of actual rectification. Besides, any moderate revision of Article 86 still conforms to the general construct of parliamentary intervention in the criminal procedure, that is, to the entrusting of judicial or quasi-judicial competence to non-judges.

If one revisits the underlying claims in favour of an exceptional legal framework for ministerial criminality, it becomes apparent that their 'utilitarian' requirements can also be met otherwise, even to the extent of completely abandoning the corresponding outlook. The perspective of abolishing all parliamentary interference and leaving the investigation and adjudication of ministerial offences exclusively to the hands of prosecutors and judges seems more appropriate and efficient.

This is by no means a radical or an unusual hypothesis. As far back as 1891, when Harilaos Trikoupis—a true cornerstone of Greek political history who served seven terms as prime minister—was contesting a motion filed for alleged financial irregularities by 20 MPs of the rival governing party, he eloquently stated:

Ministerial criminal liability in the Greek legal order   169

I will stand accused before the judiciary. Before you, I am but a Member of the Parliament, and as a Member of the Parliament I have come to review your deeds and reprimand those who manage our matters.

(Soleintakis 2005, p. 108)

Similar views have also been conveyed by a number of jurists and legal experts. The abolition of Article 86 in its entirety has been suggested, as

> it does not add anything substantial to the guarantee already acknowledged to MP's in Article 62 para. 1 (i.e. immunity from criminal proceedings). If a former minister (given that such criminal liability primarily refers to former ministers) continues to be actively involved in political life . . . then he would normally carry the MP status, and, in lack of Article 86, permission of the House would certainly be required prior to prosecution. What is more, once the appointment of non-parliamentary ministers is disallowed, there will be no issue of extending legal protection beyond the limits of said immunity.[6]

Similarly, Professor of Constitutional Law George Kasimatis (2013) has offered this advice:

> Immediately abolish the current privileged prosecution system for members of the Cabinet and, in its place, ordain that ministers will now be prosecuted and tried as every other citizen, save for an absolute prioritization to ensure a prompt conclusion to the political limbo which harms democracy.[7]

Androulakis argues that Article 86 establishes 'an unacceptable regime of *forum speciale* and extraordinary criminal liability' and asks 'why Ministers should be exempt from the ordinary criminal procedure', concluding that '[this legal framework] should be annulled by way of a constitutional amendment' (1989, pp. 63–64). Others vouch in favour of parliamentary abstinence from the criminal procedure against ministers (e.g., Charalambakis 2009, p. 777). It has also been questioned whether 'a constitutional provision can denote disbelief against the institution of Justice' and proposed that 'competence to handle these criminal proceedings should be awarded to the ordinary judiciary, to senior prosecutors or even to a collective body' (Vlachopoulos 2013).

Initiatives along these lines reinstate equality before the law, as the indictment of secretaries and undersecretaries will not be arbitrarily assessed by their peers but by a judiciary with institutional competence over legal matters. Juvenal's classic '*quis custodiet ipsos custodes*' deadlock also finds proper practical resolution, and the separation of powers is likewise restored. This would similarly serve as a symbolic token for the consolidation of social peace, as it will verify that

---

6 For this issue, see Chrysogonos' (2011) study.
7 As articulated in his 2013 interview.

170   *Eugenia Kopsidi and Ioannis A. Vlachos*

democracy trusts in the functioning of the institutions that it has established and are quintessential to its subsistence. Describing Article 86 as 'an unconstitutional provision of the Constitution', Koukiotis remarks:

> The equality principle established in Article 4 of the Constitution and the separation of powers according to Article 26 . . . can render Article 86 paras. 1–3 *invalid* and *non-applicable*, and, therefore, lead to the prosecution of Ministers under the ordinary criminal procedure.
>
> (2010, p. 1049)

Moreover, it is quite challenging to grasp how politicians are expected to operate as apt and equal substitutes of judges without typically having any relevant experience, while many even lack a rudimentary legal background, which is the bare minimum to merely comprehend the intricacies inherent in the criminal procedure. Therefore, on rare occasions when the parliamentary intervention does not practically lead to impunity, such practices innately debase the administration of justice. Of course, it would be simplistic to argue that judges and prosecutors are politically or otherwise completely unbiased, but they still remain significantly better alternatives to MPs.

A certain degree of parliamentary armistice and serenity is another beneficial derivative of this proposal. Liberated from this (at best, controversial) capacity, the MPs will concentrate more on their primary duties of lawmaking and representation in the political discourse and practice. To a certain extent, this will facilitate both the detachment of political responsibility from criminal liability at the parliamentary scrutiny level and the alleviation of the infamous 'penalization of the political life' (or perhaps, the politicisation of the criminal life). The mongers of petty micropolitical feuds and their schemes will have fewer opportunities to turn the house into a public showground of ambiguity and nebulous innuendos, which acutely violate the presumption of innocence and fuel popular distrust in the political system by and large.

Of course, the suggested model should not neglect the legitimate concerns in defence of governance and politics. It is true that criminal procedures for ministerial offences are intrinsically 'sensitive', as their expected publicity and nationwide awareness put political systems, parties, and societies to a strenuous test. Although such crimes typically require long and sophisticated investigations and may involve numerous witnesses or suspects and procedural lags, neither the political system nor society as a whole should be required to endure lengthy intervals of unrest and instability. This would only perpetuate a vicious cycle and thus defeat the purpose of ensuring an inclusively effective regime.

Immediate procedural prioritisation of such indictments and exceptional competence of experienced prosecutors and investigating magistrates could provide a solid foundation to moderate the harmful by-products of criminal procedures against political figures. Indictment for ministerial misdemeanours could be handled by public prosecutors to the Court of Appeals and should always entail mandatory preliminary investigation. In the case of felonies, a Supreme Court judge

Ministerial criminal liability in the Greek legal order 171

should be appointed as investigating magistrate, and a deputy public prosecutor assigned to the Supreme Court should order the investigation and draft the summons. A judicial council comprising five Supreme Court judges will then resolve possible disputes between the investigating magistrate and the prosecutor and irrevocably decide to refer the case before the Special Court, cease prosecution, not press charges, or request supplementary investigation.[8]

As envisaged in Article 86 of the Constitution, the Special Court carries sufficient guarantees to pass irrevocable judgement on ministerial offences, that is, to 'adjudicate at the first and final instance', as typically expressed in Greek legal jargon. The implied prohibition to appeal the Special Court's decision has been amply discussed regarding its compatibility with Article 2 of Protocol 7 to the Convention for the Protection of Human Rights and Fundamental Freedoms, which Greece ratified by virtue of Law 1705/1987. The article, titled 'Right of Appeal in Criminal Matters', stipulates in its first paragraph:

> Everyone convicted of a criminal offense by a tribunal shall have the right to have his conviction or sentence reviewed by a higher tribunal. The exercise of this right, including the grounds on which it may be exercised, shall be governed by law.

The prevailing opinion—as also articulated in case law[9]—holds that a balanced interpretation of the stipulation found in the second paragraph of Article 2 resolves the issue in favour of conformity by introducing an exception to the respective right 'in cases in which the person concerned was tried in the first instance by the highest tribunal'. Therefore, given that the Special Court is staffed by judges to the Supreme Court and the Council of State, it substantially fulfils the 'highest tribunal' clause, and the exception validly applies.

Additionally, given that no reference to transparency is incorporated in Article 86 of the Constitution or in its explanatory remarks, inclusion of such a clause would streamline the charter's animus to reflect current international developments in the field and could prove beneficial as an interpretative mechanism towards observing the respective principle.

In a nutshell, our proposal encourages a paradigm shift which endorses parliamentary disengagement from all judicial powers and the establishment of a different procedural system to better fit the necessities of everyday politics without paying a hefty price in terms of compromising fundamental principles and the rule of law. In doing so, the authors consider that the constitutional provisions relating to the Special Court can still prove useful, effective and justifiable;

---

8 Anagnostopoulos has recently proposed that the Plenary of the Athens Court of Appeals (a collective body envisaged in Art. 28 of the Code of Criminal Procedure and comprising about 200 appellate judges serving in Athens) should replace the house as the competent body to decide by vote on ministerial prosecutions. See Mandrou (2019).

9 See Decision no. 69/1992 (Special Court in Art. 86 of the Constitution; *Epitheórisi Evropaïkoú Dikaíou*, (1992), pp. 149ff.).

172 *Eugenia Kopsidi and Ioannis A. Vlachos*

therefore, an amendment to Article 86 of the Constitution ranks ahead of an abolition—at least for the time being. Unfortunately, the constitutional amendment of November 2019 did not seize the opportunity to move forward with a bolder agenda on the issue, limiting itself to the (fair) effacement of the extinguishing deadline in Article 86. According to Article 114, para. 6, this means that any possible further improvements would have to wait for at least five years and might even require broader consensus by 180 out of 300 representatives. Moreover, if the degree of parliamentarian concord during the recent amendment carries any predictive value, it leaves more to be desired regarding a future wider consent. Meanwhile, our aspirations as the authors are that the political system will mature in the years to come and that such cases will be handled with a solemn commitment to seriousness and a sense of duty to observe the fundamental principles and to improve society and democracy.

References

Anagnostopoulos, I. (2011). Issues on the prosecution of Ministers and accomplices. *Piniká Khroniká*, 61.

Androulakis, N. K. (1989). *On Ministerial Criminal Liability, Statute of Limitations-Accomplices*. Athens, Greece: Ant. N. Sákkoulas.

Aravantinos, I. (1880). *On the Responsibility of Rulers and Ministers*. Athens, Greece: Típis Io. Kouvélou and A. Trími. Available from: https://anemi.lib.uoc.gr/php/pdf_pager.php?rec=/metadata/2/2/5/metadata-421-0000022.tkl&do=197449.pdf&lang=en&pageno=1&pagestart=1&width=444&height=644&maxpage=384 [Accessed 10 November 2020].

Besila-Vika, E. (1985). *The Institution of Ministerial Criminal Liability in the Greek and Comparative Constitutional Law*. Athens: Sakkoulas.

Charalambakis, A. (2009). Ministerial criminal liability. *Piniká Khroniká*, 59.

Chrysogonos, C. (1997). Constitutional aspects of the criminal liability of Ministers and Deputy Ministers. *Iperáspisi*.

Chrysogonos, C. (2003). *Constitutional Law*. Ed. A. Sakkoulas. Athens: Komotini.

Chrysogonos, C. (2011). *A Rough Plan for Democratization: Twelve Thoughts for a Different Revision*. Available from: www.constitutionalism.gr/2056-shediasma-ekdimokratismoy-dwdeka-skeceis-gia-mia-a/ [Accessed 27 January 2020].

Feloutzis, K. (2005). *Conflicts of Competence between Ordinary and Special Criminal Courts in Cases of Relatedness and Complicity to Crime*. Athens: Sákkoulas.

Jescheck, H. H. and Weigend, T. (1996). *Lehrbuch des Strafrechts. Allgemeiner Teil*. Berlin: Duncker & Humblot.

Kalogirou, N. and Galetsellis, P. (2009). *Political and Criminal Responsibility of Members of the Government*. Athens, Greece: Nomikí Vivliothíki.

Kasimatis, G. (2013). We have democracy without . . . demos. *Eleftherotipia*. Available from: www.enet.gr/?i=news.el.article&id=340796 [Accessed 28 January 2020].

Koukiotis, D. (2010). Ministerial criminal liability and Article 86: An unconstitutional provision of the Constitution. *Pinikí Dikaiosíni*, Vol. 8-9, p. 1048.

Loverdos, A. (1995). *The Criminal Liability of the Ministers and Deputy Ministers in the Parliamentary System*. Athens, Greece: Ant. N. Sakkoulas.

Ministerial criminal liability in the Greek legal order 173

Magkakis, G. A. (1984). *Criminal Law: General Part Diagram.* Athens, Greece: Papazisi.

Mandrou, I. (2019). Seminar held in the Athens Bar Association on the new legislation on ministerial responsibility. *Kathimerini.* Available from: www.kathimerini. gr/1054778/gallery/epikairothta/ellada/hmerida-ston-dikhgoriko-syllogo-a8hnwn-gia-ton-neo-nomo-peri-ey8ynhs-ypoyrgwn [Accessed 28 January 2020].

Mantzoufas, P., Margaritis, L. and Symeonidou-Kastanidou, E. (2014). *The Criminal Liability of Ministers.* Athens, Greece: Nomikí Vivliothíki.

Margaritis, L. (2011). Ministers and deputy ministers: Passive bribery and money laundering. *Piniki Dikaiosíni.*

Neppi Modona, G. (2012). *Venice Commission: External and Internal Aspects of the Independence of the Judiciary: Report CDL(2012)049.* Available from: www.venice. coe.int/webforms/documents/?pdf=CDL(2012)049-e [Accessed 10 November 2020].

Soleintakis, N. (2005). *Ministers before the Special Court (1821–2000).* Athens: N. Soleintakis.

Spyridakis, I. S. (2014). Ministerial criminal liability. *Nomikó Víma,* 62.

Symeonidou-Kastanidou, E. (2011). The scope of the special provisions on ministerial criminal liability. *Piniki Dikaiosíni.*

Venizelos, E. (1993a). A draft for the amendment of Article 86 of the Const. 1975/1986 and the regulation of ministerial criminal liability. In: Manoledakis, I. and Venizelos, E. eds. *Ministerial Criminal Liability (Disadvantages of the Current Provision: Revision Proposals).* Athens, Greece: Ant. N. Sakkoulas.

Venizelos, E. (1993b). Ministerial criminal liability in the juxtaposition between archaic and progressive characteristics of a parliamentary system. *Iperáspisi.*

Vlachopoulos, S. (2013). *Ministerial Criminal Liability.* Available from: www. constitutionalism.gr/wp-content/uploads/2013/06/2013IstameVlahopoulos. pdf [Accessed 28 January 2020].

10 Transparency and accountability of the Italian public administration in the context of public procurement

The case of below-threshold contracts

Francesca Sgrò

10.1 Introduction

The principles of transparency and accountability have entered the Italian legal system relatively recently. In fact, their recognition is the result of the modernisation process in public administration (PA) that originated in the 1990s and was accelerated by the 'institutional' use of the internet and the increasingly frequent application of e-government models in several areas of public activity.

According to Italian law, transparency is the total accessibility of information about the organisation and the activity of PA. Closely linked to the principle of transparency is the accountability of PA, which implies the obligation to explain and justify the performed activity, public spending, and the pursued objectives.

Since their first applications, transparency and accountability have been considered instrumental principles for the implementation of the principle of impartiality in PA, enshrined in Article 97 of the Italian Constitution. In particular, Italian doctrine and jurisprudence have recognised *ab origine* the necessary functional relation between transparency and accountability on one hand, and impartiality on the other hand, which has predominantly connoted the identity of the two examined principles.

The objective of this research is to verify whether transparency and accountability have progressively developed autonomous relevance, detaching themselves from strict adherence to the principle of impartiality alone, and whether they can be considered independent principles/values oriented to the protection of the community, which in fact—due to transparency and accountability instruments—can exercise a democratic check on the PA action. The chosen field of investigation is the subject of public contracts, which represents the privileged scope of application of the transparency and accountability principles, since it is precisely through their instruments that it is possible to check whether the PA's choice of contractor is legitimate. The research focuses on the examination of the particular area of public procurement that concerns contracts whose economic costs are below the threshold of European relevance in order to outline the evolutionary

Italian public administration 175

parabola of the legal significance of transparency and accountability regarding public contracts with lower values.

This research is therefore aimed at verifying whether transparency and accountability are only projections of the principle of impartiality, as historically recognised by Italian doctrine and jurisprudence, or whether they have developed a more marked identity with multiple functionalities. In fact, transparency and accountability also significantly contribute to the fight against corruption, avoiding any conflict of interest and promoting compliance with legality in the area of public contracts (Fratini 2018). Moreover, transparency and accountability tools contribute, albeit indirectly, to the efficiency of decision-making processes because they allow the partial liberalisation of public evidence procedures to be constantly subject to the inspection of the National Anti-Corruption Authority (ANAC), stakeholders and partners. From this perspective, transparency and accountability seem to partially detach themselves from the exclusive identification with the principle of impartiality in order to progressively open up to the other two constitutional principles that have to guide PA (again in accordance with Art. 97 of the Italian Constitution), that is, good performance and administrative legality.

The survey method used is based on the study of the legislative discipline on public procurement below the threshold. Through this focus and with an inductive approach, the study aims to define the current physiognomy of the principles of transparency and accountability (i.e., the research problem). In particular, the study of public contracts below the threshold intends to demonstrate that Italian legislators now consider transparency and accountability instruments the main bastions that are able to counterbalance some political-legislative choices (risky in some aspects), aimed at simplifying procedures and relaunching the economy, as they allow administrative legality to be always ensured.

In this sector, transparency and accountability seem to become the crossroads of the different constitutional principles that characterise administrative action— not only impartiality but also good performance, legality, and democracy. It can be deduced that transparency and accountability have attained legal maturity, becoming autonomous principles/values and instruments to bring citizens closer to PA.

The legal concepts of transparency and accountability, which may be perceived as two sides of the same coin, are briefly described in Section 10.2. In Section 10.3, the application of these principles in the context of Italian public procurement is examined, focusing on the transparency and accountability obligations that are imposed on the contracting authority in service and supply contracts below the threshold. In the context of below-threshold contracts, an attempt is made to identify the importance of the principles of transparency and accountability, taking into account Italian legislators' current choice to simplify public procurement procedures. In particular, the transparency and accountability obligations that the legislators have differentiated according to a proportionality criterion on the basis of the value of the public contract are examined in Sections 10.4 and 10.5. Finally, this chapter ends with some constitutional considerations

176 Francesca Sgrò

that aim to detect the alleged evolution of the principles of transparency and accountability from the Italian perspective. From principles closely linked to the impartiality of PA, they seem to emancipate themselves into some autonomous principles/values in order to provide guidelines for both the protection of the legality of administrative action and the good performance of PA (Section 10.6).

10.2 Transparency and accountability as two sides of the same coin

Transparency is the total accessibility of information about the organisation and the activity of PA. It aims to promote a widespread check on the implementation of institutional functions and the use of public resources.

The principle of transparency—which in Italy was already enshrined in Administrative Procedure Law no. 241/1990 and subsequently specified in Legislative Decree no. 33/2013—entails the obligation to publish administrative acts, and by means of this, PA reveals and defines its accountability. In particular, each action of PA must be disclosed through the publication of relevant acts on institutional websites, specifically in the Transparent Administration section (which is specifically dedicated to this purpose), to allow anyone to access the administrative documents that have external relevance. Transparency is not achieved through the mere communication of information, but it requires the flow of information to be rational and understandable. This means that information and communication must be organised and decoded in order to make the recipients (citizens, judiciary, and guarantee authorities) truly aware of the administrative choices.

Along with the publishing rules that are imposed on PA, the duty to provide reasons also represents the most traditional expression of the principle of transparency (Masucci 2015). Acknowledged as a general principle of administrative action by Article 3 of Law no. 241/1990, it covers the obligation of PA to communicate the reasons for its decisions and concerns all public measures that have external relevance. In particular, PA provides the justification for administrative decisions, stating the relevant facts and evidence and citing the relevant legal norms and showing how they fit each other. The function of this justification is to ensure the transparency of administrative action and therefore to endorse a general check on public choices. The duty to provide reasons in fact offers a rational reconstruction of the administrative activity by explaining the logical and legal arguments followed by PA to reach its final decision. In this way, the duty to give reasons has become a fundamental guarantee for citizens (Torchia 2016).

Closely linked to the principle of transparency is accountability of PA, which implies the obligation to explain and justify the undertaken activity, the public spending, and the pursued objectives. In fact, accessibility to PA information is an instrumental requirement to give an account of the PA choices in terms of consistency with the pursued objectives, the achieved usefulness, and the justification for public spending (Opdebeek and De Somer 2016). This supervision ensures the public authorities' compliance with the principles embedded in administrative laws.

There is a circularity between transparency and accountability because of their close relation. In particular, transparency is the *objective connotation* of administrative action and has its own reflection in accountability, which connotes PA as a *subjective attribute*. They are the two sides of the same coin, and both are functional in achieving direct impartiality and indirect legitimacy of administrative decision-making.

Accountability—which today represents a typical prerogative of every PA—is not only tightly connected to the principle of transparency but is also instrumental to the principles of efficiency and effectiveness of administrative action. By means of accountability tools, PA declares and demonstrates the usefulness of any administrative action, reports the results achieved, and explains the main steps of the administrative proceedings. In this way, it is induced to act legitimately, use public resources proportionately to the results to be achieved, and satisfy the public interest.

In the context of public procurement, accountability has a high value. In fact, public economic resources allotted to the functioning of administrative bodies are largely available, increasing the risk of creating a grey area that may cause the occurrence of abuse, violations of rights, conflicts of interest, and, in the more serious cases, infiltrations by criminal organisations aimed to illegally appropriate public money through public procurement. This explains the enhancement of PA accountability in the field of public procurement, as shown by the legislative reforms over the last few years, aimed to strengthen the tools that allow PA to give an account and justify its action. In this sector, PA is required to disclose and justify the functionality of a contract as being for the public interest, the choice of the economic operator, and the consequent public expenditure.

The Italian regulation on public procurement, whose core lies in the Public Contract Code (CCP; Legislative Decree no. 50/2016), has been reformed many times to simplify the administrative procedures in order to promote the public works necessary for the development of the country and thereby to increase economic investments (Caringella and Giustiniani 2019). In low-value contracts, the objective to speed up and streamline the procedures has led to the simplification (as much as possible) of the award procedures or even the exclusion of the call for tenders, with the aim of ensuring effective and rapid action that is functional for PA efficiency. CCP promotes the approval of public contracts whose values are inexpensive, reducing some caution, but has always guaranteed the procedures' transparency, the contracting authority's accountability, and the protection of the competition of economic operators interested in negotiating with PA.

In this chapter, the aim is to analyse the most recent physiognomy of the principles of transparency and accountability of Italian PA through the study of specific innovations introduced by the recent reform of CCP (i.e., the Unblocking Construction Sites Reform approved in 2019). This investigation is limited to the contract awards for supplies of goods and services whose values are less than the threshold of the value that marks the European relevance of the awards (and also includes the awards for public works of equal value). The reason is to verify how Italian legislators have intended to compound the multiple interests relating to

178   *Francesca Sgrò*

public procurement when the level of public spending is not high and therefore the risk of illegality is low. Regarding this category of awards, the recent CCP reform has in fact marked a new balance among the different principles involved in this field. This reform aims to promote PA efficiency, which implies speed and economy of choices, while the need to prevent illegal behaviour and corruption practices is met by means of transparency and accountability tools that are provided in every step of the public procedure. In essence, the analysis is intended to outline the current meaning of these principles in the light of their most recent applications in Italy in the context of public procurement, particularly regarding the contract awards for services and supplies with values below the threshold of European relevance (and works with the same value).

10.3 Transparency and accountability in the context of Italian public procurement

According to Article 1655 of the Italian Civil Code, procurement is 'the contract by which a party undertakes to perform a work or render services, with the organisation of the necessary means and with management at its own risk, in return for compensation in money'. When PA launches calls for tenders for the contract awards for works, supplies, or services for the performance of its institutional activity, it is necessary to follow a public procedure. This procedure aims to identify the counterpart of the contract that the PA will enter into and is based on the fundamental principles of administrative activity: legality, impartiality, good performance, transparency, economy, and accountability.

The legal framework of public procurement appears metaphorically as a leviathan, that is, an imposing corpus whose members make up the different sectors involved in public contracts, distinct but in any case, united by a single identity matrix, which they contribute to shaping. In fact, public contracts include heterogeneous contract categories (works, services and supplies, concessions, etc.).

These categories are subjected to a partially different regulation, which is nonetheless characterised by the development of the same decision-making process, beginning with the 'decision to contract', continuing with the award, and ending with the stipulation and the execution of the contract. It is a complex, composite, and constantly evolving regulation, which is set up in a partially different way, based on the object of the contract and the subject/PA that leads the public procedure. The regulation of public contracts for works, supplies, or services was set out in Legislative Decree no. 50 of 18 April 2016 and subsequent amendments (CCP), and over time it has been integrated in many aspects by the interpretations proposed by ANAC in its guidelines. This complex regulatory architecture provides both the public phase, which starts with the publication of the contract notice and ends with the award, and the subsequent contractual phase, which begins with the stipulation of the contract and after its execution, terminates with the payment for the activities carried out by the economic operator.

Many constitutional interests are relevant in the field of public procurement and need to be guaranteed through their rational balancing. In particular, the

Italian public administration 179

need to adopt a wide range of guarantees to safeguard *impartiality* and *transparency* in choosing contractors must be coordinated with the objective of *good performance* of PA in terms of simplification, speed, and maximum functionalisation of efficiency and care for the pursued public interest without compromising equal treatment and free competition in the reference markets (Corrado 2019). From this perspective, transparency and accountability are direct expressions of the constitutional principles of impartiality and good functioning of PA, as established in Article 97 of the Italian Constitution. This explains the legislators' continued interest in the Public Contract Code (CCP), which has been frequently updated, most recently due to the passing of Law no. 55 on 17 June 2019 (conversion of Decree Law no. 32/2019, i.e., the Unblocking Construction Sites Reform Decree) and Law no. 58 on 28 June 2019 (conversion of Decree Law no. 34/2019, the so-called Growth Decree).[1]

The general principles governing administrative activity in public procurement are established in Article 30, p. 1 of CCP. This article ('Principles for the Award and Execution of Procurements and Concessions') integrates and coordinates the traditional principles of administrative action with the rules of primary law contained in the European Union (EU) treaties that apply to all public contracts (regardless of their economic values). This provision states:

> The award and execution of works, services and supplies contracts and concessions . . . shall ensure the quality of the performances and shall be carried out with respect to the principles of cost-effectiveness, efficacy, timeliness and correctness. In awarding contracts and concessions, the contracting authorities shall also respect the principles of competition, non-discrimination, transparency, proportionality, as well as publicity, according to the modalities indicated in this Code. The principle of cost-effectiveness may be derogated, within the limits in which it is expressly allowed for in current legislation and in this Code, by criteria, provided in the call for competition, inspired to social exigencies, as well as to the safeguard of health, environment, cultural heritage and the promotion of sustainable development, also under an energy standpoint.
>
> (Legislative Decree no. 50/2016 art 30)

In particular, CCP moves along four directions. First, it is oriented towards simplifying and speeding up procedures. Second, it aims to promote free competition in the reference markets. Third, it aims to protect transparency and prevent corruption practices and infiltrations by criminal associations. Fourth, it enhances

---

1 This chapter does not examine Law no. 120 dated 11 September 2020 (conversion of Decree Law no. 76 dated 16 July 2020 (the so-called Simplifications Decree), which introduced a temporary regime in the derogation of Art. 36, para. 2 of CCP for procedures starting on 31 December 2021. This change is limited in time and is aimed at encouraging public investment in the infrastructure and public service sector and addressing the negative economic effects of the containment measures and the global health emergency due to COVID-19.

180 *Francesca Sgrò*

environmental and social protection. The latest trends in public procurement—expressed by the recent CCP reform (the Unblocking Construction Sites Reform)—testify to a partial change of perspective. This reform aims to promote the principles of simplification and transparency, also reducing the weight of the criterion of economy (even if the latter is mentioned before the others in the succession of the principles pursuant to Art. 30 of CCP). This solution is adopted in the name of the unprecedented acceleration of procedures, which is directed towards increasing the construction of public works (unlocking those that are already ongoing) and the growth of the country on one hand, and reducing procedural obligations when the value of the contract is irrelevant on the other hand. Indeed, a dual regulatory approach is established at the European level, which identifies and distinguishes between two contract categories based on their economic values. All the procurement rules derived from European law are in fact directed towards uniformly regulating only those contracts with significant economic values, whose amounts exceed specific thresholds established by the European Commission.[2] For these contracts, detailed regulations and particularly stringent requirements for both contracting authorities and economic operators are provided. This discipline aims to define a uniform set of rules within the EU territory, which allows economic operators in all member states to participate in public tenders wherever permitted in the EU. Otherwise, for public contracts whose values are less than the threshold of European relevance (below-threshold contracts), a less rigorous procedural regime is allowed. This is possible because the national legislation is subject (only) to compliance with the general principles inferred from the European treaties in the field of public procurement, while the legislation in detail is left to the autonomy of each state.

In Italy, the first version of CCP (Legislative Decree no. 163/2006, the so-called De Lise CCP)—which transposed the provisions of Directives no. 2004/17/EU and no. 2004/18/EU—disregarded that distinction and adopted a similar regulation for below-threshold contracts and for contracts with values equal to or greater than the European thresholds. The current version of CCP

---

2 The values of the European threshold are updated every two years by means of the European Commission's decisions, which have been directly applied since the date of their publication in the Official Journal of the EU. The most recent update of the threshold was made by means of the Commission Delegated Regulations (EU) no. 1827–1828–1829–1830 of 30 October 2019, effective on 1 January 2020. The thresholds of EU relevance are as follows: (a) EUR 5,350,000 (replacing the previous value of EUR 5,548,000) for public work contracts and concessions; (b) EUR 139,000 (replacing the previous value of EUR 144,000) for public supply and service contracts and public design contests awarded by contracting authorities that are central governmental authorities; (c) EUR 214,000 (replacing the previous value of EUR 221,000) for public supply and service contracts and public design contests awarded by sub-central contracting authorities; and (d) EUR 750,000 for social service and other specific service contracts. In the special sectors, the thresholds of EU relevance are as follows: (a) EUR 5,350,000 (replacing the previous value of EUR 5,548,000) for work contracts; (b) EUR 428,000 (replacing the previous value of EUR 443,000) for supply and service contracts and design contests; and (c) EUR 1,000,000 for social service and other specific service contracts.

(Legislative Decree no. 50/2016)[3]—especially after the latest reform in 2019[4]—inverts this trend and differentiates between the two categories to simplify the award procedures for below-threshold contracts. To counterbalance this simplification, CCP reinforces the impact of some general principles deemed essential, such as accountability and transparency of PA, as well as the protection of competition and equal treatment of economic operators.

Definitely, the current setting of CCP aims to enhance the fluidity of the transactions conducted by PA in order to streamline procedures and reduce burdens on both contracting authorities and economic operators. This recent perspective explains the raising of the thresholds that allows the direct award of contracts. Essentially, a simplification intent characterises contracts whose values are below the threshold of European relevance. This purpose is achieved through the enhancement of the tools aimed at selecting the best bid by means of an easier and faster procedure.

10.4 Procurement of services and supplies with economic costs below the threshold of European relevance after the recent reform of the Italian Public Contract Code (CCP)

Without prejudice to the sequence of activities that characterise a tender (decision to contract, selection of the best bid, award, stipulation, and execution), some significant diversifications in the public procedure are laid down and are aimed to simplify it in cases of contracts with low economic values. As noted, the difference in the procedures depends on the economic value of the contract, that is, if the contract's amount (estimated net of value-added tax) is greater or less than specific thresholds set out by the European Commission and indicated in Article 35 of the Italian CCP. Limiting the analysis to public procurement of services and supplies whose values are lower than the threshold of European relevance (as indicated, for the two-year period 2020–2021, this is equal to EUR 139,000 for contracts stipulated by central state administrations and EUR 214,000 for other

---

3 The Legislative Decree no. 50/2016 has transposed into Italian legislation the provisions of Directives no. 2014/23/EU, no. 2014/24/EU, and no. 2014/25/EU of the European Parliament and of the Council of 26 February 2014.

4 The Unblocking Construction Sites Reform (Law no. 55 on 17 June 2019 amending Legislative Decree no. 50/2016) provides for a return to traditional sources because these sources, being rigid, guarantee legal certainty. The provision of a single government regulation, to be issued soon (within 180 days from the reform's entry into force, unless extended), which will collect and rationalise some of the most important guidelines of ANAC, implies the downsizing of the 'soft law' system that was enshrined in the original version of the Italian CCP. The soft law system in the field of public procurement is mainly based on these guidelines, which have certainly produced significant benefits in terms of flexibility and adaptation to the changing needs deriving from application practices but have also caused some problems. In fact, this system has generated several uncertainties in the practical applications of the legislative provisions and many difficulties in framing the guidelines within the traditional system of internal sources.

182 *Francesca Sgrò*

sub-central administrations, such as local authorities) makes clear the legislators' willingness to promote simplification and speed for below-threshold contracts, without sacrificing transparency and impartiality in managing the procedure. Pursuant to Article 36, CCP defines an autonomous regulation for below-threshold contracts and provides the generalised use of direct awards, which replaces public competition among multiple economic operators in a completely innovative way. Specifically, for below-threshold contracts, the contracting authorities can use the simplified procedures set out in Article 36, p. 2 of CCP, which are the so-called pure direct award (Art. 36 (a), p. 2) and hybrid or mixed direct award (Art. 36 (b), p. 2). There is always the possibility of using the ordinary procedures if the market requirements suggest maintaining a competitive comparison.

A detailed analysis of the current procedure for below-threshold procurement of services and supplies (referring to other studies for an in-depth treatment of the whole subject) shows that the most innovative aspect concerns the replacement of the tender with the direct award in favour of the bidder that the contracting authority (through the official who manages for the procedure) deems worthy to be awarded the contract, in light of the general principles concerning the matter. This is a high-impact political choice based on the use of the direct award as a flexible legal instrument that guarantees the simplification and timeliness of administrative action.

It is also a choice that partially contradicts the rules governing public contracts that exceed the threshold value of European relevance. In fact, over time, the public procurement system in Italy has been amended by several reforms, aimed to avoid the risk of corruption in the transactions between PA officials and economic operators. In this context, the objective of impartiality in the choice of the contractor has been pursued through both the minute details of the public procedure and the provision of stringent transparency and publicity obligations for the activities carried out in each phase. This set of solutions seems indispensable, not only to discourage corruption practices but also to ensure the accountability of the contracting authorities and therefore of PA. The publicity of the acts supporting each procedural step and the knowledge of the reasons that justify public choices allow a formal verification from both the public authorities (judiciary) and the guarantee bodies (ANAC), as well as from economic operators wishing to enter into an agreement with PA and from citizens who can exercise democratic checks on the administrative activities through the advertising.

Stated differently, the legislative policy to simplify the procedures in below-threshold contracts—carried out through the generalised use of direct awards—entails conferring immense discretionary power on the contracting authorities that are legitimised to enter into the agreement directly (without competition) with the bidder deemed more convenient, only in light of the general principles governing PA, outside the strict burdens and the guarantees characterising the tender for above-threshold contracts. It could be a reckless choice in the context of Italian public procurement. Indeed, in the latest reform, Italian legislators relaxed those constraints imposed on the public procedure and conferred greater discretion to the contracting authorities in consideration of the low values of these service and supply contracts (and works of the same amount). In this sector of public contracts, a particular delineation of PA efficiency has been privileged, which mainly tends to simplify and speed up administrative activities, even at the risk of reducing the principle of economy that simultaneously characterises the administrative actions, because the absence of competition among several competitors sacrifices the possibility to obtain superior goods or services at lower costs.

10.5 The case of the so-called pure direct award (for contracts whose amounts are lower than EUR 40,000)

Public contracts for services and supplies with amounts less than the threshold of European relevance are examined as constituting a paradigmatic case of the strategy with which Italian legislators intend to connect the simplification of administrative procedures with the principles of PA transparency and account-ability. Within this category of contracts for which the direct award has replaced the tender, a further sub-distinction, ratione valore, has been established, and the procedural constraints have been proportioned so that additional proce-dural duties have been required for the most expensive contracts. In particular, when the contracting authority is a central administration, CCP provides for a sub-distinction and distinguishes the awards whose amounts are less than EUR 40,000 (Art. 36(a), p. 2) from the awards whose amounts are equal to or exceed EUR 40,000 and less than the thresholds that are now set at EUR 139,000 for supplies and services (Art. 36(b), p. 2). In the first case, the procedure is certainly more streamlined because the contracting authorities can grant direct awards, 'also without prior consultation of two or more economic operators or for works in direct administration' (Art. 36(a), p. 2).

Normally, the procurement procedure starts with a decision to enter into an agreement (decision to contract) that contains the essential elements of the ten-der, such as the public interest to be satisfied, the selection criteria for economic operators and offers, the object of the award, and the amount. In below-threshold contracts, the decision to contract directly produces a binding agreement on the subsequent award. In fact, it also indicates the supplier, the reasons for the selec-tion of the supplier, the supplier's capability to fulfil the general requirements, and technical and professional requirements (if applicable). This is the so-called decision in a simplified form (pursuant to Art. 32, p. 2 of CCP), which is pre-ceded by an informal investigation conducted by the contracting authority by means of the activity of the official responsible for the procedure, specifically designated for each award.

In this phase, it is possible to use market analyses (preferably, but not neces-sarily, on the electronic markets of PA) or consult the lists of economic operators (previously drawn up by the contracting authority) to identify not only the costs of the goods or the services and the specific solutions proposed in the market but also the most reliable economic operator. In this context, liberalisation and

184 *Francesca Sgrò*

simplification are achieved because the contracting authority, on one hand, is not required to formally consult multiple economic operators in order to compare different offers, and on the other hand can award the supply or the service contract to a freely identified economic operator without providing any justification for this choice in the award decree (Biancardi 2020).

Regarding the duty to cite the reasons for the direct award, it is necessary to acknowledge the progressive change of opinion that has occurred over the last few years. According to the original approach of CCP (2016), the contracting authority was required to give 'adequate reasons' in the event that the contract had been directly awarded without a tender. By means of Guideline no. 4,[5] ANAC confirmed this approach and (in point 4.3.1) clarified that the contracting authority should have an 'adequate' motivation behind its choice, specifying in detail the bidder's capability to meet the general and the special requirements, the offered goods' or services' compliance with the public interest, any areas for improvement proposed by the bidder, the fairness of the price in relation to the quality of the goods or services, and compliance with the principle of rotation. However, to simplify the below-threshold procedures, the contracting authority was allowed to fulfil its duty of reason giving through the comparison among the price quotations to justify the award. Legislative Decree no. 56/2017 (the so-called Corrective Decree)—with a significant change with respect to the ANAC positions—directly reformed CCP and repealed the duty of reason-giving for direct awards whose amounts were less than EUR 40,000 (pursuant to Art. 36(a), p. 2 of CCP). The Unblocking Construction Sites Reform (2019) substantially confirmed this position. There is thus a trend reversal compared with the original approach of CCP (supported by the interpretation of ANAC); currently, the contracting authority is not required to provide any justification for direct awards with very low values. Apparently, the legislators seem to have given up a very effective transparency and accountability tool. Indeed, even without any explicit requirement, the duty of reason giving for direct awards is derived from the general principles of good performance, impartiality and transparency of PA, from Article 3 of Law no. 241/1990 (and subsequent amendments), which requires a proper and full justification for all administrative acts that produce external legal effects, as well as from Article 32, p. 2 of CCP, which states that the decision to enter into an agreement must always indicate, albeit in a simplified form, the reasons for the selection of the supplier.

In this case, the justification is not absent; it can be found in the 'decision in a simplified form' that precedes and legitimises the direct award, while only the subsequent award decree (that is, the final act of the public procedure) may not contain any explicit reason.

---

5 Guideline no. 4 ('Procedures for the award of public contracts for amounts less than the thresholds of European relevance, market analyses and management of the lists of economic operators') was approved with the resolution of ANAC no. 1097 of 26 October 2016 and (after the Unblocking Construction Sites Reform) was most recently updated with the resolution of ANAC no. 636 of 10 July 2019.

Italian public administration 185

Definitely, the contracting authority must always justify (albeit briefly) its choice of the economic operator and specify the correspondence of the operator's offer to the public interest, the fairness of the price in relation to the quality of the service (with any areas for improvement offered by the contractor), and compliance with the rotation principle or the reasons for its derogation.[6] However, the goal of simplification entails that these reasons shall be synthetic and contained only in a single act, which is the decision to contract.

On this point, it is noted that alongside the general principles governing public procurement pursuant to Article 30, p. 1 of CCP (cost-effectiveness, effectiveness, timeliness, fairness, free competition, non-discrimination, transparency, proportionality, and advertising), in the below-threshold contracts, the principle of rotation is greatly enhanced, expressly provided by Article 36, p. 1 of CCP. This principle represents the concrete implementation of free competition, intended as both an equal treatment of the economic operators that access the public procurement market and an effective possibility for participation of micro, small, and medium enterprises in cases of low-value contracts. The principle of rotation aims at avoiding the consolidation of advantageous positions by the bidders who have already been awarded the previous tenders (the so-called outgoing operators) or have participated in previous procedures without being awarded. In fact, having already obtained information on the management of the procedure by the contracting authorities, these operators would be privileged over others in the market.[7] The rotation applies only to the award immediately preceding the one that is currently granted ('one jump'), provided that the object of the awards (previous and current) belongs to the same product or service category and that their values are equivalent.

The principle of rotation is not absolute because the contracting authority may derogate from it in exceptional circumstances, but in this case, it is required to provide adequate justification. Obviously, a more stringent reason is necessary if the derogation concerns the rotation of the awards. In this case, the contracting authority shall justify the award to the outgoing operator based on objective data, such as the particular structure of the market and the absence of alternatives and competitive operators. Another motivating factor behind the choice of the outgoing operator may be its subjective profile, that is, its reliability, deduced from the degree of satisfaction recorded in the previous contractual relationship in light of the quality of its service and its compliance with the agreed delivery date

6 To prove the fairness of the price, the contracting authority may use a comparison with market price lists, with offers previously presented for identical or similar goods and services or with prices charged to other administrations. Certainly, the comparison among multiple offers, although no longer expressly requested, still represents a best practice that is useful for ensuring competition, transparency, and accountability without sacrificing the simplification of the award procedures.

7 The principle of rotation is applied to both the bidders (aimed to exclude the outgoing economic operator from the tender) and the invitations (aimed to exclude not only the outgoing economic operator but also the other economic operators invited in the previous tender although unsuccessful bidders).

186 *Francesca Sgrò*

and costs. Otherwise, only an essential and concise justification is required in the case of derogation from the rotation of the invitations. In this case, the contracting authority may justify its invitation addressed to the previous bidder (albeit not awarded), referring to the expectation derived from previous contractual relationships or other reasonable circumstances, about the operator's reliability and suitability to perform consistent with the expected cost and quality levels.

Actually, the legislators diversify the transparency burdens based on the real needs arising during the procedure, as evidenced by the flexibility of the duty to give reasons for the award. The direct award for any work, service, and supplies amounting to less than EUR 40,000 does not require an express justification. However, the justification for the award is not entirely excluded but results aliunde, not from the award decree but from the decision (in a simplified form) to contract that legitimises the public procedure. In fact, pursuant to Article 32, p. 2 of CCP, the decision to contract shall include the reasons that explain and justify the award to a specific economic operator. The award decree is therefore strictly consequential to the decision to contract and refers to it for the reasons behind the choice made by the contracting authority. In this way, the duty to give reasons, which is a general principle (pursuant to Article 3 of Law no. 241/1990), remains safe and can be satisfied *per relationem*.

Stated differently, the duty to give reasons once again becomes an imperative obligation that must be expressed explicitly and fully in the event that the contracting authority derogates from one of the fundamental principles governing the procedure, as in circumstances where it cannot respect the rotation and decides to award the contract to the outgoing operator (in legitimate cases). In such cases, the contracting authority is required to explain the legitimacy of its derogation from the principle of rotation, and the duty of reason giving becomes the main accountability tool[8] to explain the legitimacy and the impartiality of the administrative choice and the proper functioning of PA.

10.6 The case of the so-called hybrid or mixed direct award (for contracts whose amounts are from EUR 40,000 up to the level of European relevance)

As noted, contracts for supplies and services whose amounts are equal to or exceed EUR 40,000 and less than EUR 139,000, which is currently the threshold of European relevance, can also be directly awarded. In this case, the more consistent values of the contracts have led legislators to introduce additional procedural burdens to protect impartiality, transparency, and accountability, which require enhanced protection due to the increase in public spending. For

---

8 In 2005, Koppell presented five 'conceptions of accountability': transparency (revealing the facts about the performance), liability (facing the consequences of the performance), controllability (acting in line with the principal's desires), responsibility (following the rules) and responsiveness (meeting expectations). These five conceptions provide a framework for analysing accountability concerns and priorities (Koppell 2005).

this category, the public procedure is featured by the direct award, with prior consultation, where existing, with at least five economic operators for services and supplies (three for works of the same value), identified on the basis of market analyses or lists of economic operators, in accordance with the criterion of rotation of invitations (pursuant to Art. 36(b), p. 2 of CCP). According to this new procedure—introduced by the Unblocking Construction Sites Reform (2019) and qualified by the first commentators as a hybrid or mixed direct award—the contracting authority shall carry out a thorough investigation before awarding the contract. In particular, it is required to carry out market analyses or consult official lists of economic operators and then select different operators to be invited to the competition. The competitive comparison among the bids determines the choice of the contractor. The hybrid or mixed direct award is therefore based on the comparison among various offers, and although simplified forms and procedures are used, it does not sacrifice but enhances the obligation of publicity aimed at protecting transparency and accountability. Indeed, the new regulation requires the acquisition of at least five bids in the sector of services and supplies; in this regard, the contracting authority is required to consult various operators to acquire different offers, among which a comparison is made. This seems to be an element of stiffening and aggravating the procedure (despite the intentions of the reform), which is nonetheless justified to safeguard the impartiality of public choice. The procedure starts with the decision to contract, which can be adopted in a simplified form (pursuant to Art. 32, p. 2 of CCP) and contains information similar to that provided for the pure direct award (pursuant to Art. 36(a), p. 2 of CCP). Subsequently, the procedure is divided into three phases: (1) 'selection of economic operators' to be invited to the competitive comparison, which are identified by means of market analyses or consultation of lists; (2) 'invitation' to the selected economic operators to submit an offer; and (3) 'competitive comparison' among the bids submitted, with the choice of the successful bidder. The operators invited to the procedure are selected in a non-discriminatory way, whose number is proportional to the amount and the relevance of the contract and in any case, at least equal to five (for services and supplies) on the basis of the criteria defined in the decision to contract, as well as in compliance with the principle of rotation of the invitations. Even in the hybrid or mixed direct award (similar to the pure direct award), the invitation addressed to the outgoing contractor is exceptional and shall be adequately motivated. To guarantee the transparency of the choice and the efficiency of the procedure, the contracting authority can adopt a regulation to govern the comparison of the invited economic operators.[9] The tools assigned to the contracting authority to perform its investigation are both market analyses and operator lists, which are subject to stringent publication

---

9 The regulation may indicate (a) the methods of conducting market analyses, possibly grouped by amount range; (b) the methods of establishing the lists of suppliers, possibly grouped by category and amount range; and (c) the criteria for choosing the subjects that will be invited to submit an offer.

requirements. The market analysis has an exploratory function, aimed at identifying the economic operators that are present on the market, meet the requirements set by the contracting authority and are interested in participating in the tender. In this way, the contracting authority will gain in-depth knowledge of the reference market and the conditions that are generally applied and obtain important information concerning both the features and the quality standards of the requested goods and service, plus the charged costs. The contracting authority has the broad freedom to choose the methods and the criteria to perform market analyses and can diversify its modus operandi based on the value of the award or the type of the requested goods or service. As a rule, the most used method is the consultation of catalogues of the electronic market. The start of the investigation activity is disclosed by publishing a notice on the contracting authority's website (Transparent Administration section) for at least 15 days (which can be reduced in cases of particular necessities). In this notice, the elements that will be included in the subsequent invitation to the competition are substantially moved up. These elements are the value of the award, the essential components of the contract, the requirements of professional suitability, the minimum requirements of cost-effectiveness and financial capacity, the level of technical and professional ability, the minimum number (not less than the number indicated by law) and possibly the maximum number of operators that will be invited to the competitive comparison, the selection criteria, and the modality for communicating with the contracting authority.

As an alternative to the market analyses, the group of economic operators to be invited may be identified by the contracting authority, which will select them from specific lists that were previously drawn up. In particular, the contracting authority will publish a notice in the Transparent Administration section of its institutional website. In the notice, the contracting authority will declare its decision to set up official lists, grouped under product categories from which it will select the operators to be invited to the public procedures, and will highlight the requirements for the registration of the operators on these lists. In particular, the notice will establish the general requirements (pursuant to Art. 80 of CCP) that the operators must fulfil, the criteria for selection, the categories of the awards and the ranges of the amounts, based on which the contracting authority has divided the lists, and any minimum requirements for registration. The contracting authority will assess the requirements and check the information provided by the operators. At the end of this selection, the final lists of the selected economic operators will be published. These lists—which will implement a quality 'vendor rating' system—are subject to periodic reviews to verify the providers' consistent fulfilment of the requirements over time. By consulting the lists, the contracting authority will have a list of operators whose seriousness and professionalism have already been verified. Moreover, having asked to be included in these lists, these operators have expressed their willingness to participate in the award procedures, so they are more reliable. Subsequently, when the public procedure takes place, the contracting authority will simultaneously invite some of the providers to the tender by selecting them from these lists and then choosing the best bid based

Italian public administration   189

on the award criteria (pursuant to Art. 95 of CCP): the lowest price or the most economically advantageous tender.

10.7 Final considerations on balancing the principles of transparency and accountability with the aim of simplification in the context of below-threshold contracts

In Italy, the urgent demand to carry out public works and infrastructures and speed up the execution of administrative activities has led to the promotion of simplification and celerity regarding public contracts that have low economic values, as evidenced by the recent reform of public procurement. The Unblocking Construction Sites Reform (2019) mainly involves the contract awards for works, goods, and services that have reduced values, which are strictly instrumental to the administrative activities. In such cases, the level of public spending is low; therefore, the risk of illegal conduct is reduced. For these reasons, legislators have adopted a sort of 'liberalisation of procedures', giving up some anti-corruption precautions and allowing the contracting authorities to enter into an agreement without an ordinary tender but only by means of a direct award. Indeed, in the context of below-threshold contracts, the latest reform aims to achieve a balance among different interests and therefore promotes gradual liberalisation, diversifying the procedural obligations based on the economic value of the public contract. For the awards whose amounts are less than EUR 40,000, a highly simplified procedure applies, and the contracting authority can freely choose the successful bidder, provided that the general principles are complied with (including the principle of rotation). For simplification purposes, in a direct award (that is pure), the duty of reason giving is not required, although the reasons that justify it can be deduced aliunde and in any case, are always expressed in the decision to contract (which legitimises the whole procedure). Certainly, the duty to give reasons expands and becomes an indispensable element in the event that the contracting authority derogates from the legislative procedure, as in the case of the award to the outgoing operator (in legitimate cases) by way of derogation from the principle of rotation. In this hypothesis, this derogation from the legislative framework increases the demand for transparency so that the duty to give reasons becomes the main accountability instrument because it allows the contracting authority to justify the legitimacy of the applied derogation.

For services and supplies (and works of equal value) whose amounts are equal to or exceed EUR 40,000 and less than EUR 139,000, the procedural sequence is more complex, and each measure aimed at simplification is overseen by a corresponding transparency tool. When the value of the contract increases, the legislators consider it appropriate to introduce some caution in ensuring impartiality in the management of the award and provide for a competition, albeit simplified, based on the comparison among different bids. In this case, the obligations of publicity increase because of the demand to disclose the investigation acts supporting the choice of the operators to be invited to submit an offer. In essence,

190 *Francesca Sgrò*

the reinforced proceduralisation of the administrative action does not concern the evaluation of the submitted offers (i.e., the final sequence of the award procedure) but the previous and preparatory phase focused on market analyses and official lists of reliable providers. This is the most significant phase of this procedural sequence because it is when the preliminary selection occurs, which is able to bind the shortlist of final competitors. This is also the phase that the legislators have intended to enrich with additional obligations of publicity, precisely because in a maximally simplified competition, this preliminary selection largely influences the final choice.

Transparency and accountability characterise the entire regulatory framework of public procurement. The proceduralisation of administrative activity and the publicity of each decision are necessary tools of legality, and they fight against corruption but risk becoming factors of complexity in case they are not proportional to the interests involved. Nevertheless, to unblock a sector that is traditionally affected by delays and slowness, it is necessary to promote the simplification of procedures for public contracts whose amounts are not within the threshold of European relevance. The recent reform of the Italian CCP has promoted a sort of liberalisation based on the simplification of procedures and the increase of discretionary power entrusted to the contracting authorities. At the same time, it has placed important protective tools alongside each 'deflationary' measure—the duty to provide reasons and publish the most relevant documents—to safeguard transparency and accountability. These measures follow a proportionality criterion; in fact, there is a gradation of transparency burdens because they increase not only when the value of the contract increases but also whenever the simplification measures and the related increasing discretionary power may create a grey area in the administrative action. The advertising obligations become crucial tools in the most significant phases of the procedure, such as when the contracting authority derogates from the ordinary procedure outlined by legislators or, in general, adopts relevant decisions for the public choice. There is a graduality of the advertising obligations because the administrative documents are published on the basis of real and effective needs for transparency and accountability. An excess of information is avoided because, although it discourages corrupt practices, it may foster 'bid-rigging' agreements among the economic operators.

To promote a groundbreaking balance among different principles and opposing public interests, the regulation of below-threshold contracts (especially after the Unblocking Construction Sites Reform) is tied to the principles/values of transparency and accountability, which represent a guarantee of legality, good performance, and impartiality. Transparency and accountability have close functional relations for the full achievement of other constitutional principles, but over time, they have acquired autonomous ontological relevance. The protection of transparency and accountability not only influences the legal obligations imposed on PA but also shapes the PA's modus operandi, currently oriented to giving account of any choice made, especially whether its activity is carried out by the exercise of discretionary power. Transparency and accountability are mentioned among the general principles that govern PA and guarantee the balance in the management of administrative power. They aim to ensure both impartiality in the choices and good performance in the effects; they also contribute to making PA efficient and responsible. Finally, they implement the democratic principle because they allow a democratic check on administrative decisions.

An examination of the latest legislative reforms has revealed the Italian legislators' willingness to exclude tenders among several economic operators and to opt for direct awards in low-value contracts. In terms of the value, this intention is reflected in the choice to underrate both the principle of competition that pervades the subject of public procurement in European legislation and the principle of cost-effectiveness that traditionally characterises domestic legislation. The downgrading of these principles is justified by the pressing need to make PA more efficient and speed up public procurement contracts of lesser value but may generate the risk that corrupt conduct will be fuelled precisely because of the lack of the guarantees that the tender ensures. However, it should be noted that to counterbalance this choice, the legislators have only used transparency and accountability tools, which therefore become predominant in order to avoid the risks of corruption and illegality that may arise from the absence of tenders among several operators. In addition to the principle of competition, the choice of opting for direct granting of contracts below the threshold also downplays the principle of cost-effectiveness, which historically puts the subject of public contracts under some stringent accounting constraints. The absence of competitive tendering eliminates the possibility that through competition among several contenders, PA may purchase goods or services under the best economic conditions. In this case as well, it is a sacrifice decided by the legislators to hasten the process of choosing the contractor for contracts below the threshold. On one hand, it is offset by the compliance with the principle of rotation of credit facilities (mentioned above); on the other hand, it is supervised by the transparency and accountability obligations provided for at each stage of the procedure.

The accountability of PA that—in the role of the contracting authority—uses public resources strengthens the community's participation in public governance and provides a new direction, which is based on disclosing the public choices and reporting the results. In this way, whether there is clarity of intent and prompt information disclosure, those grey areas that favour corruption and illegality cannot be created in the delicate and risky public procurement sector.

If the conceptual autonomy granted to the principles of transparency and accountability and the strengthening of the instruments for the implementation of these principles are really suitable for counterbalancing the simplification and guaranteeing the full legality of the administrative action, only the evidence of facts, and therefore a subsequent diachronic investigation, can confirm it. It is certainly clear that Italian legislators are proceeding with caution, and such uncertainty is explained in light of the particular domestic situation and Italy's chronic exposure to corruption risks in the public procurement sector. However, this does not diminish the autonomous legal importance that is now ascribed to the principles of transparency and accountability, considered essential in the management of any public procurement procedure.

192 Francesca Sgrò

References

Biancardi, S. (2020). *Servizi e forniture. Manuale per la gestione degli appalti sopra e sotto soglia comunitaria*. Santarcangelo di Romagna: Maggioli, pp. 83–119.

Caringella, F. and Giustiniani, M. eds. (2019). *Il Decreto Sblocca Cantieri*. Roma: Dike.

Corrado, A. (2019). *La trasparenza negli appalti pubblici, tra obblighi di pubblicazione e pubblicità legale. Federalismi.it—Rivista di Diritto Pubblico Italiano, Comparato, Europeo* [Online], 1, pp. 1–16. Available from: www.federalismi.it/nv14/articolo-doc umento.cfm?Artid=35526&content=&content_author [Accessed 3 January 2020].

Fratini, M. (2018). *Manuale Sistematico di Diritto Amministrativo*. Roma: Dike.

Koppell, J. (2005). Pathologies of accountability: ICANN and the challenge of 'multiple accountabilities disorder'. *Public Administration Review*, 65(1), pp. 94–108.

Masucci, G. (2015). *Motivazione*. In: Clarich, M. and Fonderico, G. eds. *Procedimento Amministrativo*. Milanofiori Assago, MI: Wolters Kluwer, pp. 89–114.

Opdebeek, I. and De Somer, S. (2016). Duty to give reasons in the European legal area: A mechanism for transparent and accountable administrative decision-making? A comparison of Belgian, Dutch, French and EU administrative law. *Rocznik Administracji Publicznej* [Online], 2, pp. 97–148. Available from: www.ejournals.eu/RAP/2016/2016%20(2)/art/7581/ [Accessed 12 October 2016].

Torchia, L. (2016). Il nuovo codice dei contratti pubblici: Regole, procedimento, processo. *Giornale di Diritto Amministrativo*, 4, pp. 605–612.

11 Transparency and government accountability in Brexit negotiations[1]

Natalie Fox

11.1 Introduction

On Thursday, 23 June 2016, the United Kingdom (UK) decided to leave the European Union (EU) in a process called 'Brexit'. The in-out referendum on the EU membership was held in accordance with the European Union Referendum Act 2015. The British voters were asked whether the UK should remain in or leave the EU.[2] The referendum result has given rise to the most profound constitutional change in decades. Nevertheless, the exclusively politically binding decision of British society could not naturally result in reversing the processes that had shaped the UK's systems in an evolutionary manner for decades. Holding a referendum was not a constitutional or legal requirement. In accordance with the British constitutional law, the parliament in its sovereignty could have decided to withdraw (or not) without using this form of direct democracy. UK constitutional law scholars (e.g., Barnett 2017, p. 153) emphasise that 'referendums in the UK have always been considered to be "advisory" rather than legally binding'. Nonetheless, this does not mean that the purely advisory character of the referendum is a hindrance in British political practice to the meaningful impact of the majority of voters' unambiguous opinion on the conduct of a given policy. Thus, the UK's withdrawal from the EU was made to depend on the future result of a referendum, which had a purely advisory character in the strict legal sense but was binding in the political sense (Allen 2018, p. 106).

From a legal point of view, before the Brexit negotiations formally commenced, the court was confronted by a legal challenge. As a result, a ruling was issued on the power of the UK Government under the royal prerogative to trigger Article 50 of the Treaty on the European Union (TEU), the first step in the process of the UK's withdrawal from the EU. Thus, the Supreme Court's intervention was necessary in order to define the constitutional role of Westminster in this scope.

---

1 This chapter presents the results of Research Project No. 2018/29/N/HS5/00685, financed by the National Science Centre (Poland).
2 See Article 1(4) of the European Union Referendum Act 2015. The result showed 51.89% voting to exit the EU and 48.11% opting to remain (no minimum percentage of the vote was required for a binding decision). In contrast, in the 1975 referendum, two-thirds (67.23%) of UK voters favoured continued European Community membership.

194 *Natalie Fox*

This chapter provides an analysis of the EU/UK approach to transparency, which was being used as a tactic in the Brexit negotiations and is of particular interest. Taking into account the nature of the issue, it would be rational to expect the EU and UK political parties to adopt a common approach to transparency, which would result in increased responsibility. Openness and transparency are key elements in ensuring accountability in the decision-making process. The UK Government embraced the Brexit talks in a particular way. On the one hand, the UK sought to avoid the scenario called the 'no-deal Brexit'; on the other hand, it consistently exposed a tough line on the issues where it was difficult to reach an agreement, although it would result in the 'hard Brexit'.

Moreover, the UK constitutional structure also influences transparency in the Brexit negotiations through the role of Westminster (and its EU Select Committees). A key component of democratic governance is clarity of responsibility, enabling voters to accurately hold politicians to account for their actions. In this context, an important aspect of the current research is the question of how accountable the divorce process from the EU should be construed. The analysis is complemented by a brief examination of the doctrine of parliamentary sovereignty from political and legal perspectives in the context of the Brexit negotiations. It is widely known that the UK's membership in the EU resulted in a progressive limitation of Westminster sovereignty. In legal terms, it is also questioned whether the decision on the withdrawal from the EU will result in a 'renaissance' of the traditional sovereignty doctrine, per A. V. Dicey (1982). Thus, this chapter links the processes taking place at the international level with those on the domestic plane.

The following research hypotheses were adopted. First, the result of the 2016 EU referendum took on a particular political role because its effect made it impossible for the UK Parliament to disregard the will of the people. Second, the outcome of the so-called Miller I case showed that the courts had been forced again to draw the boundaries of constitutional competence between the executive and the parliament, in the sense that they had consistently backed Westminster. Third, the more open the Brexit process was, the more responsible the government became. Therefore, maintaining control over the dissemination of information, especially regarding disputes among cabinet ministers as to what form Brexit should take and how long it should last, was of paramount importance to the stability of the government. Fourth, in legal terms, the objective of this chapter is to present the argument that the expected results of the process of the UK's withdrawal from the EU will not lead to restoring the traditional doctrine of parliamentary sovereignty but may only apparently result in the revitalisation of the current status quo of individual state institutions.

11.2 The UK's exit from the EU

11.2.1 The conduct of the UK's foreign affairs—a brief outline

In the UK, it is commonly known that the capacity to conclude and denounce treaties is a matter of royal prerogative. However, in practice, the process of negotiating, signing, and ratifying treaties is conducted by the currently ruling government on behalf of the Crown (see, e.g., Higgins 2009, p. 550). Consequently, the responsibility for concluding and terminating treaties involving the UK lies with the Secretary of State for Foreign, Commonwealth and Development Affairs. In turn, a government department, the Foreign, Commonwealth and Development Office is responsible for all aspects of foreign and EU policies concerning the conclusion of treaties and the decision-making process in formal and procedural issues. In this light, it is obvious that the British system draws a clear demarcation line between the strictly international sphere, which is immanently a part of royal prerogative (Leyland 2016, p. 87; Loveland 2015, p. 93) and implemented by the executive authority with the prime minister at its head, and the domestic plane, which is the internal effectiveness of international obligations (Gillespie and Weare 2015, pp. 94–95).

11.2.2 *Triggering of Article 50(2) of the TEU without parliamentary authorisation*

The sovereign's will, as expressed in the 2016 EU referendum, became the political basis for the government's decision to withdraw the UK from the EU. However, from the legal point of view, following the events, the main concern of both British scholarship and case law was the triggering of Article 50 of the TEU procedure. The cited provision is the legal basis for such an action because pursuant to the regulations contained therein, 'any Member State may decide to withdraw from the Union in accordance with its own constitutional requirements'.[3] A member state wishing to withdraw from the EU is obliged to formally notify the European Council of its intention to conduct negotiations and conclude a withdrawal agreement.[4] It is important to note that neither the method nor the form of notification has been specified in the EU Treaties' provisions. In this context, the matter of proper procedure should be considered in the case of the UK's withdrawal from the EU structures. In British constitutional practice, two important issues related to this matter emerged. First, owing to the uncodified British Constitution, it was necessary to define unequivocally the British 'constitutional requirements' in this respect. Second, there arose the fundamental question—triggering a discussion both politically and doctrinally and requiring judicial intervention—of whether the government had independent competence to trigger Article 50(2) of the TEU, ergo what role the parliament should play in this respect. Against this backdrop, the decoding of the normative content of Article 50(2) of the TEU, whose provision determines the starting point of the Brexit, is identified with the act of submitting an application (notification of

---

3 See Article 50(1) of the TEU. As it appears, this formulation is autonomous, while its content should particularly consider the manner of participation of a member state in supranational organisations, especially regarding the form and the manner of terminating international agreements.
4 See Article 50(2) of the TEU.

196 *Natalie Fox*

intention) to withdraw from the EU. Undoubtedly, in accordance with the political tradition of the UK, this competence (on the exercise of prerogative power) in practice is bestowed on the government. However, against this background, there arose the legal question of whether the executive government could use the Crown's prerogative powers to give notice of the withdrawal without parliamentary authorisation.

Initially, the answers to one of the most important questions related to the Brexit process were sought in the scholarship views. For example, Barber et al (2016) argued that prior consent was required in the statutory form to take further necessary steps in the withdrawal procedure (in this context, see also Phillipson and Young 2018). An additional confirmation of this thesis is the role of the parliament established in the literature and practice, measured by its significance for the political system. As pointed out by Bradley and Ewing (2003, p. 77):

> Parliament's importance within British government depends less on absolute legislative power than on its effectiveness as a political forum in expressing public opinion and in exercising control over government.

In this connection, an interesting aspect of the discussed issue was the impact of the results of the referendum of 23 June 2016 on the future decision of Westminster.

Two circumstances need consideration here. First, as indicated in the scholarship, despite the non-binding nature of the referendum outcome, overall, the UK Parliament respects the position expressed by the citizens, which results simply from the contemporary realities of political life. Due to its unequivocal character, the outcome of the referendum did not leave any room for a decision in terms of the parliament's reinterpretation of the will of the nation (despite a slight majority of votes). In the public opinion, it was emphasised that the parliament should deem itself bound by the result of the advisory participation of voters.[5] Therefore, in political terms, the result of the 2016 referendum took on a particular role because its effects made it impossible for the parliament to disregard the will of the people. Second, it is impossible not to refer briefly to the method of the implementation of EU legislation within the UK legal system, which was relevant in the Brexit process. It should be emphasised that the principle of dualism existing in the British constitutional law means that in addition to legal acts constituted by national authorities, if international agreements and other international acts (including those established by the authorities of international organisations) would be applied, then in the understanding of the UK doctrine of parliamentary sovereignty, international legal acts require appropriate, separate, and independent 'anchoring' in domestic law. Thus, it is necessary to apply the appropriate procedures to transform the norms of international law into provisions of the

---

5 As Matthews (2017, pp. 604–607) points out, the increased practice of referenda has consolidated 'the pattern of constitution-by-consent', creating a competitive source of legitimacy and authority.

British legal system. Since foreign affairs in the UK are generally conducted on behalf of the Crown by ministers as part of prerogative power, on this basis, both negotiation and ratification of treaties may take place without any consultation with the UK Parliament, which does not play any direct role in the process of concluding international agreements. However, it is worth noting that international agreements necessitate obtaining the consent of the relevant legislative body in order to enter into force. This means that simply signing and ratifying agreements are not synonymous with their transformation into the domestic structure of British law. Thus, in terms of the British legal system, the significance for the characteristics of the specifics of the process of implementation of EU legislation is that an international agreement subject to ratification (or one that is not subject to ratification) does not become an internal part of the UK law until it first takes on the form of a primary legislation (Barnett 2017, p. 128; Lang 2017; Oliver 2003, pp. 81–82; Feld 1972, p. 251). Thus, without the approval of the legislative branch, the executive branch may not change an applicable law, meaning that on each occasion, it is necessary to issue a special statute incorporating treaty provisions into the national legal system.

In the above context, the Brexit negotiations allowed the discernment of a certain systemic contradiction manifested in two instances. On the one hand, UK constitutional law scholars expressly believed that it was impossible to make the British institution of the referendum binding. On the other hand, the government of Theresa May claimed the right to trigger Article 50(2) of the TEU and thus set the course of the procedure for withdrawing the UK from the EU structures without the parliament's consent. It should therefore be stated that de facto, as a result of the EU referendum, the freedom of parliamentary decision was curtailed and the referendum lost in practice its *strict* consultative nature (e.g., Ewing 2016, p. 293). Thus, the de facto paramount status of popular sovereignty was further emphasised by the conflict over Article 50 of the TEU, which could only be resolved by making a judicial decision.

11.2.2.1 Miller I case judgement

In the case of *R (Miller) v. Secretary of State for Exiting the European Union*,[6] the UK Supreme Court, sitting for the first time en banc on 24 January 2017, answered a legal question for which the constitutional requirements were legally unspecified. The case required a determination on whether the government's triggering of Article 50(2) of the TEU procedure required approval from the parliament. In other words, the main question in this case was whether, under royal prerogative, the Crown (the executive) had the power to initiate the withdrawal process from the EU. The decision was issued, following an appeal against the High Court of Justice judgement of 3 November 2016,[7] which maintained

---

6 [2017] UKSC 5; hereinafter Miller I case.
7 *R (Miller) v. Secretary of State for Exiting the European Union* [2016] EWHC 2768 (Admin).

198 *Natalie Fox*

that the case might be subject to a judicial review and that there was no prerogative power to trigger Article 50(2) of the TEU. The prerogative of either concluding or denouncing treaties, which operates entirely at the international level, cannot be exercised in relation to the EU treaties, particularly if there is no applicable basis in this respect, expressed in the primary legislation. Against this background, the European Union Referendum Act 2015 provided the legal basis for the referendum itself but did not authorise the government to trigger Article 50 of the TEU. The Supreme Court acknowledged that the established constitutional requirements did not authorise the government to initiate the procedure of leaving the EU without conferring this power by the UK Parliament through the adoption of a relevant statute. The key problem in the so-called Miller I case concerned the determination of the extent to which the scope of the prerogative power was subject to a judicial review. The ruling confirmed that the prerogative power might be limited or waived by the primary legislation. The Supreme Court referred to the views of one of the leading lawyers of the 20th century, Sir H. W. R. Wade (1980, p. 47), who wrote that most of the powers that constituted the royal prerogative had just been limited or abolished in this way. He pointed out that a statutory limitation or revocation of a prerogative right might occur by express words or by necessary implication. Since the EU legislation was implemented in the British legal order under the European Community Act 1972, on this basis, any national legislation had to comply with the EU law. Thus, ministers have no power to make any changes to the applicable sources of law, unless they are effectively authorised to do so by the legislator. Then, as a result of the Miller I case judgement, the European Union (Notification of Withdrawal) Act 2017 was adopted on 16 March 2017, containing the statutory consent of the parliament, authorising the prime minister to refer to Article 50(2) of the TEU. Therefore, this series of actions marked the formal and legal start of the Brexit procedure. Thereby, the law enforced the notification to be carried out in accordance with regulations.

11.3 The EU and the UK positions in the Brexit negotiations and the impact of the principle of transparency

On 29 March 2017, Prime Minister Theresa May submitted a document to the president of the European Council, Donald Tusk, notifying him of the UK's intention to withdraw from the EU, as a consequence of invoking Article 50(2) of the TEU, after the passing of the European Union (Notification of Withdrawal) Act 2017, following the UK's EU membership referendum on 23 June 2016. This had a twofold effect. First, the formal process of the Brexit negotiations was given the green light. Brexit talks were conducted in the light of the guidelines provided by the European Council. Second, the goal was to conclude an agreement that would set out the arrangements for the UK's withdrawal, taking into account the framework for its future relation with the EU. That agreement shall be negotiated in accordance with the procedure set out in Article 218(3) of the Treaty on the Functioning of the European Union (TFEU).

The first aspect of the Brexit negotiations was the timing, which was considered of paramount importance. The withdrawal procedure from the EU stipulates that from the date when the UK Government sends the European Council a formal notification of its intention to withdraw from the EU, the two-year period will start to apply, during which the negotiations will be held in order to reach a formal deal. Thus, the withdrawal was then planned to occur on 29 March 2019 (Exit Day 1), two years after the date of notification, as specified by Article 50(3) of the TEU. Moreover, the normalisation of this in effect also technically allows the extension of the two-year period, but only if the EU-27 agree unanimously. Therefore, on this legal basis, due to a number of emerging problems, the Brexit deadline was initially extended to 12 April 2019, and then again to 31 October 2019 (Exit Day 2). As is well known, the third extension stipulated the Brexit deadline of 31 January 2020. The fact that the UK decided to leave the EU did not automatically mean that the EU institutions, procedures, and regulations already in operation would no longer apply and that it would be possible to defy them. They remained binding for the UK, and their impact on British law was still considerable until the end of the implementation/transition period (on 31 December 2020).

The second important aspect was the representation, which referred to who was able to lead the Brexit negotiation process. Obviously, the UK was represented by its government, notably by Prime Minister Theresa May (and subsequently by Prime Minister Boris Johnson), but an important role was also assigned to David Davis, the UK's Secretary of State for Exiting the European Union. From 14 July 2016 to 31 January 2020, the Department for Exiting the European Union was also appointed, whose main responsibilities were overseeing the negotiations to leave the EU and establishing the future relation between the UK and the EU. However, this issue was more complicated on the EU side. The EU Treaties vest the European Council (i.e., the heads of the member states) with the ultimate negotiation power. The European Council shall issue the EU's negotiation guidelines and nominate the EU negotiator; it also has the authority—subject to the European Parliament's consent—to finally conclude any Brexit agreement on behalf of the EU (Hacke 2017, p. 106). The European Council chose the European Commission as the EU lead negotiator. The European Commission was responsible for the negotiations and was in close contact with the European Council, which provided political leadership and oversight.

Third, the complexity of the Brexit talks mainly entailed developing the legal framework of the Withdrawal Agreement and determining the terms of the UK's future relation with the EU. This involved the adoption of appropriate negotiating techniques on the sides of both the UK and the EU. In this connection, it is essential to portray how the Brexit negotiations were held and what negotiation strategy was adopted during this process.

200 *Natalie Fox*

11.3.1 Brexit negotiation strategy

Owing to the fact that the UK remained a full member of the EU until its actual withdrawal from the latter (which took place on 31 January 2020), the aim of the Brexit negotiations was a proper and suitable preparation for the formal withdrawal. However, the initial reaction of the British government was Prime Minister May's refusal of a 'running commentary' on the Brexit negotiations. In the first place, it was triggered by the fear of revealing the British negotiating position prematurely and the necessity to gain time in order to determine a particular approach. In turn, the EU was the first party to start publishing documents delineating the adopted negotiating position, which somewhat forced the UK to react appropriately and promptly. Hence, the UK could not keep postponing the publication of the necessary documents and the presentation of its negotiating position, including the withdrawal agreement and the post-Brexit settlement. Moreover, it soon became evident that the British government did not intend to issue any information on the withdrawal negotiation plan, as it simply lacked one. It was argued that the decision made in the EU referendum came as a surprise, as the government headed by the then Prime Minister David Cameron did not expect such a result. As a consequence, the later approach to the negotiations of Prime Minister May, who became responsible for managing the government and obliged it to withdraw the country from the EU, began to be challenged. It was particularly problematic that a conservative manifesto from 2015 obliged the party to respect the outcome of the referendum, and the campaign was conducted in this spirit, and the Cameron government (to which May then belonged) quickly adopted the electorate's decision. Despite campaigning to remain in the EU, when she became prime minister, May had to fulfil her promise of respecting the will of the people, emphasising that 'Brexit means Brexit'. It could be observed that in the initial period of her term in office, the prime minister demonstrated caution, but at the same time, she strenuously and incessantly strived for the withdrawal. She consistently tried to ensure that her government and party (Conservative) had the sense of taking the proper direction in the tumultuous aftermath of the referendum and managed to overcome the initial challenge of putting its outcome into effect.

The information on the intentions of the British government in the context of the negotiations was provided in a fragmentary but controlled manner and presented in a notification letter sent to the President of the European Council. Moreover, the Government White Paper provided the parliament and the country with a clear vision of what the government was seeking to achieve in negotiating Brexit and the new partnership with the EU. Prime Minister May set out the government's approach to the discussions, clearly emphasising the fact that the UK would strive for the deep and special partnership that takes in both economic and security cooperation. Additionally, it was clearly stressed that the Brexit process should be used in such a way that the objectives were achieved in a fair and orderly manner and with as little disruption as possible on each side. It was also strongly underlined that although the UK was leaving the EU, but not Europe, it wanted

Transparency and accountability in Brexit 201

to remain committed partners and allies of the UK's friends across the continent at the same time. In the opinion of Prime Minister May, the cessation of the accession to the EU structures was not intended to weaken the EU's position. The EU referendum of 2016 was a vote to restore national self-determination, and the notification of the intention to act was to give effect to the democratic decision of the people of the UK. Hence, the priority goal was to agree on the terms of a future partnership alongside those of the withdrawal from the EU.

The UK Government proposed principles that could help shape forthcoming discussions. First of all, from the outset, it was declared constructively and respectfully, in the spirit of sincere cooperation. The government wanted to achieve the best possible result of leaving the EU and build a new ambitious and special future partnership between the UK and the EU. Agreeing on a high-level approach to the issues arising from the UK's withdrawal was an early priority. Government officials realised the challenge to reach such a comprehensive agreement within the two-year period set out for withdrawal discussions in the TEU. At the early stage of the negotiations, an important aspect was the setting of the implementation period in order to adjust to the new arrangements in a smooth and orderly manner. The deep and special partnership was supposed to contribute towards the prosperity, security, and global power of the European continent. Most of all, the UK did not want to lose the regulatory alignment, the trust in one another's institutions, and the spirit of cooperation stretching back for decades. Moreover, from the beginning of the negotiations, it was realised that the Article 50 exit procedure was intended to put member states (in this case, the UK) at a disadvantage when leaving the EU. Therefore, even before a formal notification was given, other EU governments were called upon to indicate which demands could be accepted in order to avoid their rejection at the formal start of the withdrawal procedure. However, the EU's position in the Brexit negotiations was based on the largely united approach of the four freedoms of the single market (goods, capital, services, and labour), which are indivisible in nature and cannot be 'cherry picking' (Taylor 2017). The EU representatives repeated the claim of indivisibility and that the best cannot be chosen among the four freedoms. Moreover, it was assumed that the UK's leaving the EU would have consequences, such as losing its influence on rules, which in turn would affect the European economy. Thus, in the face of the upcoming exit talks on the withdrawal, the EU has adopted a tough line, refusing 'pre-negotiations'.

It cannot be denied that the most desired and expected solution would be the so-called soft Brexit, in which the UK would remain a participant in the European Economic Area and the single market. Nonetheless, what was feared the most was that if talks would break down or the UK would leave the EU without having completed an agreement, then there would be the so-called hard Brexit, which was the scenario that seemed the most likely from the beginning of the Brexit talks. It is true that both politicians and EU officials are used to the conservative and traditional mindset. However, the real reason for the adopted position in the negotiations should be viewed as out of the fears that if the UK would achieve a 'special status' and negotiate an agreement based on its own institutional solutions,

202　*Natalie Fox*

then other countries—inside or outside the EU—might ask for equivalent deals. This would entail a weakening of the institutional structures of the EU and could even lead to its disintegration. Therefore, undoubtedly, when analysing the Brexit negotiations, it can be concluded that they were mainly based on preventing the collapse of the EU so that other member states would not start moving towards the British withdrawal decision. Thus, the UK's withdrawal from the EU had to be an example of demonstrating that making such a decision must entail significant ramifications. Officially, in March 2017, the European Council authorised the opening of the Brexit negotiations and adopted the negotiating guidelines. From then on, the EU required the members of the European Parliament to approve both the Withdrawal Agreement (negotiated under Article 50 of the TEU) and a free trade agreement regulating future relations between the UK and the EU.

11.3.2　*The EU/UK approach to transparency in the Brexit negotiations*

The Brexit negotiations represented a striking example of the rising importance of the concept of transparency. The credibility of the EU and the British government depended on the transparency of their negotiation activities. It constituted an important component to signal to the public and external entities that the information offered by the EU/UK was indeed reliable. Transparency is perceived as a factor that reinforces cooperation between states and contributes to solving collective action problems. It is also a key feature of democracy, which is the government's constant response to the preferences of its citizens (Grigorescu 2003, pp. 644–646). Transparency is understood as comprising the features of public and disclosed activities, where their condition and course are available to anyone interested; therefore, nothing is hidden, uncertain, unclear, or doubtful. Thus, it is used in relation to various aspects related to information flow. Informing the public opinion about the undertaken activities and intentions is meant to increase the public confidence of citizens. It should be stated that the emphasis on transparency was evident in the narrative around Brexit; however, it is necessary to analyse how this system was implemented in practice. To this end, it requires ascertaining the EU/UK approach to transparency in the Brexit negotiations.

Originally, the principle of transparency was not entrenched in the founding treaties; however, it was developed in the case law of the European Court of Justice (ECJ). Eventually, transparency was enshrined in Article 1(2) of the TEU, which makes openness one of the defending characteristics of the EU, opening a 'new stage in the process of creating an ever-closer union among the people of Europe, in which decisions are taken as openly as possible and as closely as possible to the citizen'.[8] In sequence, Article 15 in the third subparagraph of the TFEU provides that

---

8 Declaration No. 17 on the right of access to information, annexed to the Final Act of the TEU, signed in Maastricht on 7 February 1992, recommended steps to improve public access to information in order to accomplish transparency in decision-making processes.

Transparency and accountability in Brexit 203

each institution, body, office or agency shall ensure that its proceedings are transparent and shall elaborate in its own Rules of Procedure specific provisions regarding access to its documents, in accordance with the regulations referred to in the second subparagraph.[9]

Therefore, the principle of transparency was implemented within the EU, the main piece of legislation being Regulation (EC) No. 1049/2001 of the European Parliament and of the Council of 30 May 2001 regarding public access to the European Parliament, Council, and Commission documents.[10] Article 2(4) of the Transparency regulation creates a baseline of the right to access the documents of the institutions. Moreover, in implementing the transparency policy, the EU negotiator acts within the limits of the EU law and respects the European Commission's legal obligations regarding the protection of information as defined in Article 4(1) of the Transparency regulation. Consequently, the transparency regime at the EU level foresees a number of exceptions to the default position, as highlighted in the case law, which is of openness, although subject to a strict proportionality test in relation to the aim sought.[11] This was recognised in Article 4(1)(a) of the Transparency regulation, which establishes an absolute exception from the transparency system, inter alia, in international relations. Against this background, the political importance of the negotiations determines the scope of the freedom to disclose documents and sometimes leads to a different level of transparency, consisting of keeping a certain degree of secrecy in external (international) relations. The main argument for this is the need to leave the parties some room for manoeuvre in diplomatic and political negotiations. Additionally, maintaining a strong and well-functioning government more often than not leads to limited information disclosure.

In the course of the negotiations, both the EU and the UK published a considerable number of documents outlining the details of the negotiating positions taken. It is important that the party that publishes first (in this case, the EU) and the most is in some way better prepared and as such, has a higher likelihood of achieving a more favourable outcome in the negotiations. While trying to suppress the growing criticism in the initial phase of Brexit (and not decreasing later; Elgot and Asthana 2017) and following the EU's example, the UK Government began to publish various pieces of information with some delay (e.g., published position papers, in particular by the newly created Department for Exiting the European Union), issued statements, and made speeches and announcements. All European Commission negotiating documents made available to the EU member states, the European Council, the European Parliament, the Council of

---

9 The right of access to documents is placed among the treaty provisions that have general application (Article 15(3) of the TFEU) as a principle of good governance, and it is regarded as a fundamental right, guaranteed under Article 6 of the TEU and in Articles 41 and 42 of the Charter of Fundamental Rights of the EU (CFREU).

10 31 May 2001 OJ L 145/44; hereinafter the Transparency regulation.

11 Case C-353/99 P *Council v. Hautala* [2001] ECR I-9565, para. 28.

the European Union, national parliaments, and the UK were also released to the public. The EU published a number of negotiating documents, including agendas for negotiating rounds, EU position papers, non-papers, EU text proposals, and regularly updated factsheets. The transparency policy was regularly reviewed to ensure that it fulfilled its objective and had no negative impact on the integrity of the negotiations.

As the EU negotiator, the European Commission was committed to ensuring the maximum level of transparency as a response to the unprecedented situation of the UK's withdrawal from the EU. In the Brexit negotiation process, a tailor-made approach to transparency was embraced. Transparency is also the EU's core principle applicable in the Brexit negotiations, according to the European Council's guidelines adopted on 29 April 2017. Generally, the EU approach to openness in this process was crucial. Additionally, it is an indispensable principle in achieving the EU's constitutional goals of ensuring the accountability of decision makers, supporting legal certainty, and strengthening the rule of law (Art. 2 of the TEU) and the general principle of equality. In fact, transparency ensures a more effective management system, which is also more accountable to citizens, facilitating participation in public activities, providing access to information and resources, and enabling participation in the management process (Kendrick and Sangiuolo 2017, p. 4).

Additionally, the Terms of Reference (ToR) adopted on 19 June 2017 by negotiators in both the EU and the UK, which provide the negotiations' structure, dates and priorities, include an entire section on transparency. However, these provisions are concise and not very transparent. They stipulate the duty of the two parties to cooperate to ensure that the 'default position of transparency' is followed, but they also allow both parties to treat the negotiation documents in accordance with their respective laws. They grant each party the power to apply restrictions on the distribution of documents but impose the obligation to consult the other party in advance before disclosing them.[12] They also exclude public participation in actual negotiations between the EU and the UK, stating that each round of negotiations should only involve public officials from both sides.[13] The default position on transparency agreed in the ToR was tactically implemented by both negotiating parties and effectively relieved the UK from the legal consequences of transparency obligations under EU law.

In the Brexit negotiations, the UK Government adopted an alternative strategy befitting its own constitutional requirements. Initially, the negotiations led to distrust among the general British public as they were conducted in a rather vague manner. Although the EU referendum was a factor that legitimised the government's approach to the negotiations, the referendum question did not include a description of the importance of Brexit. First of all, in an unprecedented manner, the Miller I case (2017) questioned the government's power to assign a

---

12 See paragraphs 11 to 14 of the ToR.
13 See paragraph 5 of the ToR.

prior role in the negotiation process. Second, the authority of the May Government was challenged on many occasions, which particularly resulted from the inability to reach an agreement by working out a compromise solution on the Withdrawal Agreement, which in turn led to the pursuit of the so-called hard Brexit. This resulted particularly in undermining the UK's position in the Brexit negotiations on the international arena and on the domestic plane. It was believed that the government was divided and did not know what it actually wanted to achieve as a result of the ongoing negotiations. This led to the belief that the executive may not have sufficient constitutional power to agree on the terms of the UK's withdrawal from the EU. Hence, there was the need to approve any withdrawal agreement that would be settled with the EU, and there was even the idea of holding a second withdrawal referendum (Bogdanor 2017). Thereby, the divisions and disagreements in the cabinet regarding the direction of the Brexit negotiations hindered the adoption of a transparent approach. Third, the public narrative around Brexit was largely shaped by the media. On the one hand, the government's initial reluctance to publish its positions in a manner similar to that adopted by the EU was received by the media with an element of hostility, which placed the EU in a more favourable position in shaping public opinion. On the other hand, after the High Court in the Miller case ruled on 3 November 2016 that the government needed parliamentary approval to trigger Article 50(2) of the TEU, the three judges who expressed their opposition (Lord Reed, Lord Carnwath, and Lord Hughes) were verbally attacked by some people who believed that the decision to withdraw had already been made in a referendum. Grossly misleading press articles in such newspapers as the *Daily Mail*, *Daily Express*, and *Daily Telegraph*, which campaigned for the UK to leave the EU, described the judges as 'having blocked Brexit' and as 'enemies of the people'.[14] The negotiations were also complicated by the fact that instead of trying to dispel the various rumours that appeared solely through the publication of documents presenting a uniform (common) position, there were many occasions of alleged 'leaks' to the press from several cabinet ministers.

On many occasions in the UK, it was also noticeable that the choice of information to be released depended largely on the public interest, and the government did not always keep the parliament informed of its intentions when it seemed desirable to achieve an effective negotiation result. It cannot be denied that the constitutional foundations of the British system conditioned the government's behaviour. Thus, under the UK's constitutional arrangements, it was up to the government, specifically the cabinet, to determine the outcome that the UK wanted to achieve from the Brexit negotiations. Nonetheless, some constitutional conventions and practices in the UK Constitution promote the principle of transparency. First, since the outcome of the negotiations was essentially a question of a national political compromise, conducted under the convention of

---

14 See "We Must Get Out of the EU' (*Daily Express*, 4 November 2016); 'Enemies of the People' (*Daily Mail*, 4 November 2016); 'The Judges versus the People' (*Daily Telegraph*, 4 November 2016).

206 *Natalie Fox*

collective ministerial responsibility, which requires uniform public involvement of ministers, misunderstandings should be resolved confidentially, as it was advisable to keep all objections private. Second, an important role was played by the parliament's informing function, assigned by Bagehot (1981, p. 101), and in practice exercised by the UK's Select Committees. The British Constitution places the control of the information related to the Brexit negotiations in the hands of the government. However, the extent to which the government will succeed in controlling this information depends on its majority in the House of Commons. After the general election on 8 June 2017, the government (and the Conservative Party) lost its parliamentary majority. This required cooperation with opposition parties to work out a compromise, but they did not necessarily share similar views on the importance of Brexit and the shape that the Withdrawal Agreement should take.

Undoubtedly, Brexit talks were chaotic. They did not proceed smoothly and were characterised by a rather constant source of uncertainty for British politics, the economy, and the entire British law. This was largely due to the fact that the British side did not immediately present a coherent plan of what it would like to achieve when the negotiations started. Some political pundits also argued that in view of the fact that the government was unprepared for Brexit, the negotiation process was performed disastrously (Powell 2020). Such a view is not surprising, since from the very beginning, before the formal start of the Brexit negotiation process, it had sparked basic constitutional dilemmas. It was not clear how this process should be shaped according to the British constitutional requirements, since it was difficult to anticipate the outcome of the EU referendum. A dispute over triggering Article 50 of the TEU arose, resulting in a fight against the background of scholars, but above all, the political views between the Brexiteers and those who were planning to stay, that is, the Remainers, ultimately resulting in a judicial intervention in the Miller I case, where the judiciary had no option but to discipline the executive branch. Then, the Brexit negotiations focused only on establishing the conditions for the withdrawal and led to reaching a consensus on the so-called Withdrawal Agreement, which would outline the future shape of British constitutional law by setting out the terms of the UK's exit and the Political Declaration on the framework for the future EU–UK relation.

11.4 The Brexit negotiations and the UK Government's accountability

The constitutional objectives in the Brexit negotiations could only be accomplished by ensuring accountability in the decision-making process by the government. The parliament has an obligation to monitor and control the negotiation process as a matter of accountability. However, to be effective, the negotiations should be held in an atmosphere of mutual trust, which naturally requires, first, secrecy and second, minimum public or parliamentary scrutiny to maximise the chances of their success. Against this background, what needs to be determined is how accountability in the divorce process from the EU should be construed.

Taking into account the meaning of the concept in question, constitutional scholars emphasise that accountability is 'a complex and chameleon-like term' (Mulgan 2000, p. 555). A classic scholar of British constitutional thought is A. V. Dicey; while writing about a 'balanced constitution', he presented the idealised concept of the rule of law, claiming two pillars—the political responsibility of ministers to the parliament and the personal legal liability of all public officials before the ordinary courts of the land (1982, pp. 115–116). The distinction between these two forms of responsibility is crucial. Furthermore, when delving into the classic British constitutional theory, this chapter's author originally came across the term 'responsibility', which means 'the relations between Ministers of the Crown with, on the one hand, their departments and, on the other one, Parliament' (Harlow 2002, p. 6). In turn, the concept of 'accountability' gained importance relatively recently, although it was already ingrained in the classic British constitutional theory. It was delineated as

> a framework for the exercise of state power in a liberal-democratic system, within which public bodies are forced to seek to promote the public interest and compelled to justify their actions in those terms or in other constitutionally acceptable terms (justice, humanity, equity); to modify policies if they should turn out to have been ill conceived; and to make amends if mistakes and errors of judgment have been made.
>
> (Oliver 1991, p. 28)

Eventually, Mulgan (2000, p. 555) observed:

> A word which a few decades ago was used only rarely and with relatively restricted meaning (and which, interestingly, has no obvious equivalent in other European languages) now crops up everywhere performing all manner of analytical and rhetorical tasks and carrying most of the burdens of democratic 'governance'.

There is no doubt that the doctrine has a considerable variety of conceptual definitions of accountability relating to various aspects of its functioning (Oliver 2003; Pyper 1996). However, in the context of Brexit negotiations, attention will be paid only to the effects that government transparency may have on accountability. The literature indicates that transparency has been considered an important factor contributing to the accountability of a democratic government (Grigorescu 2003, p. 644). In the context of the negotiations on the UK's withdrawal from the EU, a greater level of transparency resulted in increased responsibility. Openness and transparency are key elements in ensuring accountability in the decision-making process. The more open the Brexit process was, the more responsible the government became. Therefore, maintaining control over the dissemination of information, especially regarding disputes among the cabinet ministers on what form Brexit should take and how long it should last, was of paramount importance to the stability of the government.

208 *Natalie Fox*

In the British Constitution, the actions of the government (ministers and their departments) are mostly regulated by constitutional conventions (see, e.g., Leyland 2016, pp. 25–43; Ellis 2004; Marshall 1987); that is, the repeated and followed rules of established structural practice that define the way that the government operates and the exercise of royal prerogatives, as well as regulate the manner of incurring responsibility.[15] When thinking about accountability, one should distinguish between political and legal accountability. The UK model of the constitution takes as the paradigm form of accountability the practice that ministers are answerable to the parliament. In this context, the ultimate form of political accountability in British constitutional law is a general election, prompted either by timing (one must be held every five years)[16] or by the cabinet's loss of the support of the majority of the members of parliament (MPs) in the House of Commons. The legislative and executive branches can maintain their independent existence through the two ways in which an election can be triggered before the end of the five-year term: (1) if a motion for an early general election is agreed on, either by at least two-thirds of the house or without a division; and (2) if a motion of no confidence is passed by a simple majority and no alternative government is found. Between elections, it is important that the central government be called on to explain its actions, inactions, and failures in several different ways (e.g., discussion of the annual Queen's/throne speech, budget exposé, debate on a specific goal of a government policy in the House of Commons, or the inquiry procedure *questions*). Therefore, against this background, a key role in the political responsibility of the government is played, on the one hand, by the will of the people, and on the other hand, by the principle of responsible government, manifested in the principle of the convention of collective ministerial responsibility, or the position of the constitutional system of the head of government, regulated only by way of conventions. Ministers before the parliament are only responsible for the way in which they carry out their functions in terms of efficiency and the overall course of action. The government is required to have a substantially united front. Therefore, disputes have to be discussed in confidential meetings of the cabinet. Thus, public statements represent a collective stance, while the government's policy is defended, irrespective of any different opinions expressed by the ministers (Kendrick and Sangiuolo 2017, p. 10). This convention is designed to ensure the government's stability and its ability to inspire confidence in the House of Commons. Generally, during the Brexit negotiations, it was of utmost importance that the government (and the majority Conservative Party) maintained the confidence of the House of Commons at all costs. However, the manner in which the referendum campaign was

---

15 A. V. Dicey understood conventions of the constitution as 'maxims or practices which, though they regulate the ordinary conduct of the Crown, of ministers, and of other persons under the constitution, are not in strictness laws at all'. They are characterised by a non-legal and informal character, regulating systemic issues belonging to the area of constitutional matters (1982, pp. 70, 277).

16 See Article 1(3) of the Fixed-Term Parliaments Act 2011.

conducted or the two early general elections held at that time (2017, 2019) only revealed different views in the cabinet.

The specificity of British constitutional law also influenced the transparency of the Brexit negotiations through the role of the parliament. As already emphasised, the legitimacy of the government's actions in the Brexit negotiations resulted from the referendum (Bogdanor 2016, p. 314). Thus, in political terms, the result of the 2016 referendum took on a particularly political role because its effects made it impossible for the parliament to disregard the will of the people. Moreover, from the initial stage, the role of Westminster was significantly reduced in the Brexit procedure, which had already been demonstrated in the context of the lack of statutory consent to trigger Article 50(2) of the TEU, which was eventually decided in the Miller I ruling. Furthermore, in relation to the Brexit negotiations, special attention should be paid to the role played in this process by the EU Select Committees functioning in the parliament and exercising control over the implementation of the provisions of the laws by the government. Although the parliament is not responsible for implementing legislation, in a post-legislative scrutiny, its special committees can investigate how well an act (e.g., in such case the European Union (Withdrawal Agreement) Act 2020 or the European Union (Future Relationship) Act, and other statutes associated with the process of exiting the EU) is being implemented by the government and the effect that the new law is having.

11.4.1 The role of the UK's Select Committees in influencing the EU decision-making process

One important issue of European integration has been the requirement to establish appropriate parliamentary bodies and procedures to ensure that the national legislative bodies of the member states have a real voice in the EU decision-making process. Thus, the intensification of integration processes has resulted in the need to strengthen the UK parliamentary scrutiny in the areas under EU competence (see, e.g., Oliver 2003, pp. 85–87). The UK membership in the EU structures and the Brexit process had increased the importance of the parliamentary EU Select Committees as a link between EU legislation and the UK Parliament. The two houses of the parliament developed individual scrutiny procedures. The core subject of scrutiny was the process by which, in accordance with the agreed ToR, legislative proposals and other EU documents had been analysed and the financial, administrative, legal, and political consequences that might have arisen for the UK, as a result of the adoption of the submitted legislative proposals, had been taken into account (Cygan 2017). Undoubtedly, the obligation to inform Westminster about European affairs has helped enable the UK Parliament to scrutinise the legislative processes undertaken at the EU level.

In 1974, EU Select Committees were set up in both houses of the UK Parliament for the purpose of scrutinising draft legislative acts at the initial stage of the EU legislative process. In the House of Commons, three EU Select Committees had been set up, called European Committees, with their formal and legal basis for operation laid down in Section 119 of the Standing Orders of the House of Commons 2018. Informing the parliament or its houses of the political and legal significance of individual EU documents and deciding which of those would require further examination were the tasks of the European Scrutiny Committee, whose remit is defined in detail in Section 143 of the Standing Orders of the House of Commons. The committee analysed draft EU legislation and reported to the house on the legal and political importance of each document. Its tasks also included monitoring and analysing government positions within the Council of Ministers and drawing up appropriate reports (Ryan 2019, p. 362). During the transition period, the European Scrutiny Committee analysed how the EU regulations and policies could still exert an influence on the UK after its exit from the EU and what changes would be required in the current control system, which has largely remained unaltered since the accession. Key issues that the European Scrutiny Committee addresses in its inquiry include (a) how the UK's exit from the EU will affect the current system for scrutinising EU laws and policies and what changes might be needed; (b) whether and how EU laws and policies might affect the UK after Brexit; (c) what the purpose of the scrutiny of EU laws and policies should be in a post-exit world; (d) what action the government should take to support and facilitate a strong parliamentary scrutiny process post-exit; and (e) what form of scrutiny should be taken to maximise its effectiveness.

The other two European Committees in the House of Commons are responsible for matters relating to the decision to withdraw the UK from the EU. The European Statutory Instruments Committee is tasked with the selection ('sifting') of the proposed negative statutory instruments resulting from the European Union (Withdrawal) Act 2018 amended by the European Union (Withdrawal Agreement) 2020, which empowers the ministers to issue regulations on 'deficiencies in retained EU law'. In turn, the Exiting the European Union Committee was responsible for examining the expenditure, administration, and policy of the Department of Exiting the European Union, established in 2016 (by Prime Minister May), and evaluated as well as monitored its work (including the established office of the Secretary of State for Exiting the European Union). This department was disbanded with the official completion of Brexit at the end of January 2020. In turn, in the beginning of March 2020, the Exiting the European Union Committee was transformed into the Committee on the Future Relationship with the European Union, responsible—as the name suggests—for negotiating and determining future British relations with the EU.

In turn, in the upper house of the parliament, the EU Select Committee was established by virtue of Section 64 of the Standing Orders of the House of Lords 2016, which coordinates the policies and actions of the British government in relation to the EU and considers EU documents submitted to the House of Lords by ministers and other matters concerning the EU (Ryan 2019, p. 362). The EU Select Committee assisted the house in the procedure for the submission of 'reasoned opinions' and represented the house in the interparliamentary cooperation within the EU as appropriate (it was responsible for the proper representation of the House of Lords in contacts with the EU institutions and EU-27).

Both houses of the parliament used similar parliamentary methods to scrutinise legislation and other EU affairs. The main methods of operation included (1) hearings of government ministers, (2) debates, and (3) investigative work by the EU Select Committees. In each house, reports were made by the committees on selected issues, and government ministers might be called on to respond to the findings and to provide explanations regarding the conduct of the negotiations in the European Council and on the legislative proposals made. The model of scrutiny exercised by the committees was based on documentary analysis. The work of the EU Select Committees covered both legislative proposals and non-legislative documents. The types of documents that were subject to scrutiny (to be 'deposited') were agreed between the two houses of parliament and the government and included all legislative proposals, together with a number of other documents published by the EU institutions.

One of the effective instruments for the parliamentary scrutiny of EU legislation was the so-called parliamentary scrutiny reserves. The parliament had certain powers to review and express opinions on EU draft legislative acts and any other documents falling within the remit of the EU Select Committees of both houses of parliament. The government supported the principle of effective scrutiny of European legislation, and both houses adopted appropriate resolutions on scrutiny reserve, which were published together with the Standing Orders (of the House of Commons or the House of Lords). On this basis, no minister of the Crown should agree to the adoption of EU legislation that had not yet been approved by the European Scrutiny Committee of the House of Commons or by the EU Select Committee of the House of Lords. In general, these were acts or documents for which the scrutiny process had not yet been completed, as they were referred to the committee for debate. Thus, until the parliamentary scrutiny by the houses was completed, it was not possible for the government to accept the legislative proposals or other documents presented by the EU that had not been recommended by the EU Select Committees.

The scrutiny process formally started when the government deposited an EU document in the UK Parliament; that is, it was sent to the relevant EU Select Committee in the House of Commons or the House of Lords for further scrutiny. The government then drew up an Explanatory Memorandum (EM) on each document submitted within 10 working days, in the course of which it analysed the legal basis and the political consequences that might result from its adoption. After the committee received the EM from the government, the committee chair (with the support of legal advisers) decided which documents should be subject to more detailed scrutiny (Rogers and Walters 2015, pp. 351–352). It was then up to the committee to decide on the angle of review of the document, selecting one of four possible solutions. First, the committee might refrain from undertaking further scrutiny of the document, thus 'clearing the document from scrutiny'. Second, the committee might ask the government to forward a document for review to the competent minister, requesting further information in writing. Third, there was the possibility to hold evidence sessions or seminars with the stakeholders. The committee should have organised one or two meetings to hear the views of

212   *Natalie Fox*

witnesses or stakeholders before requesting clarification from the government. Fourth, with regard to particularly important proposals, the committee might launch a full investigation, after which a report would be published, to which the government was required to respond within two months, and which was then discussed in the house. In the third and the fourth cases described, correspondence between the committee and the government was continued until the committee was 'satisfied'. The final stage of the scrutiny procedure by the committee should be included in the decision stating that the EU document was officially cleared from scrutiny. This was possible once the government had fully explained its position and the document itself was 'approaching' its adoption. It should then take the form of a legislative act acceptable to the UK Parliament; otherwise, it was definitively rejected. However, when a document had been the subject of a full investigation, it should automatically be cleared from scrutiny when the final report presented by the committee was discussed in a house session.

It should be noted that it was also possible for the ministers to altogether repeal the scrutiny reserve resolutions adopted by the committees when there were specific reasons for doing so. In such a case, at the first possible opportunity, the government representatives should explain to the committee the reasons for this course of action. Most of the repeals occurred in situations of dynamically evolving yet sensitive policy areas, such as the decision to impose sanctions or when exceptional policy measures were required. However, it should be emphasised that the resolutions adopted by the houses regarding parliamentary reservation for the duration of the review were not in fact intended, after the audit process had been completed, to prevent the ministers from giving their consent to the adoption of new EU commitments, even when the select committees in both houses had expressed reservations about the proposed directives, regulations, or decisions. Nevertheless, there was considerable political pressure on the ministers who should take the reports presented by the committees into account, as they were responsible for the decisions made before the parliament. The formal scrutiny of EU draft legislation primarily served a constitutional function by strengthening the parliamentary accountability of the executive branch of government. Its aim at the restriction of scrutiny thus carried out, together with the opinion expressed by the UK Parliament, should restrict the activity of the ministers exercising their legislative role in the Council of the European Union. Against this backdrop, the EU Select Committees undoubtedly served a crucial function for Westminster, which did not play a direct role in the EU legislative process, and thanks to their work, had the ability to exercise a scrutiny function towards the government by its commitment to explain and justify its actions and expenditures in the EU.

However, as a result, the EU Select Committees only seemingly formed an effective mechanism to ensure that the UK Parliament could influence the EU decision-making and scrutinise government actions on the international stage. Notably, their twofold role was to act as subsidiary bodies of the British Parliament, focused primarily on providing opinions and scrutinising government actions regarding European affairs and to grant the national legislature influence on the EU decision-making process by providing access to information on legislative proposals. However, it would be a mistake to claim that the scrutiny of EU legislative proposals was fully complete and did not raise any particular doubts. Although it was a part of British constitutional law, the EU law was not created by the national legislator but was the result of a legislative and political process over which Westminster had no direct control. Therefore, the scrutiny of EU legislative proposals and other documents in both houses of parliament provided two potential opportunities for the UK to influence the decision-making process of the EU. The first possibility had the direct effect of influencing the ministers themselves through pre-legislative scrutiny. On this basis, one of the objectives of the scrutiny was to hold the UK ministers accountable, resulting in the possibility to ensure that Westminster's position was fully taken into account before negotiations in the European Council. The second possibility of parliamentary influence on the EU legislation was ensured by the institution of parliamentary reservation for the period of review; within this framework, it was possible to issue reasoned opinions, expressed directly by the houses, on the legitimacy of adopting the proposed EU legislation. However, unlike the scrutiny of the executive branch, the latter form of scrutiny was less precise in terms of its importance, due in practice to the lack of a clear consensus between the two houses regarding the number of positions to be taken on the issuance of reasoned opinions (Cygan 2017). Scrutiny reserve resolutions were perceived as tools to ensure that sufficient time was available to obtain information on EU legislative projects, but they were not intended to change the views of the cabinet members. The MPs in the UK had an important tool in their hands, but they did not use it to become political players. Detailed information regarding the negotiation process allowed the MPs to inform the government at an early stage about potential problems in its negotiating position. Furthermore, the relevant literature (Auel et al. 2012, pp. 5–6) indicates that the system of parliamentary reservations was the result of a debate in the legal discourse on the consequences of the UK's membership in the EU, arising from the doctrine of sovereignty of the parliament. It is noted that this system can be perceived as a form of compensation for the restrictions imposed on Westminster as a result of its participation in EU structures. However, parliamentary reservations could contribute to the development of informal cooperation between the parliament and the government at both political and administrative levels (Cygan 2007). Moreover, the interparliamentary dialogue in the negotiations with the EU was necessary to try to break the Brexit impasse.

11.4.2 The process of constitutional change in 'regaining' the UK Parliament's sovereignty

As a matter of the constitutional law of the UK, the institutional embodiment of legal accountability is judges, who also define the scope and limits of the powers of the government branches, including the executive. Judicial review of the lawfulness of the ministers' actions is an exclusive competence of the courts in this respect. The practice of judicial control of executive power, including ministers' illegal actions, was developed from common law and case law. The development

214 *Natalie Fox*

of judicial activism in the second half of the 20th century was due to the stronger political position of the executive branch and its dominance over the parliament (mainly owing to the UK's membership in the EU). This led to a certain activation of the courts as a factor guaranteeing balance in the constitutional system of the UK. The courts took full responsibility for verifying the legality of the executive branch's actions after the impeachment procedure was discontinued. In the case of *M. v. Home Office and Another*,[17] Lord Donaldson drew attention to the obligation of the executive authority to respect the courts' powers to adjudicate on illegal activities of ministers, referring to the principle of separation of powers. In this context, the Miller I case judgement described above was an important aspect of legal liability in the Brexit procedure. The outcome of this case demonstrated that the courts had been forced again to draw the boundaries of constitutional competence between the executive branch and the parliament, in the sense that they had consistently backed the parliament. The main argument of the pro-Brexit campaign was to 'take back control' and consequently, regain sovereignty. This was due to the fact that the British constitutional scholars have long referred to certain legal and political arguments concerning the constraint on the doctrine of parliamentary sovereignty since the accession to the European Community (currently the European Union).

Against this backdrop, the conceptualisation of the doctrine of sovereignty of the British Parliament and the clarification of its constitutional significance require a distinction between legal and political sovereignty. It is often not an easy task to distinguish its forms, since the lack of a clear distinction between politics and law is largely due to the unwritten nature of the British Constitution. More specifically, the difference between political and legal sovereignty is that the issue of political sovereignty refers to the highest political power in the state, which belongs to a collective entity—the people. It is related to a representative and accountable government whose members, based on their mandate, can exercise power and implement their election promises. In contrast, legal sovereignty refers to the highest legislative authority in the country, whose subject is the monarch in the parliament. Formally speaking, therefore, it means that the parliament can make norms with no limits in terms of their substance. Undoubtedly, the classic definition of sovereignty, borrowed from constitutional law and not derived from a judicial perspective, is the one presented by Dicey (1982), that is, it is necessary to separate political and legal issues and to recognise that in the current situation, legal sovereignty rests with the parliament, although there may be political constraints that effectively limit the exercise of these powers. From this perspective, it can be observed that the theoretical approach to the principle in question is currently limited by its practical application (Allan 2013, p. 72).

Indeed, one of the manifestations of the modification of the doctrine of parliamentary sovereignty was the EU law. It was caused by the impossibility of enacting provisions inconsistent with the directly effective European

---

17 [1992] QB 270, 314.

Community law (as a result of the enactment of two implementing statutes, i.e., European Community Act 1972 and European Union Act 2011). The reasons behind this are observed first and foremost in the process of the harmonisation of legislations and the inclusion of the UK territory under the jurisdiction of the EU institutions. Both the principle of direct effectiveness and efficiency of the EU law and the quasi-binding nature of the referendum do not adhere to the fundamental principles of the British political system and the principle of parliamentary sovereignty.[18] Pointing to the reason for such a state of affairs, in the *Factortame* case,[19] Lord Bridge rightly stated that the reduced sovereignty resulting from the EU membership was not a consequence of the court decisions issued but the result of political decisions with the UK's accession to the European Community's structures. In the first place, the courts expressly accepted the primacy of the EU law and the modification of the approach to the traditional (orthodox) doctrine of sovereignty presented by Dicey (1982), which meant (among others) the inability to apply the doctrine of implied repeal to constitutional statutes.[20] Second, the UK courts kept existing constitutional law in line with actual constitutional practice. In this respect, the principle of sovereignty should also be analysed in connection to the existing relation between the parliament and the judiciary. This particular boundary between the two branches of government, as well as the notion that the courts may be forced to deviate from the strict doctrine of supremacy in the face of threats to the fundamental principles of democracy, has been the subject of the ongoing debate.

In this respect, the literature on the subject portrays two distinct approaches to the above issue. The first is based on the assumption that the sovereignty of the parliament was permanently changed through the UK's membership in the EU structures; the UK's withdrawal from the EU will not change this at all and will not restore the traditional doctrine presented by Dicey (1982). Brexit will not remove the judicial threat to parliamentary sovereignty caused by the so-called judicial activism; on the contrary, it will actually further deepen its erosion (Gee and Young 2016, pp. 146–147; Gordon 2016a, pp. 409ff.; Gordon 2016b, p. 335; Bogdanor 2012, pp. 179ff.). The second position emphasises that one of the arguments for Brexit was that leaving the EU would reinvigorate Britain's centuries-old parliament, strengthening its position towards a doctrinal interpretation of the principle of sovereignty (Ewing 2017, pp. 713, 725–772; Bellamy 2011, pp. 93ff.; Goldsworthy 2010, pp. 12ff.).

---

18 On the lack of coherence between the above-mentioned phenomena and the principle of supremacy of the British Parliament, see Loveland (2003, pp. 676–678). According to Dicey, a referendum is essentially a form of limiting the principle of sovereignty (1982, p. 138).

19 *R v. Secretary of State for Transport, ex parte Factortame Ltd (No. 2)* [1991] 1 AC 603, per Lord Bridge.

20 However, in practical terms, it is obvious that certain statutes are of special constitutional significance, for example, ECA 1972, EUA 2011, or the Human Rights Act 1998 (see especially *Thoburn v. Sunderland City Council* [2002] EWHC 195 (Admin)).

216 *Natalie Fox*

The flexible formula of the British Constitution results in a relative openness to external influences. Prima facie, therefore, the decision to withdraw from the EU should result in a 'renaissance' of the doctrine of Westminster sovereignty, per Dicey (1982). However, the continued validity of the European Convention on Human Rights (incorporated based on Human Rights Act 1998) and the irreversible consequences of the devolution of competences in the UK for Wales, Scotland, and Northern Ireland are factors that hinder the possible restoration of such sovereignty. Thus, it is not entirely possible to reverse the effects of the 'soft' modification of the foundations of the UK's system, which has often occurred in the sphere of the practical implementation of the competences of particular branches of government. It is widely known that the UK's membership in the EU structures resulted in a progressive limitation of the UK Parliament's sovereignty, and the significant modification of the relation between the judiciary and the parliament strengthened the role of the courts. In the case of the UK's membership in the EU, a political necessity has brought about the situation, recognised by the UK judiciary, in which European Community law prevails over inconsistent national legislation (see the *Factortame* litigation). Now the UK's return to the Diceyan traditional (orthodox) doctrine of parliamentary sovereignty—as emphasised by Bradley and Ewing (2003, p. 77)—would scarcely compensate for the disadvantages of an isolationist policy within Europe. In legal terms, the expected results of the process of the UK's withdrawal from the EU will not lead to the restoration of the traditional doctrine of parliamentary sovereignty but may only apparently result in the revitalisation of the current status quo of individual state institutions. Although that doctrine has been modified (see, e.g., Gordon 2017, p. 151)—which is not in doubt at present—it should be stressed that it remains a key constitutional foundation that continues to shape the public law superstructure that it supports (Irvine 2003, p. 184). In the current legal and political reality, it is too early to unequivocally determine *pro futuro* the post-Brexit situation in this regard.

11.5 Conclusion

The process of the UK's withdrawal from the EU has resulted in some modifications at both legal and political levels. The 2016 EU referendum and its aftermath have exposed the extent to which the foundations of the British Constitution have been eviscerated. While some scholars perceived the decision to hold a referendum on EU membership as triggering a severe constitutional crisis, others argued that the political and democratic dilemmas arising from Brexit were symptoms of a broader and constitutionally complex issue, with roots reaching far beyond the 2016 EU referendum. On the one hand, controversy was stirred by the simple fact that the British people made the decision in favour of Brexit, as Prime Minister Cameron had counted on referendum voters' rejection of the proposal for withdrawal, which did not in fact happen. On the other hand, in

Transparency and accountability in Brexit 217

legal circles, there emerged a rekindled interest in the topic of a newer and still fragile constitutional convention, stating that

> decisions of fundamental importance bearing on the constitution of the UK should be preceded by holding a referendum, regional or national, before legislation is introduced and passed into law by the national Parliament.
>
> (Lord Windlesham 2007, p. 103)

As a form of direct rather than parliamentary democracy, a referendum on questions of exceptional national or regional significance has not been typical in British constitutional practice. However, in recent years, new uses have been made of this process, which is increasingly becoming a more frequently applied systemic solution classified as a form of direct democracy, which significantly affects the British legal order.

The 'unprecedented nature' and implications of the UK's withdrawal from the EU have required an assortment of unequalled measures. International negotiations are based on diplomatic methods of operation and the pursuit of a compromise to reach the necessary agreement. In the Brexit negotiations, the high level of unity between the EU-27 and the EU institutions was a consequence of the strong negotiating position presented by the EU, which adopted a maximum level of transparency as a core principle. The UK Government embraced the Brexit talks in a particular way. On the one hand, the UK sought to avoid the scenario called the 'no-deal' Brexit. On the other hand, it consistently and accordingly exposed a tough line on the issues where it was difficult to reach an agreement, although it would result in the 'hard Brexit'. In this context, the analysis presented in this chapter allowed the formulation of three important conclusions. First, transparency as a public audit tool was a key element in enhancing democratic legitimacy. The arguments in favour of openness were the demonstration of unity and strength by each side to increase awareness and create bonds with the society. Second, Brexit as a hybrid phenomenon, that is, both legal and political, is the next stage in the debate on the place and the role of the EU. Third, the use of the principle of transparency as a negotiating technique has increased the level of accountability of the government.

As emphasised in this chapter, the UK Parliament had an obligation to monitor and control the negotiation process as a matter of accountability. This procedure required democratic scrutiny of the executive branch's actions to ensure that the conditions under which political power would be exercised would not be subject to unlimited discretion. In Brexit talks, this was the only way to bring about government accountability and, consequently, for the legislature to fulfil its fundamental constitutional obligation. After all, without maximum access to government information on how the Brexit decisions were being made, there was no effective way to monitor the exercise of the government's power and hold it accountable. Subsequently, it also contributed to the partial revision of the parliament's position in relation to the executive branch, which was confirmed in the

218 *Natalie Fox*

Miller I case. So far, national courts had tended to yield to the executive branch regarding international affairs, trying to keep themselves out of a field they perceived as unsuitable for judicial decision-making. Moreover, in the case of the UK, the analysis of the impact of its withdrawal from the EU had to be correlated with the issue of great importance for British constitutionalism: the doctrine of parliamentary sovereignty. Undoubtedly, this principle affects the essence of the functioning of the branches of government in the UK and determines their legal nature. As demonstrated by the expected result of the process of the UK's withdrawal from the EU, it will not lead to the restoration of the traditional (orthodox) doctrine of parliamentary sovereignty presented by Dicey (1982).

The Brexit process has been the most protracted issue in recent years. However, it should be stressed that the entire political class in Britain is characterised by a certain cautiousness and restraint concerning rapid changes and the respect for tradition; as a result, there is also no social consent for radical actions to be taken. The Brexit negotiations had such a chaotic and unpredictable character that sometimes, speculations about what could happen in the near future as a result of the withdrawal seemed pointless. The situation was changing very dynamically, and it was not certain until the end whether this process would draw to a close and when. At this moment of the history of the UK, the Brexit process is done. On 31 January 2020, the UK left the EU, 47 years after its accession.

References

Allan, T. R. S. (2013). *The Sovereignty of Law: Freedom, Constitution and Common Law*. Oxford: Oxford University Press.

Allen, N. (2018). 'Brexit means Brexit': Theresa May and post-referendum. *British Politics*, 13, pp. 105–120. Available from: https://link.springer.com/article/10.1 057%2Fs41293-017-0067-3 [Accessed 7 September 2020].

Auel, K., Rozenberg, O. and Thomas, A. (2012). *Lost in Transaction? Parliamentary Reserves in EU Bargains*. OPAL Online Paper Series, 10, pp. 4–29. Available from: https://core.ac.uk/download/pdf/35301397.pdf [Accessed 17 November 2020].

Bagehot, W. (1981). *The English Constitution*. Glasgow: William Collins & Co.

Barber, N., Hickman, T. and King, J. (2016, 27 June). Pulling the Article 50 'Trigger': Parliament's indispensable role. *U.K. Constitutional Law Blog* [Online]. Available from: https://ukconstitutionallaw.org/2016/06/27/nick-barber-tom-hickman-and-jeff-king-pulling-the-article-50-trigger-parliaments-indispensable-role/ [Accessed 7 September 2020].

Barnett, H. (2017). *Constitutional & Administrative Law*. London: Routledge.

Bellamy, R. (2011). Political constitutionalism and the Human Rights Act. *International Journal of Constitutional Law*, 9(1), pp. 86–111.

Bogdanor, V. (2012). Imprisoned by a doctrine: The modern defence of parliamentary sovereignty. *Oxford Journal of Legal Studies*, 32(1), pp. 179–195.

Bogdanor, V. (2016). Brexit, the constitution and the alternatives. *King's Law Journal*, 27(3), pp. 314–322.

Bogdanor, V. (2017, 3 August). A second Brexit referendum? It's looking more likely by the day. *The Guardian* [Online]. Available from: www.theguardian.com/

commentisfree/2017/aug/03/second-brexit-referendum-case-getting-stronger-political-deadlock-life-raft [Accessed 14 September 2020].

Bradley, A. W. and Ewing, K. D. (2003). *Constitutional and Administrative Law.* 13th ed. Harlow: Longman.

Cygan, A. (2007). EU affairs before the United Kingdom Parliament: A case of scrutiny as substitute sovereignty? In: Tans, O., Zoethout, C. and Peters, J. eds. *National Parliaments and the European Democracy: A Bottom-Up Approach to European Constitutionalism.* Groningen: Europa Law Publishing, pp. 75–96.

Cygan, A. (2017). Parliamentary scrutiny of EU affairs by the UK Parliament: The primacy of ministerial accountability. In: Cornell, A. J. and Goldoni, M. eds. *National and Regional Parliaments in the EU-Legislative Procedure Post-Lisbon: The Impact of the Early Warning Mechanism.* Oxford and Portland, OR: Hart Publishing, pp. 271–290.

Dicey, A. V. (1982). *Introduction to the Study of the Law of the Constitution.* Indianapolis: Liberty Fund.

Elgot, J. and Asthana, A. (2017, 5 January). Theresa May plans major speech to defuse Brexit criticism. *The Guardian* [Online]. Available from: www.theguardian.com/politics/2017/jan/05/theresa-may-plans-major-speech-defuse-brexit-criticism [Accessed 14 September 2020].

Ellis, E. (2004). Sources of law and the hierarchy of norms. In: Feldman, D. ed. *English Public Law.* Oxford and New York: Oxford University Press, pp. 44–96.

Ewing, K. D. (2016). Editor's introduction. *King's Law Journal,* 27(3), pp. 289–296.

Ewing, K. D. (2017). Brexit and parliamentary sovereignty. *Modern Law Review,* 80(4), pp. 711–726.

Feld, W. (1972). Legal dimensions of British entry into the European Community. *Law and Contemporary Problems* [Online], 37, pp. 247–264. Available from: https://scholarship.law.duke.edu/cgi/viewcontent.cgi?article=3363&context=lcp [Accessed 7 September 2020].

Gee, G. and Young, A. L. (2016). Regaining sovereignty? Brexit, the UK Parliament and the common law. *European Public Law,* 22(1), pp. 131–148.

Gillespie, A. A. and Weare, S. (2015). *The English Legal System.* 5th ed. Oxford: Oxford University Press.

Goldsworthy, J. (2010). *Parliamentary Sovereignty: Contemporary Debates.* Cambridge: Cambridge University Press.

Gordon, M. (2016a). Brexit: A challenge for the UK Constitution, of the UK Constitution? *European Constitutional Law Review,* 12(3), pp. 409–444.

Gordon, M. (2016b). The UK's sovereignty situation: Brexit, bewilderment and beyond . . . *King's Law Journal,* 27(3), pp. 333–343.

Gordon, M. (2017). *Parliamentary Sovereignty in the UK Constitution: Process, Politics and Democracy.* Oxford and Portland, OR: Bloomsbury.

Grigorescu, A. (2003). International organizations and government transparency: Linking the international and domestic realms. *International Studies Quarterly,* 47, pp. 643–667.

Hacke, A. (2017). Brexit negotiations: Process proposal. In: Armour, J. and Eidenmüller, H. eds. *Negotiating Brexit.* München: C. H. Beck, Oxford: Hart and Baden-Baden: Nomos, pp. 105–109.

Harlow, C. (2002). *Accountability in the European Union.* Oxford: Oxford University Press.

Higgins, R. (2009). *Themes and Theories: Selected Essays, Speeches, and Writings in International Law.* Oxford: Oxford University Press.

220 Natalie Fox

Irvine, D. (2003). *Human Rights, Constitutional Law and the Development of the English Legal System: Selected Essays*. Oxford and Portland, OR: Hart Publishing.

Kendrick, M. and Sangiuolo, G. (2017). Transparency in the Brexit negotiations: A view from the EU and the UK. *Federalismi.it*, 18, pp. 2–22. Available from: www.sipotra.it/old/wp-content/uploads/2017/09/Transparency-in-the-Brexit-negotiations.-A-view-from-the-EU-and-the-UK.pdf [Accessed 26 September 2020].

Lang, A. (2017, 17 February). *Parliament's Role in Ratifying Treaties* [Online]. House of Commons Library. No. 5855. Available from: https://researchbriefings.parliament.uk/ResearchBriefing/Summary/SN05855 [Accessed 7 September 2020].

Leyland, P. (2016). *The Constitution of the United Kingdom: A Contextual Analysis*. 3rd ed. Oxford and Portland, OR: Hart Publishing.

Lord Windlesham. (2007). Britain and the European Constitution. *Parliamentary Affairs*, 60(1), pp. 102–110.

Loveland, I. (2003). Britain and Europe. In: Bogdanor, V. ed. *The British Constitution in the Twentieth Century*. Oxford: Oxford University Press, pp. 663–688.

Loveland, I. (2015). *Constitutional Law, Administrative Law, and Human Rights: A Critical Introduction*. Oxford: Oxford University Press.

Marshall, G. (1987). *Constitutional Conventions: The Rules and Forms of Political Accountability*. Oxford: Oxford University Press.

Matthews, F. (2017). Whose mandate is it anyway? Brexit, the Constitution and the contestation of authority. *The Political Quarterly*, 88(4), pp. 603–611.

Mulgan, R. (2000). Accountability: An ever-expanding concept? *Public Administration*, 78, pp. 555–573.

Oliver, D. (1991). *Government in the United Kingdom: The Search for Accountability, Effectiveness and Citizenship*. Milton Keynes: Open University Press.

Oliver, D. (2003). *Constitutional Reform in the United Kingdom*. Oxford: Oxford University Press.

Phillipson, G. and Young, A. L. (2018, 10 December). What would be the UK's constitutional requirements to revoke Article 50? *U.K. Constitutional Law Blog* [Online]. Available from: https://ukconstitutionallaw.org/2018/12/10/gavin-phillipson-and-alison-l-young-wightman-what-would-be-the-uks-constitutional-requirements-to-revoke-article-50/ [Accessed 7 September 2020].

Powell, J. (2020, 30 December). 5 reasons the UK failed in Brexit talks. *Politico*. Available from: www.politico.eu/article/5-reasons-uk-failed-brexit-talks/ [Accessed 26 September 2020].

Pyper, R. (1996). *Aspects of Accountability in the British System of Government*. Eastham: Tudor.

Rogers, R. and Walters, R. (2015). *How Parliament Works*. 7th ed. London and New York: Routledge.

Ryan, M. (2019). *Unlocking Constitutional and Administrative Law*. 4th ed. London: Routledge.

Taylor, R. (2017, 27 November). Brexit, the four freedoms and the indivisibility dogma. *LSE* [Online]. Available from: https://blogs.lse.ac.uk/brexit/2017/11/27/brexit-the-four-freedoms-and-the-indivisibility-dogma/ [Accessed 14 September 2020].

Wade, H. W. R. (1980). *Constitutional Fundamentals*. London: Stevens & Sons.

Index

accomplices 165–166
accountability 1–3, 5, 9–10, 12–13, 46, 63, 80, 156, 102–104, 121, 166, 174 –177, 190–191, 207
administrative justice 108
administrative review 110, 118
administrative rule-making 104
administrative simplification 184, 189–190
algorithms 17
artificial intelligence 11
audit institutions 33, 49, 51–52, 109; *see also* SAI (State Audit Institution)
automated means 17, 22
award 182–185, 186

balanced budget rule 29
balanced constitution 207
balancing (judicial) 11
below-threshold contracts 180
bias (algorithmic) 14, 17
Brexit 193–210, 213–218
British Constitution 195, 206, 208
British constitutional law 193, 196, 206, 208–209, 213
budget 30, 34, 51; act 34, 37, 43; adoption 30; bill 29, 31, 34, 35–38, 42; concept 29; control 30, 33, 55; deficit 2, 29, 35, 38–40, 55, 148; execution 30, 34, 36; funds 51; inspection 55–56; preparation 30; process 29–33, 43

censorship 14–15
central bank: reform 41–42; role 2, 28–29
community standards 24
Comptroller-Generals 108–109, 116
constitutional conventions 208
constitutional court: general 29, 36–37; Germany 30; Italy 85, 87, 91, 94, 96–98; Poland 38–39, 68; Romania 145–147; Slovenia 30; Spain 35, 38, 39
constitutional values 13, 29, 36
content: moderation 11–12, 18; removal 11, 23
Copyright Digital Single Market Directive 22
counter 83
Court of Justice of the European Union 20–21, 69, 71
COVID-19, 28
criminal offences 157–158

debt *see* public debt
decision-making process 194–195, 206–207, 209, 213
deficit *see* budget deficit
digital: constitutionalism 13–15; governance 10, 12; Services Act 22
disciplinary: chamber of the Supreme Court 71–77; commissioners 73–74; court(s) 73; liability (judges, judiciary) 63, 65–66, 69, 77; misconduct 66–67; penalty (panelties) admonition 70; proceedings 75–76; tort(s) 66, 69–70
discrimination 2, 22, 179
dismissal: from the office 69–70; power 136, 144
doctrine of parliamentary sovereignty 194, 196, 213–216, 218
due process 15–16
duty: of care 21; to give reasons 176, 186, 189

E-commerce directive 12, 20, 22
economic crisis 28–29, 33–40, 43, 144, 158; *see also* global financial crisis

222 *Index*

equality 14, 22, 158, 165, 168–170, 204
EU referendum 193–196, 200–201
European law 19, 33–35, 180
European Union 12, 21, 39, 49, 130, 193, 197–199, 203–204, 209, 212, 214–215, 210
exceptional regime 158, 162
expenditure 37–38, 46, 105, 116, 177, 210
external audit 53, 58
extinguishing deadline 158, 164–165
extraordinary renditions 96–98

Facebook (Oversight Board) 12
Factortame judgment 215–216
financial accountability 3, 46–47
financial responsibility 30
free competition 179, 185
freedom of expression 2, 13, 20
fundamental rights 19

global financial crisis 28

horizontal accountability 103
human moderator 18

illegal content 22–23
immunity 4, 72, 88, 96, 157, 159, 164, 169
income 37, 69–70
independence 64–65, 121
integrity branch of government 107
intelligence services 87–95
internal audit 48–50
internal financial control 47, 52
internal review 90
IT platforms 22–23

Johnson, Boris 199
judicial activism 214–215

Latin America 102, 105
Law and Justice (political party) 63
legal accountability 103
legality 112–113, 119, 175
legality review 109–112
liability 21–22, 63, 66, 156–157, 169

May, Theresa 197–199
Miller I case judgment 194, 197–198, 204, 209, 214, 218
ministerial criminal liability 156, 163

minister of justice 69, 73–76, 86
monetary powers 29, 41

National Council for the Judiciary 68
non-judicial accountability 104

openness 194, 202–204, 207, 217

parliamentary: dissolution 32, 136, 164; scrutiny 206, 209–213; sovereignty 193–194, 214–216, 218; term 164
political responsibility 4, 156, 170, 207–208
presidential: election 24; powers 132, 134, 138, 142; system 132; *see also* semi-presidentialism
primary legislation 197–198
Prime Minister 129, 132–133, 143–144, 146, 148, 198, 200
prioritisation of content 18
private entities 14, 22–23
prosecution 157, 164–165, 169
public debt 2, 29, 32, 39–42; *see also* budget
public procurement 178–179, 182, 190
public sector institutions 47–50

Queen's/throne speech 208

report, final account 48, 50–51
reprimand 69, 169
responsibility 194–195, 206–208, 214
royal prerogative 193–198, 208
rule of law 71, 159, 204, 207

SAI (State Audit Institution) 33, 43, 48, 50–56, 57
secondary legislation 105, 110, 112
self-regulation 15
semi-presidentialism 134–138
separation of powers 1, 4, 64, 77, 132, 145, 158–159, 165, 167–168, 170, 214
social cohesion 24
Special Court 162–163, 171
speech: hate 17, 20; moderation 11, 17; online 15; presidential 149
state secrecy 88, 93–94
statute of limitations 162, 164–165

terrorism 3, 90, 95–96, 98
transparency 2, 5, 10, 57, 80–81, 174–177, 190–191, 202–203, 207

Treaty on European Union 5, 193
Treaty on the Functioning of the
European Union 39, 138, 199
Trump, Donald 9, 24

use of terms 23

withdrawal agreement 195,
198–200, 202, 205–206,
209–210

Ziobro, Zbigniew 72, 74
Zuckerberg, Mark 10

Printed in the United States
by Baker & Taylor Publisher Services